Adam Green

DESTINED FOR EQUALITY

DESTINED FOR EQUALITY

THE INEVITABLE RISE OF WOMEN'S STATUS

ROBERT MAX JACKSON

HARVARD UNIVERSITY PRESS

CAMBRIDGE, MASSACHUSETTS, AND LONDON, ENGLAND 1998

Library of Congress Cataloging-in-Publication Data

Jackson, Robert Max.
    Destined for equality : the inevitable rise of women's status /
Robert Max Jackson.
        p.   cm.
    Includes bibliographical references and index.
    ISBN 0-674-05511-X (alk. paper)
    1. Women's rights—History.   2. Women—Economic conditions.
    3. Women—Social conditions.   4. Women—Legal status, laws, etc.   I. Title.
HQ1236.J33   1998
305.42'09—dc21   97-52359

To my daughter
Maia Ruth Brown-Jackson

ACKNOWLEDGMENTS

Since the 1960s, writers have filled library shelves with books that ably, sometimes brilliantly, relate the history of women in diverse classes, ethnicities, occupations, regions, and periods. Women's social status has so colored their experience that these histories of women are all histories of gender inequality. These histories serve as the invaluable foundation on which this book builds.

Over the past decade many colleagues, scholars, and students have offered criticism, suggestions, and goodwill that improved the manuscript through many revisions. Those whose comments led to significant changes include Kathleen Gerson, Joan Huber, Jerry Jacobs, James Jasper, Iona Mara-Drita, Jane Poulsen, Robin Tamarelli, Charles Tilly, Melissa Wilde, and the participants in the Workshop on Gender and Inequality at New York University. To the many others who generously offered comments and support over the years I am extremely thankful. This book also owes much to the extraordinary editorial skill of Joyce Seltzer at Harvard University Press.

CONTENTS

DESTINED FOR EQUALITY

THE EGALITARIAN IMPULSE

Over the past two centuries, women's long, conspicuous struggle for better treatment has masked a surprising condition. Men's social dominance was doomed from the beginning. Gender inequality could not adapt successfully to modern economic and political institutions. No one planned this. Indeed, for a long time, the impending extinction of gender inequality was hidden from all.

In the middle of the nineteenth century, few said that equality between women and men was possible or desirable. The new forms of business, government, schools, and the family seemed to fit nicely with the existing division between women's roles and men's roles. Men controlled them all, and they showed no signs of losing belief in their natural superiority. If anything, women's subordination seemed likely to grow worse as they remained attached to the household while business and politics became a separate, distinctively masculine, realm.

Nonetheless, 150 years later, seemingly against all odds, women are well on the way to becoming men's equals. Now, few say that gender equality is impossible or undesirable. Somehow our expectations have been turned upside down.

Women's rising status is an enigmatic paradox. For millennia women were subordinate to men under the most diverse economic, political, and cultural conditions. Although the specific content of gender-based roles and the degree of inequality between the sexes varied considerably across time and place, men everywhere held power and status over women. Moreover, people believed that men's dominance was a natural and unchangeable part of life. Yet over the past two centuries, gender inequality has declined across the world.

The driving force behind this transformation has been the migration of economic and political power outside households and its reorganization around business and political interests detached from gender. Women (and their male supporters) have fought against prejudice and discrimination throughout American history, but social conditions governed the intensity and effectiveness of their efforts. Behind the very visible conflicts between women and male-dominated institutions, fundamental processes concerning economic and political organization have been paving the way for women's success. Throughout these years, while many women struggled to improve their status and many men resisted those efforts, institutional changes haltingly, often imperceptibly, but persistently undermined gender inequality. Responding to the emergent imperatives of large-scale, bureaucratic organizations, men with economic or political power intermittently adopted policies that favored greater equality, often without anticipating the implications of their actions. Gradually responding to the changing demands and possibilities of households without economic activity, men acting as individuals reduced their resistance to wives and daughters extending their roles, although men rarely recognized they were doing something different from their fathers' generation.

 Social theorists have long taught us that institutions have unanticipated consequences, particularly when the combined effect of many people's actions diverges from their individual aims. Adam Smith, the renowned theorist of early capitalism, proposed that capitalist markets shared a remarkable characteristic. Many people pursuing only their selfish, private interests could further the good of all. Subsequently, Karl Marx, considering the capitalist economy, proposed an equally remarkable but contradictory assessment. Systems of inequality fueled by rational self-interest, he argued, inevitably produce irrational crises that threaten to destroy the social order. Both ideas have suffered many critical blows, but they still capture our imaginations by their extraordinary insight. They teach us how unanticipated effects often ensue when disparate people and organizations each follow their own short-sighted interests.

Through a similar unanticipated and uncontrolled process, the changing actions of men, women, and powerful institutions have gradually but irresistibly reduced gender inequality. Women had always resisted their constraints and inferior status. Over the past 150 years, however, their individual strivings and organized resistance became increasingly effective. Men long continued to oppose the loss of their privileged status. Nonetheless, although men and male-controlled institutions did not adopt egalitarian values, their actions changed because their interests changed. Men's resistance to women's aspirations diminished, and they found new advantages in strategies that also benefited women.

Modern economic and political organization propelled this transformation by slowly dissociating social power from its allegiance to gender inequality. The power over economic resources, legal rights, the allocation of positions, legitimating values, and setting priorities once present in families shifted into businesses and government organizations. In these organizations, profit, efficiency, political legitimacy, organizational stability, competitiveness, and similar considerations mattered more than male privileges vis-à-vis females. Men who had power because of their positions in these organizations gradually adopted policies ruled more by institutional interests than by personal prejudices. Over the long run, institutional needs and opportunities produced policies that worked against gender inequality. Simultaneously, ordinary men (those without economic or political power) resisted women's advancements less. They had fewer resources to use against the women in their lives, and less to gain from keeping women subordinate. Male politicians seeking more power, businessmen pursuing wealth and success, and ordinary men pursuing their self-interest all contributed to the gradual decline of gender inequality.

Structural developments produced ever more inconsistencies with the requirements for continued gender inequality. Both the economy and the state increasingly treated people as potential workers or voters without reference to their family status. To the disinterested, and often rationalized, authority within these institutions, sex inequality was just one more consideration when calculating strategies for profit and political advantage. For these institutions, men and women embodied similar problems of control, exploitation, and legitimation.

Seeking to further their own interests, powerful men launched institutional changes that eventually reduced the discrimination against women. Politicians passed laws giving married women property rights. Employers hired women in ever-increasing numbers. Educators opened their doors to women. These examples and many others show powerful men pursuing their interests in preserving and expanding their economic and political power, yet also improving women's social standing.

The economy and state did not systematically oppose inequality. On the contrary, each institution needed and aggressively supported some forms of inequality, such as income differentials and the legal authority of state officials, that gave them strength. Other forms of inequality received neither automatic support nor automatic opposition. Over time, the responses to other kinds of inequality depended on how well they met institutional interests and how contested they became.

When men adopted organizational policies that eventually improved women's status, they consciously sought to increase profits, end labor shortages, get more votes, and increase social order. They imposed concrete solutions to short-term economic and political problems and to conflicts associated with them. These men usually did not envision, and probably did not care, that the cumulative effect of these policies would be to curtail male dominance.

Only when they were responding to explicitly egalitarian demands from women such as suffrage did men with power consistently examine the implications of their actions for gender inequality. Even then, as when responding to women's explicit demands for legal changes, most legislators were concerned more about their political interests than the fate of gender inequality. When legislatures did pass laws responding to public pressure about women's rights, few male legislators expected the laws could dramatically alter gender inequality.

Powerful men adopted various policies that ultimately would undermine gender inequality because such policies seemed to further their private interests and to address inescapable economic, political, and organizational problems. The structure and integral logic of development within modern political and economic institutions shaped the problems, interests, and apparent solutions. Without regard to what either women or men wanted, industrial capitalism and rational legal government eroded gender inequality.

MAPPING GENDER INEQUALITY'S DECLINE

When a band of men committed to revolutionary change self-consciously designed the American institutional framework, they did not imagine or desire that it would lead toward gender equality. In 1776 a small group of men claimed equality for themselves and similar men by signing the Declaration of Independence. In throwing off British sovereignty, they inaugurated the American ideal of equality. Yet after the success of their revolution, its leaders and like-minded property-owning white men created a nation that subjugated women, enslaved blacks, and withheld suffrage from men without property.

These men understood the egalitarian ideals they espoused through the culture and experiences dictated by their own historical circumstances. Everyone then accepted that women and men were absolutely and inalterably different. Although Abigail Adams admonished her husband that they should "remember the ladies," when these "fathers" of the American nation established its most basic rights and laws, the prospect of fuller citizenship for women was not even credible enough to warrant the effort of rejection. These nation builders could not foresee that their political and economic institutions would eventually erode some forms of inequality much more emphatically than had their revolutionary vision. They could not know that this social structure would eventually extend egalitarian social relations much further than they might ever have thought desirable or possible.

By the 1830s, a half-century after the American Revolution, little had changed. In the era of Jacksonian democracy, women still could not vote or hold political office. They had to cede legal control of their inherited property and their income to their husbands. With few exceptions, they could not make legal contracts or escape a marriage through divorce. They could not enter college. Dependence on men was perpetual and inescapable. Household toil and family welfare monopolized women's time and energies. Civil society recognized women not as individuals but as adjuncts to men. Like the democracy of ancient Athens, the American democracy limited political equality to men.

Today women enjoy independent citizenship; they have the same liberty as men to control their person and property. If they choose or need to do so, women can live without a husband. They can discard an unwanted husband to seek a better alternative. Women vote and occupy political offices. They hold jobs almost as often as men do. Ever more women have managerial and professional positions. Our culture has adopted more affirmative images for women, particularly as models of such values as independence, public advocacy, economic success, and thoughtfulness. Although these changes have not removed all inequities, women now have greater resources, more choices in life, and a higher social status than in the past.

In terms of the varied events and processes that have so dramatically changed women's place in society, the past 150 years of American history can be divided into three half-century periods. The *era of separate spheres,* covers roughly 1840–1890, from the era of Jacksonian democracy to the Gilded Age. The *era of egalitarian illusion*s, roughly 1890–1940, extends from the Progressive Era to the beginning of World War II. The third period, the *era of assimilation,* covers the time from World War II to the present.

Over the three periods, notable changes altered women's legal, political, and economic status, women's access to higher education and to divorce, women's sexuality, and the cultural images of women and men. Most analysts agree that people's legal, political, and economic status largely define their social status, and we will focus on the changes in these. Of course, like gender, other personal characteristics such as race and age also define an individual's status, because they similarly influence legal, political, and economic rights and resources. Under most circumstances, however, women and men are not systematically differentiated by other kinds of inequality based on personal characteristics, because these other differences, such as race and age, cut across gender lines. Educational institutions have played an ever-larger role in regulating people's access to opportunities over the last century. Changes in access to divorce, women's sexuality, and cultural images of gender will not play a central role in this study. They are important indicators of women's status, but they are derivative rather than formative. They reveal inequality's burden.

The creation of separate spheres for women and men dominated the history of gender inequality during the first period, 1840–1890. The cultural doctrine of separate spheres emerged in the mid-nineteenth century. It declared emphatically that women and men belonged to different worlds. Women were identified with the household and maintenance of family life. Men were associated with income-generating employment and public life. Popular ideas attributed greater religious virtue to women but greater civic virtue to men. Women were hailed as guardians of private morality while men were regarded as the protectors of the public good. These cultural and ideological inventions were responses to a fundamental institutional transition, the movement of economic activity out of households into independent enterprises. The concept of separate spheres legitimated women's exclusion from the public realm, although it gave them some autonomy and authority within their homes.

Women's status was not stagnant in this period. The cultural wedge driven between women's and men's worlds obscured diverse and significant changes that did erode inequality. The state gave married women the right to control their property and income. Jobs became available for some, mainly single, women, giving them some economic independence and an identity apart from the household. Secondary education similar to that offered to men became available to women, and colleges began to admit some women for higher learning. Divorce became a possible, though still difficult, strategy for the first time and led social commentators to bemoan the increasing rate of marital dissolution. In short, women's opportunities moved slowly forward in diverse ways.

From 1890 to 1940 women's opportunities continued to improve, and many claimed that women had won equality. Still, the opportunities were never enough to enable women to transcend their subordinate position. The passage of the Woman Suffrage Amendment stands out as the high point of changes during this period, yet women could make little headway in government while husbands and male politicians belittled and rejected their political aspirations. Women entered the labor market in ever-increasing numbers, educated women could get white-collar positions for the first time, and employers extended hiring to married women. Still, employers rarely considered women for high-status jobs, and explicit discrimination was an accepted practice. Although women's college opportunities became more like men's, professional and advanced degree programs still excluded women. Married women gained widespread access to effective contraception. Although popular opinion expected women to pursue and enjoy sex within marriage, social mores still denied them sex outside it. While divorce became more socially acceptable and practically available, laws still restricted divorce by demanding that one spouse prove that the other was morally repugnant. Movies portrayed glamorous women as smart, sexually provocative, professionally talented, and ambitious, but even they, if they were good women, were driven by an overwhelming desire to marry, bear children, and dedicate themselves to their homes.

Writing at the end of this period, the sociologist Mirra Komarovsky

Table 1.1. The decline of gender inequality in American society

	1840–1890 The Era of Separate Spheres	1890–1940 The Era of Egalitarian Illusions	1940–1990 The Era of Assimilation	1990–? Residual Inequities
Legal and political status	Formal legal equality instituted	Formal political equality instituted	Formal economic equality instituted	Women rare in high political offices
Economic opportunity	Working-class jobs for single women only	Some jobs for married women and educated women	All kinds of jobs available to all kinds of women	"Glass ceiling" and domestic duties hold women back
Higher education	A few women admitted to public universities and new women's colleges	Increasing college; little graduate or professional education	Full access at all levels	Some prestigious fields remain largely male domains
Divorce	Almost none, but available for dire circumstances	Increasingly available, but difficult	Freely available and accepted	Women typically suffer greater costs
Sexuality and reproductive control	Repressive sexuality; little reproductive control	Positive sexuality but double standard; increasing reproductive control	High sexual freedom; full reproductive control	Sexual harassment and fear of rape still widespread
Cultural image	Virtuous domesticity and subordination	Educated motherhood, capable for employment & public service	Careers, marital equality	Sexes still perceived as inherently different

captured its implications splendidly. After studying affluent college students during World War II, Komarovsky concluded that young women were beset by "serious contradictions between two roles." The first was the feminine role, with its expectations of deference to men and a future focused on familial activities. The second was the "modern" role that "partly obliterates the differentiation in sex," presumably because the emphasis on education made the universal qualities of ability and accomplishment seem the only reasonable limitations on future activities. Women who absorbed the egalitarian implications of modern education felt confused, burdened, and irritated by the contrary expectations that they display a subordinate femininity. The intrinsic contradictions between these two role expectations could only end, Komarovsky declared, when women's real adult role was redefined to make it "consistent with the socioeconomic and ideological character of modern society."[1]

Since 1940, many of these contradictions have been resolved. At an accelerating pace, women have continually gained greater access to the activities, positions, and statuses formerly reserved to men.

Despite the tremendous gains women have experienced, they have not achieved complete equality, nor is it imminent. The improvement of women's status has been uneven, seesawing between setbacks and advances. Women still bear the major responsibility for raising children. They suffer from lingering harassment, intimidation, and disguised discrimination. Women in the United States still get poorer jobs and lower income. They have less access to economic or political power. The higher echelons of previously male social hierarchies have assimilated women slowest and least completely. For example, in blue-collar hierarchies they find it hard to get skilled jobs or join craft unions; in white-collar hierarchies they rarely reach top management; and in politics the barriers to women's entry seem to rise with the power of the office they seek. Yet when we compare the status of American women today with their status in the past, the movement toward greater equality is striking.

While women have not gained full equality, the formal structural barriers holding them back have largely collapsed and those left are crumbling. New government policies have discouraged sex discrimination by most organizations and in most areas of life outside the family. The political and economic systems have accepted ever more women and have promoted them to positions with more influence and higher status. Education at all levels has become equally available to women. Women have gained great control over their reproductive processes, and their sexual freedom has come to resemble that of men. It has become easy and socially acceptable to end unsatisfactory marriages with divorce. Popular culture has come close to portraying women as men's legitimate equal. Television, our most dynamic communication media, regularly portrays discrimination as wrong and male abuse or male dominance as nasty. The prevailing theme of this recent period has been women's assimilation into all the activities and positions once denied them.

This book focuses on the dominant patterns and the groups that had the most decisive and most public roles in the processes that changed women's status: middle-class whites and, secondarily, the white working class. The histories of gender inequality among racial and ethnic minorities are too diverse to address adequately here.[2] Similarly, this analysis neglects other distinctive groups, especially lesbians and heterosexual women who avoided marriage, whose changing circumstances also deserve extended study.

While these minorities all have distinctive histories, the major trends considered here have influenced all groups. Every group had to respond to the same changing political and economic structures that defined the opportunities and constraints for all people in the society. Also, whatever their particular history, the members of each group understood their gender relations against the backdrop of the white, middle-class family's cultural preeminence. Even when people in higher or lower-class positions or people in ethnic communities expressed contempt for these values, they were familiar with the middle-class ideals and thought of them as leading ideas in the society. The focus on the white middle classes is simply an analytical and practical strategy. The history of dominant groups has no greater inherent or moral worth. Still, except in cases of open, successful rebellion, the ideas and actions of dominant groups usually affect history much more than the ideas and actions of subordinate groups. This fact is an inevitable effect of inequality.

THE MEANING OF INEQUALITY AND ITS DECLINE

We will think differently about women's status under two theoretical agendas. Either we can try to evaluate how short from equality women now fall, or we can try to understand how far they have come from past deprivations.

Looking at women's place in society today from these two vantage points yields remarkably different perspectives. They accentuate different aspects of women's status by altering the background against which we compare it. Temporal and analytical differences separate these two vantage points, not distinctive moral positions, although people sometimes confuse these differences with competing moral positions.

If we want to assess and criticize women's disadvantages today, we usually compare their existing status with an imagined future when complete equality reigns. Using this ideal standard of complete equality, we would find varied shortcomings in women's status today. These shortcomings include women's absence from positions of political or economic power, men's preponderance in the better-paid and higher-status occupations, women's lower average income, women's greater family responsibilities, the higher status commonly attached to male activities, and the dearth of institutions or policies supporting dual-earner couples.

Alternatively, if we want to evaluate how women's social status has improved, we must turn in the other direction and face the past. We look back to a time when women were legal and political outcasts, working only in a few low-status jobs, and always deferring to male authority. From this perspective, women's status today seems much brighter. Compared with the nineteenth century, women now have a nearly equal legal and political status, far more women hold jobs, women can succeed at almost any occupation, women usually get paid as much as men in the same position (in the same firm), women have as much educational opportunity as men, and both sexes normally expect women to pursue jobs and careers.

As we seek to understand the decline of gender inequality, we will necessarily stress the improvements in women's status. We will always want to remember, however, that gender inequality today stands somewhere between extreme inequality and complete equality. To analyze the modern history of gender inequality fully, we must be able to look at this middle ground from both sides. It is seriously deficient when measured against full equality. It is a remarkable improvement when measured against past inequality.

These differences in perception raise an important question. What does inequality mean? To some people, past and present inequality between women and men seems self-evident; to others, gender inequality has always been questionable. To some people, the improvements in women's status over the past two centuries are obvious; to others, they are illusory. Inequality obviously entails differences among people or their circumstances. But not all difference is a manifestation of inequality.

Gender inequality has depended on the relationship between two distinct types of inequality. Some systems of inequality divide positions or roles within major social institutions, for example, giving managers authority over staff. Other systems of inequality divide groups defined by personal characteristics, for example, benefiting one race to the disadvantage of another. In practice, these two kinds of inequality intermingle; people do not experience them separately. Nonetheless, they have distinctive causes and effects, their relationship is changeable, and the dynamics between them have critically influenced the modern history of gender inequality.[3]

Positional inequality refers to relationships *between social positions,* defined by their roles and functional identity within some social structure.[4] Positional inequality defines two (or more) structural positions rendered unequal by their integral rights and resources. These characteristics do not depend on the identity of the people who occupy the positions; the structural inequality between positions persists even when the people change. Positional inequality makes people unequal if they occupy unequal positions in some working social structure and the amount of inequality between them reflects the resources and rights characterizing their structural positions. Examples of structures include the economy, the polity, the military, and most organizations. Examples of structurally unequal groups include managers and machine operators, government officials and ordinary citizens, and military officers and enlisted soldiers. Sometimes the structures define a specific relationship between positions, such as authority relationships within an organization. Sometimes the structures define the inequality between positions indirectly, by attaching variable amounts of resources (for example, income, authority, influence, and visibility) to positions. The general inequality between high-status, high-paid occupations and low-status, low-paid occupations is an example.

The defining relationships of positional inequality are always between *positions,* not between people. The characteristic inequality between two positions does not change with the coming and going of people who temporarily occupy those positions. People become, for example, low status and disadvantaged by occupying low-status, disadvantaged positions in the structure. In contrast, positions do not gain or lose authority (or privileges or status) according to the identity of the person who takes them. Skills, connections, or group identity may cause one person to do better or to do worse than others in the same position. Still, such variations in the performance of duty do not alter the position.

In contrast, *status inequality* refers to relationships *between different types of people,* who distinguish themselves by personal characteristics and exclusionary practices. Like the integral personal characteristics defining these groups, their unequal statuses cling to people through changes or variations in the positions they hold. Status inequality occurs because people use group identities for social solidarity and for social selection, and the amount of status inequality between people reflects the differences in opportunities available to their reference groups. Age, sex, race, and education exemplify the personal characteristics that sometimes mark pervasive inequality. The distinguishing characteristics have no inherent, necessary relationship to functioning social processes. Status inequality reflects the relationship between two groups, not the particular personal characteristics that differentiate them. Under a system of status inequality, these characteristics become selection criteria, rewarding some types of people with status-confirming social positions, consigning other types to demeaning ones. For example, those in higher-status groups have more access to political power, receive preferential treatment by law, and get better education and better jobs. The distinguishing characteristics defining the unequal groups also typically demarcate the boundaries of group solidarity (although that solidarity may be obstructed by other conditions). Those in the high-status group identify themselves as different and better, and their solidarity motivates and sustains their discrimination against others.

The defining relationships of status inequality are always between people, not between positions. The inequality between two groups distinguished by their members' personal characteristics is preserved as people depart and join the groups. The high or low rank produced by status inequality persists even if people move between positions. The structural positions people occupy can sometimes offset the effects of status inequality. For example, although American blacks have a considerably lower status that whites, a wealthy black woman might enjoy greater influence and respect than a poor white woman. Still, the people with a low status based on personal attributes remain disadvantaged compared to those in the same structural position who have a high status.

Sex inequality is primarily a status differential because it distinguishes two kinds of people, not two kinds of positions. Male and female are not functionally related social positions, like high-status and low-status jobs. Men's and women's characteristic social standings stick to them in all the positions they fill. Occasionally, some people may *pass* as a member of the opposite sex, just as people occasionally pass as members of different races. Barring successful deceit, however, all biological males are forever associated with the male social category and all biological females with the female social category.

Although the inequality between women and men is defined by their personal characteristics, it becomes manifest largely through the unequal structural positions they occupy. The resulting congruence between gender inequality and positional inequalities makes gender inequality appear positional.

The status inequality dividing women and men depends on two analytically distinguishable factors: how much positional inequality exists in society and the degree to which gender inequality is embedded in positional inequality. Gender inequality has declined mainly through an erosion of the overlap between gender and the major forms of positional inequality. Economic and political processes have gradually reduced the degree to which gender affects the allocation of positions, although general inequality within these systems remains the same. In contrast, reducing gender inequality within households has required moving from a more hierarchical positional structure to a more egalitarian one, which explains why women's childrearing responsibilities have been lingering obstacles to greater gender equality. Restructuring the system of positional inequality within the family has been more difficult than altering the relationship between the economic and political systems of positional inequality and the gender system of status inequality. Still, widespread gender inequality in marriages cannot endure long in the absence of economic and political inequality between the sexes. The link between gender and positional inequality has been the key to women's status.

Historically, concerns about structural or institutional inequality have emphasized the divergence from three egalitarian ideals: legal equality, political equality, and equality of opportunity.[5] When applied to gender, these ideals define three ways in which women and men could be equal. Legal equality would exist if the laws and the judicial system treated women the same as men, as individuals who are equal objects of state action. Political equality would exist if the political process, which selects and influences members of government, treated women the same as men, as equal members of the polity. Equality of opportunity would exist if institutions treated women and men the same, giving them identical access to valuable resources, both as the objects of policies and aspirants to membership. Gender *in*equality is greater the more that institutions depart from these egalitarian ideals. It exists to the degree that the state treats women differently from and worse than men, that political processes grant men a greater role than women, and that institutions generally offer better opportunities to men than to women. From the institutionalist perspective, gender inequality is a characteristic of social organization in which key social processes favor men.

Some theorists have approached the problem of inequality differently, referring to three components of inequality experienced and used by individuals: power, privilege, and prestige. People with greater power have resources or social positions that let them command the behavior of others. People with greater privilege have more access to consumption goods and leisure, exhibit a more desirable lifestyle, and spend less effort and less time on drudgery. People with higher prestige have honor, esteem, or high regard that commands the respect and deference of others. Causal processes link these three components of inequality so that people usually rank similarly on all three. Even so, people, and groups, can be high on one and low on the others. From this individualistic perspective, gender inequality exists to the degree that men get more power, more privileges, and more prestige than do women. From the individualistic perspective, inequality is a characteristic of people or groups by which men have more of the things that people value and more of the resources that gain valued things.

The institutional perspective and the individualistic perspective produce complementary visions of gender inequality. The first stresses that organizations or structures controlling opportunities and resources treat men better than women and remain largely in men's hands. The second stresses that most men have more power, more privileges, and more prestige than most women. Whichever way we look at it, gender inequality means the *net* advantages of being male exceed those of being female.

If we apply these two approaches, we can map the terrain of inequality separating women and men. In modern societies, gender inequality seems normally to have included a wide range of male advantages. The legal framework has assumed that men are dominant in all spheres of life. Men have had preponderant influence over the centralized policies of the society. In modern societies, men exercised this influence through control of the state. Men have controlled most resources owned by institutions, especially those associated with organized economic, political, and military activities. Economic and political organization generally restricted this power to a minority of men. Most men have had more money, more authority, more of other resources than the women in their social milieu. Most women have depended on men to connect them to the public realm and have deferred to men's authority. Few men have similarly depended on or deferred to women. Similarly, men have usually controlled family resources and men have dominated family decision making. Men have applied the techniques of direct power to women—by physically intimidating and assaulting them—more than women have used those techniques against men. Men have had more valued opportunities than women. Men have had more liberty than women. Men and male attributes have been, on balance, more highly regarded than women and female attributes in the prevailing ideals and beliefs. Women have trailed men along each major dimension of inequality. This includes those considered both by the approach stressing institutional activity and the approach stressing the rights and obligations of individuals.

As used here, gender inequality means that men, as a group, enjoyed a net advantage over women, the composite result of their differences along varied dimensions. Gender inequality does not imply that differences between women and men have been universal or absolute in a society. Men did not have an edge in every aspect of life. Instead, inequality has implied that men did better than women in more areas or in more important areas than the reverse. Even in severely unequal societies, men have rarely had an advantage in every facet of life.

Similarly, inequality has not meant that all men have had higher status and better lives than all women (or all women worse lives than all men). On balance, men did better than women. In particular, in each group defined by class and ethnicity, men usually had clear advantages over women. Nonetheless, men's relative advantages were not universal. Usually, most men have had worse lives than the most privileged women in society (that is, some women have enjoyed more resources and better lives than most men). Some severely disadvantaged men have had worse lives than even average women (that is, even average women have had more resources and better lives than some men). These discontinuities in gender inequality have occurred because other social characteristics also influenced the quality of people's lives, particularly class, race, and ethnicity.

Also, as used here, gender inequality refers to people's social positions, not to their experiences. While we can anticipate that members of dominant groups usually have a better quality of life than people in subordinate groups, this study neither assumes nor tries to show that women's and men's lives have typically followed this prediction. One important corollary of this distinction is that improving a group's social status may not make its members happier or their lives more fulfilling.

The decline of gender inequality has meant that the differences between women's lives and men's lives have diminished. In particular, the difference between women and men has shrunk considerably for every major dimension of inequality defined by the institutional and the resource perspectives. The changes have been uneven, and we cannot reduce them to one simple, precise numeric estimate of gender inequality's overall decline. But the improvements in women's circumstances have been sufficiently widespread and consistent over time that they provide incontrovertible evidence of gender inequality's decline.

Inequality's decline has not required or meant that all aspects of women's lives improved uniformly. Gender inequality's decline has meant that women's net disadvantages (when compared to men) have declined significantly. Theoretically, a decline in inequality need not even mean that women's lives have got better, although they probably have by most people's standards. Some people believe that women's disadvantages have grown worse in some areas, such as the experience of fear in public spaces. Even if such claims were valid (and the evidence for these claims is narrow and disputable), they would not contradict the inference that general gender inequality has declined. The main historical pattern has been for women's relative disadvantages to decline, even if their lot has worsened in some areas.[6]

Further complicating inequality's decline, when women acquired more equal rights, they were not automatically able to exercise those rights. Legal equality did not imply that women had equal means to use or to abuse the judicial system. Political equality did not ensure that women had as much political power as men. Equality of opportunity did not guarantee that women had as many resources or held prestigious positions as often as men. Women were subject to the general rule that people who have lacked equal resources in one realm have usually faced a disadvantage when trying to exercise formal equality in another realm. For example, because women have had less income and property than men, they (like members of other disadvantaged groups) have found it harder to use their legal and political rights. Also, making rights and opportunities equal did not undo the manifest inequality that had accumulated in earlier times. For example, getting the rights to vote and to hold political office did not give women control of a political party, control of existing political offices, or a network of politically influential people. Still, increasing the formal equality between women and men did reduce the *direct* use of gender as part of the mechanisms deciding who gets what. When formal equality between women and men increases significantly, usually it will gradually reduce manifest inequality. Increases in formal equality have improved women's ability to compete for, use, and accumulate resources. Often, this accumulation has been slow at first, and it may become visible only after two or three generations.

Given the inherent difficulties facing any effort to measure the amount of inequality between two groups, no one can say precisely how much gender inequality has declined over the past 150 years. The rights, the opportunities, and outcomes for women and men have become more similar across a wide range of activities. Most important, this change includes women's rising part in status-conferring economic and political activities. The overall impact of these changes implies that inequality has declined significantly, even if we cannot give precise meaning to the amount of that decline.

THE FORCE DRIVING EQUALITY'S GROWTH

The theoretical perspective advanced here will unfold through the historical analyses and appear as a complete structure by the end. To produce an adequate theoretical interpretation of gender inequality's decline, we have to identify and abstract critical patterns from the endless complexity of history. One reason that good social theories are hard to create is that we have no standardized procedure to discover which patterns matter or how to abstract from them. We must mix art, artifice, and good luck with hard work and experience. In this process, the direction of theoretical development will be guided by some key decisions we make about which aspects of a phenomenon we want to explain and what kind of explanation we seek.

Several characteristics are particularly telling for the theoretical interpretation of gender inequality. Women's unprecedented and apparently irreversible progress toward complete gender equality over the past two centuries suggests that the causes of gender inequality's decline must include conditions and processes unique to modern times, and that it cannot be adequately explained through ahistorical theories meant to explain the variations in degrees of inequality across all cultures and periods.

The decline in gender inequality has been an international phenomenon. Although this study focuses on the United States, a similar pattern of declining gender inequality has appeared in all nations with modern economies and political structures. The timing, rate, and form of specific changes have varied considerably, but the fundamental pattern has been similar. This consistency suggests that the essential causes of gender inequality's decline must be conditions or processes intrinsic to the development of modern institutions. They constitute an engine of social change present in all countries moving toward a modern economic and political order. The distinctive historical events and social conditions occurring in the United States (or any other country) might explain why the path it followed to gender inequality was different from that followed in other countries, but they cannot be components of the general theoretical explanation of women's rising status.

In the United States, women's disadvantages declined in each of the past three half-century periods. The concrete social changes that reduced inequality had extremely varied specific historical antecedents. For example, at various times women's status benefited from laws passed without consideration of their effects on gender status, from self-interested policies installed by employers, from collective actions by movements representing women, and from the side effects of basic organizational dynamics. These patterns suggest that the primary causes of gender inequality's decline must have been active over the entire period,[7] that they must be loosely linked to the specific changes reducing inequality, and that they must have developed gradually. The diversity suggests a highly complex causal process in which many indirect links and contingent processes have mediated between the primary causes and the ultimate outcomes.

To take into account these key patterns of gender inequality's decline, a satisfactory theoretical analysis needs to identify an enduring engine of social change integral to modern societies. It should specify a guiding social mechanism that linked the engine of change to gender inequality and gave direction to its effects. And it should show how these long-term, fundamental processes led to and guided the many varied short-term events that altered the circumstances of women and men.

Two kinds of social conflict fueled the decline of gender inequality. The first kind concerned the antagonisms and struggles between women and men. Bound together through the social order, family obligations, and sexual tensions, divided by unequal statuses and roles, women and men have perpetually vied for advantage and ascendancy. Because mutual antagonism and sporadic strife have always characterized gender inequality, the presence of tension and conflict between the sexes cannot alone account for modern improvements in women's status. In the past, women generally failed to gain much from their struggles, and when they did succeed, their triumphs remained isolated. Their successes were individual victories that failed to spread to others or to accumulate over time.

The perpetual struggle between women and men over their domains and rights resembles the incessant squabbles between two neighboring countries over the extent of their sovereignty. Most of the time, the dispute simmers, and the boundary remains stable. They make demands, negotiate, fight, and reach accommodations every day. Who decides how to spend the family's income? Who controls the children? Which household tasks must the wife do, and which ones should the husband complete? The questions are endless. Most disputes take place along the boundary separating women's rights and duties from men's. In a traditional household, for example, a couple may argue about how much time the husband spends with their children on the weekend. This is a boundary dispute. They do not question if she or he should have major responsibility for the kids. That would be a war for dominance. As with nations, boundary disputes lead to significant shifts in the terrain women and men control only when the balance of power changes.

Still, this constant conflict between women and men was crucial to the modern decline of gender inequality. It made gender status highly responsive to changes in structural conditions. When any social changes affected either gender's bargaining power or goals, the constant struggle between the sexes translated changed conditions into shifts of social status.

The shift of power outside the household, into organizations with no distinct need or interest in preserving gender inequality, gradually altered the balance of power between the sexes. This allowed the boundary disputes to open into widespread conflict over gender status.

Agitation and collective action by women was particularly influential because it provided an active force to overcome the momentum of established patterns of inequality. The acceleration of women's movement into high-status jobs, upper-level political positions, and postgraduate education beginning in the 1960s owes much to the concerted effort of women vying for change.

A second type of conflict concerned the inconsistency between two sets of social structural imperatives, rather than two groups being at odds over conflicting interests. This conflict, which has been unfolding for 150 years or longer, concerns a rupture between the social conditions needed to sustain sex inequality and the structural conditions produced by social development. The industrial, market economy and the liberal, democratic political order have dominated social conditions in the United States. For male domination to persist, economic and political processes had to respect and bolster the boundaries between women's and men's roles. As modern organization advanced, the economic and political systems have absorbed, centralized, and magnified social power. They have rationalized relations of authority and have eradicated civil and social distinctions among ordinary people. The interests governing economic and political processes began to reward ignoring gender as a distinction in the formation of varied policies. These changes have slowly but unavoidably eroded the conditions that preserved men's advantages across generations.

Gender inequality declined because modern society transferred social power from people committed to preserving men's advantages to

institutions and people whose interests were indifferent to gender distinctions.[8] *Social power* concerns the capacity to control resources and people and to get things done. Modern economic and political structures shifted power from households into businesses and government organization. Such organizations had no inherent interest in gender inequality. Those who controlled economic and political power became increasingly ruled by those interests that perpetuated and profited the organization giving them power. While prejudices against women still ruled many actions of men with power, their institutional interests repeatedly prompted them to take actions incompatible with preserving gender inequality (often without any recognition that their actions would affect gender inequality). While most men clung to beliefs in male superiority, their individual efforts to restrict women declined as they benefited less from women's subordination and found it harder to hold women back. Lacking interests in gender inequality's persistence, the state and businesses withdrew their power from its defense, causing gender inequality to become disembedded from political inequality and economic inequality. As power and interests were reorganized, women found more and more opportunities to rebel successfully against the residual inequality, and with each improvement in women's status these opportunities increased further.

Unseen processes contributed as much to gender inequality's gradual collapse by eroding its foundations as did the overt pummeling by those seeking to knock it down. Political and economic developments favoring women did not often improve their status directly or simply. Instead, these developments changed the opportunities and interests of people (and organizations) in ways that led to improvements for women.

As opportunities opened and obstructions crumbled, women sought to better themselves, and by raising their aspirations and increasing their resources, their successes induced them to seek even more. Inequality invariably produces resistance and can endure only through continuous effort. Stable, large-scale structures of social inequality persist across generations only if they meet certain conditions. Pervasive, reliable mechanisms must transfer crucial resources exclusively to members of the advantaged group and restrain disadvantaged people's efforts to overcome the limits inequality places on their lives. When these social mechanisms that channel resources and restrain rebellion break down, as they did with gender, inequality becomes increasingly precarious.

Men pursuing their self-interests established the industrial-capitalist economy and the liberal-democratic political order. The men guiding these efforts wanted, above all else, to preserve and expand their economic and political power. These systems served those aims well. Over time these systems also followed an inherent logic of development and repeatedly demanded adaptations to the problems and needs exposed during their growth. Many of these adaptations meshed with existing gender inequality, but some did not. As these institutions' needs increasingly differed from the needs of gender inequality, their adaptations more often hindered gender inequality's persistence. Slowly but inexorably, these adjustments reduced the viability of women's subordination. The organized pursuit of economic and political inequality inadvertently created conditions favorable to gender equality.[9]

This book seeks to show both how and why gender inequality has declined, both to describe and to explain women's rising status. To achieve these goals we will examine and analyze these changes in detail from various vantage points. We will consider how the state extended greater legal and political rights to women; how women became assimilated into the economy; how individualism benefited women as it became institutionalized in education, ideas, and the family; how women have promoted (and sometimes opposed) their rising status; and how men (even as they clung to their advantages) have progressively conceded greater rights, opportunities, and status to women. Together, these analyses will develop what aims to be a general explanation of women's rising status.

CHAPTER TWO

CITIZENSHIP: GAINING EQUALITY FROM THE STATE

During the past 150 years, the state has done an about-face. Once, it stood guard over men's advantages; now it challenges the male advantages it once defended. Once, the state granted only men the right to participate in the political process and to act as independent members of civil society. Now the state not only treats women and men the same; it also actively demands that other institutions in society stop treating men better than women.

Since, until recently, men occupied most positions of political power, government actions diminishing gender inequality seem paradoxical. Men were in a position to obstruct any improvements in women's civil rights. They held most good jobs and most positions of economic power. Men were still dominant in most families. Men also held almost all police and military power. The state comprised only members of a dominant group, men, and that dominant group controlled all significant social institutions and resources. Such a state would seem unable to conceive or carry out policies favorable to a subordinate group and likely to diminish the control of the dominant group. Yet during the past 150 years the state repeatedly did grant women greater rights and statuses. These enhanced rights directly opposed male dominance as they substantially reduced the differences between women's and men's positions in society.

Government policies favorable to women's status developed in three overlapping phases. First, in the nineteenth century, state governments sought some basic, formal, legal equalities between the sexes. This occurred through changes in state laws and judicial interpretations that gradually gave married women independent control of inherited property. These changes also granted women control over any income they earned and gave them the right to make contracts. In the second phase, culminating during the Progressive Era, the state enacted formal political equality between the sexes by granting women the right to vote. In response, legislative attention to women's concerns increased, and a few women squeezed into political positions. Finally, in the third phase, the state loosely adopted the goal of formal economic and social equality. Since World War II, laws and court decisions have increasingly banned forms of discrimination that restricted women's economic and institutional opportunities. In recent years, women have risen to new prominence in political offices. During each phase, the state expanded the ways women and men received equal treatment under the law.

No consistent actor or interest was responsible for the overall trend toward legal and political equalization. Instead, the initiative behind the legal and political changes benefiting women sometimes emerged from within the state itself, sometimes from business interests, and sometimes from women's organizations. The progressive trend did not reflect the drift of popular opinion, nor was it the simple product of an enduring social division. Instead, the policy changes were sometimes uncontested and sometimes evoked great conflict. Equally, the trend did not simply mirror a direct shift in power from men to women. Women, as a group, found it difficult to accumulate power sufficient to force concessions from men.

Nor did these developments mean the government sought to make women and men truly equal. On the contrary, most men with political power wanted to preserve differences between the sexes. Here lies the crux of the intellectual and historical puzzle. Men have controlled the state, men with political power have seen the world through the lens of their dominant gender experiences, and they have largely devised state policies expecting to preserve the gender differences they valued and found familiar. Nonetheless, critical changes in state policies have gradually but unstoppably diminished men's advantages in law, in political participation, and in their treatment by organizations throughout society.

Theorists concerned with women's status have stressed the masculine-bias side of the paradox, largely viewing the state as an instrument that preserves inequality. Trying to understand how gender inequality works, feminist scholars have often stressed how the state bolsters male advantages. Differing in many details, such analyses commonly characterize the state as a masculine, patriarchal entity, inevitably expressing and defending male interests. Some suggest that the state cannot avoid seeing all issues through male eyes and masculine preferences, so that laws and government policies "constitute the social order in the interest of men as a gender," to use Catharine MacKinnon's succinct description.[1] The results have been evident in laws that granted men valuable rights denied to women, such as suffrage. The state also has sustained gender inequality through all programs that have given men preferred access to resources such as education. Less directly, the state has bolstered gender inequality through all the policies that reinforce the "traditional" sex-role division between women's childrearing and men's employment. Some suggest the state's support for conventional civil and political citizenship rights, even when formally gender neutral, sustain gender inequality because employment allows men much greater use of these rights. Some argue that women's rising political and legal status was illusory,[2] while others imply that the improvements are real but all attributable directly to women's political activity. All these theories agree on one point: the state served male power because the state belonged to men.

While these ideas have considerable merit, they fail to address the other side of the paradox. Over the past two centuries, the state has adopted policies and laws that have progressively enhanced women's status. True, laws and social policies have largely reflected the ongoing system of gender inequality. Equally true, most men controlling the government have explicitly chosen to favor male interests when legislative, judicial, or administrative issues have made gender interests salient. Notwithstanding these facts, the state has also made crucial choices that favored women. These choices have influenced historical trends more, even though they may have occurred much less often. The problem to understand is why and how the state would play this progressive role even when it was an institution largely adapted to sustaining gender inequality.

The seeming contradiction of a male-dominated state adopting policies benefiting women is not the only puzzling feature of women's rising political and legal status. If we compare different periods, places, or nations, it becomes clear that many different historical paths led to greater gender equality. Diverse, seemingly unrelated events with distinctive impinging causes have contributed to women's legal and political assimilation.

Thus, a second problem is to discover how a causal process could have given force and direction to men's legal and political concessions to women over the long run without deciding definitely when and how the changes would occur. Obviously, this question assumes that such a causal process exists, and some might deny that it does. The working assumption here is that women's legal and political status has improved in all modern societies, everywhere through similar reductions in differential treatment by the state, although the form and speed of change have varied greatly. This seems an unlikely pattern unless some common, persistent causal process is at work. Not surprisingly, no simple answer will work.

The key to the state policies that favored women's rising status rests in the multiplicity of interests and goals served by the state. When social theories discuss the state's role in directing history, they are usually referring to the state personnel who directly influence policy decisions. The modern state comprises all positions and organizations appointed, created, funded, and accountable to elected officials or to some other segment of the government.[3] Elected officials in legislative, administrative, or judicial posts and high-level bureaucrats in government organizations decide the state's agenda and strategies. Social circumstances and history constrain their actions, so that most manifest state goals are responses to the demands of the social environment, and most state strategies are adaptations to the limits of social, economic, and political conditions. Still, political processes such as elections, coalition building, and defining issues allow considerable room for unpredictable outcomes.

While many conditions have influenced the modern American state's policies, several general goals and concerns have dominated their historical development. The state has always defended the interests of the social strata with political influence, who directly or indirectly controlled entry to government office. Sometimes this oriented the state toward the small but well-heeled classes with money, capital, and managerial power. Sometimes the state was more concerned with the political impact of the less affluent but large classes that represented votes, such as workers. In both cases, the state represented group interests. While paying heed to the interest groups whose support controlled politicians' fates, the state has tried to keep society running smoothly by maintaining order and by preserving or creating the conditions needed for the effective functioning of other institutions. In its early days, the state focused on providing the external conditions needed for society to run: legality, public order, protecting the borders. Over time the state's responsibilities expanded to include creating and supporting an infrastructure (for example, roads, mail, education), fostering development (for example, opening new areas of the West), and managing crises. Simultaneously, the state has tried to protect itself and to expand its authority. Long-term officeholders found their personal interests bound to those of the state organization. These included lifelong politicians, many appointed officials (including the judiciary), and employed bureaucrats. They cared about the state's own fate, not just its effects. They also wanted to preserve their positions within the state.

In short, while men monopolized political power, government officials had to balance many goals and interests, some of which called for strategies inconsistent with gender inequality. Sometimes the state responded more to other interests, most importantly those of business, which could contradict those of male advantages. Sometimes state officials were more concerned with sustaining the society as a whole, for example, during wars and depressions. Sometimes politicians were more preoccupied with the state's stability and legitimacy, as when they abandoned some unpopular discriminatory practices. Sometimes, politicians were more worried about gaining or losing the support of female voters than of male voters.

The history of the major legal and political changes that eroded men's advantages suggests that three interwoven transitional processes were essential. Men's interests in preserving gender inequality declined. The state developed its own countervailing interests. Women gained increasing power to challenge the prevailing order. Together these transitional processes eroded the conditions necessary for preserving men's advantages. These transitions reflected the shift of social power into impersonal organizations dictated by the modern political and economic structures. Organizational interests gradually separated strategies preserving economic and political inequality from those needed to preserve gender inequality. This process assured that men's legal and political advantages would not survive intact, but it did not determine when or how they would fall to challenge and circumstance.

MARRIED WOMEN'S PROPERTY RIGHTS

In the nineteenth century the state made its first great concession to women by removing married women's legal "disabilities."[4] Formerly, marriage gave women a legal status similar to that of children, awarding the husband control over his wife's inheritance, property, and income. The burden of these restrictions varied with women's class position. Affluent women were more affected by property rights. Working-class women were more likely to suffer from a lack of control over their incomes.

By passing laws known as the Married Women's Property Acts, state legislatures gave married women the legal right to control property and income, to make contracts, and to take legal actions through the courts independently of their husbands. These laws gave married women formal legal equality with their husbands over a wide range of economic issues and reduced their legal dependence. In practice, women only gradually gained the rights promised by these laws over a period stretching well into the twentieth century. Still, the concession of these fundamental rights was a dramatic stage in the development of women's social status.

In the era of separate spheres, people and government contended with specifying legal debts, rationalizing law, and giving daughters inheritances because new economic forms had displaced preindustrial forms organized around tenancies in land. The capitalist market economy stressed transferable property and temporary contractual relations between individuals for employment and business. As Karl Marx so aptly assessed it in the middle of the nineteenth century, land and labor became commodities, to be bought and sold under prevailing market conditions. These conditions made anachronisms of feudal laws tying fictitious perpetual families to permanent tenancies or rights.

These legal barriers from the past conflicted with the realities of social life in the nineteenth century. Affluent fathers often wished to leave property to their daughters that their husbands could not touch. Working-class women who earned a wage were not likely to think of their earnings as their husbands' property. Creditors found fault with the old laws because they could complicate efforts to pry money from debtors. Businessmen were equally concerned that the old laws could make all family property vulnerable to creditors when a man's business failed. People had devised various routes around these laws to fit their real needs. Still, the old legal assumptions became progressively more burdensome and out of step with the capitalist economy.

It was in response to these issues that state legislatures gave women the right to control property and income independently of their husbands through the Married Women's Property Acts, which began to appear about the middle of the nineteenth century. The laws of the state of New York were representative. New York passed its first law in 1848 with the title "An act for the more effectual protection of the property of married women." It declared that "the real and personal property of any female who may . . . marry . . . shall continue her sole and separate property." Other acts, passed in 1860 and 1862, extended and clarified these rights, protecting married women's control over any property they inherited or income they earned, and giving them independent legal rights to make contracts, to sue, and to be sued.

Legislatures did not give women complete rights all at once. They repeatedly amended the new laws to expand the rights they granted women. The judiciary only gradually conceded ground to the new laws and social practices. The bond between husband and wife, compounded by women's general subordination and common deference to their husbands, also placed practical limits on women's use of these rights. Still, by the end of the nineteenth century women largely had legal control over their separate property and income.

This was a decisive break with the past, when the inferior political status of women reflected their legal and economic dependency. Men's political standing depended on their property holdings and legal relations to other property holders (for example, as tenants or retainers). The men who lacked property had legal and economic positions that resembled those characteristic of women, and they suffered similar exclusion from political processes and power.

The modern economic system clashed with these old practices. The new emphasis on transferable property, impermanent employment, and continuous reorganization focused on individuals, not on families. Just as modern corporations have a singular legal personality, when families were the essential units of economic organization, it was effective to focus all economic, political, and legal rights on the male head. As economic activity and power shifted into enterprises organized outside families, the old pattern became increasingly incompatible with the needs of the modern economy. In the United States, this contradiction became salient when the common-law provisions for marital property started to play havoc with commercial transactions. Debt was the primary issue.

The capitalist marketplace had changed people's views about debt. Eternal debt was once considered the unfortunate fate awaiting those driven into penury by misfortune or misdeed. Now, however, commercial transactions used debt so often, they made it an ordinary part of business. As a result of periodic recessions in capitalist economies, irredeemable indebtedness threatened all businessmen. This problem led to bankruptcy laws to protect debtors from ruin.

Women's legal disabilities did not fit debt's new role in commerce. The common law exposed women's property to creditors in circumstances that seemed unfair. For example, the law could forfeit a wife's inheritance to her husband's business failure. Conversely, it sometimes shielded indebted people's property from valid creditors by tying it up in trusts for women. The legislation enhancing married women's rights was not about women's rights. Instead, it concerned men's exposure to creditors and creditors' access to legitimate restitution. It sought to preserve a man's property gained through his wife from economic catastrophe, much as bankruptcy laws might protect his home from being sold to pay his debts.[5] Litigation referring to the marital property reform laws in New York showed this predominantly commercial interest. In the fifty years after the laws' passage, most litigation invoking the married women's property acts concerned debtor-creditor relations, not husband-wife disputes. The spokesmen for commerce had condemned the common-law doctrine that stripped wives of legal independence because it muddied the legal obligations for debt. Women's social status did not concern them.

In this period, broader legal reforms also affected marital property. A widespread movement aimed its sights at *feudal* common law. Its spokesmen argued for rationalized, commercial law dictated by the legislature rather than by the courts.[6] In 1836 the New York legislature abolished the trusts that people had been using to give property to daughters on the grounds that "by introducing two classes of rights over same lands, governed by different rules, and subject to different jurisdictions . . . they rendered titles perplexed and obscure, and multiplied litigation."[7] The movement to rationalize law derived its idealistic rhetoric from the American Revolution. Commercial interests prompted the movement's practical motives. The reformers' critique of marital property attracted special attention from the middle classes.

The common-law disposition of marital property hindered middle-class parents who wanted to give their daughters some assets. Because their wealth was not in land, the rising commercial middle class had less interest in keeping family capital intact. Because wives could not keep separate control over their property under the common law, affluent families used trusts to transfer property to daughters. In simple terms, equity law allowed families to set up trusts for daughters. A trust granted legal title to a male trustee and an equitable title to the daughter. The terms of the trust defined her rights. These could include full rights to use and dispose of the property as she wished. The chancery court enforced the trustee's obligations. This artifice became annoyingly cumbersome as more people used it. When the movement to reform property laws abolished the legal devices that families had used to keep estates in the hands of one son, even more women inherited property. In 1846 reformers in New York abolished the state's Court of Chancery as they merged common and equity law. Thus, people were using the device of equity to transfer property to daughters at an increasing rate while the procedure's legal status became ever more ambiguous. The Married Women's Property Acts ended this discord between middle-class needs and the law. With a right to hold property separate from their husbands, daughters could inherit freely. The overuse of equity stopped.

Coincidentally, social conditions supported new beliefs favoring greater rights for women. Yet in the early debates over the changing laws few voiced concern for women's rights. The general ideal of natural rights associated with the American Revolution seemed to be the most radical idea most could tolerate. Still, ideas about women's rights had begun to win notoriety. Most people knew about the movement to educate women. When the first marital property acts were passed, at midcentury, few legislators seem to have known much about the nascent feminist movement. However, politically active women's claims for greater rights were well known in the following decades when married women's property rights were being solidified. Both movements' ideologies challenged married women's legal disabilities under the common law. Legislators found it hard to devise convincing reasons to explain why ideals of natural rights did not apply to women. These new ideas about women's rights appeared in the legislative debates. They defined one side of the discussion in the news media. While practical concerns motivated most efforts to change the law, new conceptions of women's rights probably helped to dampen opposition.

Apparently, legislators found that women's common-law status was an old-fashioned cog that disrupted the legal machinery of the modern economy. Legislators abandoned women's complete legal dependency on husbands because it had the wrong form, not because such dependency was unjust.[8] They found that the common-law definition of marital property increasingly hindered social and economic progress.[9] It burdened debtor-creditor relations; it hindered women's new role as wage laborer; it was inconsistent with rationalizing the law; it encumbered parents' efforts to leave property to daughters; and it contradicted the state's ideology of republican liberty. By coincidence, the needs of the economic and political order served women's interests.

In the period of separate spheres spanning the middle of the nineteenth century, the major legal changes that benefited women fell to them as had the apple to Newton, propelled by forces they might discern but could not influence. The law served economic interests. Married women's legal disabilities did not. The law also tried to regulate and smooth the workings of kinship that extended into public life. The economic reorganization of family life conflicted with common-law property rights. No reasons remained to enforce women's legal disabilities other than a simple wish to preserve male dominance and a fear of change. These concerns slowed the legislation granting married women property rights and delayed their full application, but could not halt them.

WOMEN'S FORMAL POLITICAL EQUALITY

Suffrage was the second outstanding legal and political change affecting women. Women gained suffrage rights after a struggle lasting more than a half-century. *How* women got the vote contrasts dramatically with the process that gave women the Married Women's Property Acts. Women received property rights from the state as a kind of institutional largesse. For the vote, they organized and agitated against the state until they had won. Yet, despite the contrasting transition processes, the reasons *why* women's rights expanded had some important similarities.

In the United States, the struggle over woman suffrage spanned seven decades, from the Civil War through World War I. It nominally began in 1848, when those attending the Seneca Falls Convention demanded the vote for women. It ended in 1920, when the U.S. constitutional amendment for woman suffrage was finally ratified.[10] What started as a small band of progressive thinkers grew to a massive popular movement. The suffrage movement won women the vote after many years of agitation—lecturing, lobbying, meeting, distributing leaflets, and demonstrating in the streets. Many women fought long and sacrificed greatly for this movement. The movement, as much as its success, was an extraordinary accomplishment.

To understand their achievement fully, we must uncover what made this widespread movement possible and why it succeeded. Women had suffered political marginality for centuries. Why did their political status become such a salient issue during this period? What led so many to fight so long? And why did the state respond favorably to their demands?

Suffrage was a volatile issue in the nineteenth century, not only for women, but also for men without property, naturalized citizens, and members of minorities. In Europe, the suffrage for working-class men remained a hotly fought issue throughout the century. In the United States, working-class men received voting rights in the early nineteenth century, when most men without property were the young or old dependents of a kinsman who did have property. The permanent working class was a small minority in a nation dominated by farmers and small businessmen. In 1870 the suffrage was extended further when black American men gained the formal right to vote through the Fifteenth Amendment (although discriminatory practices and laws effectively barred most blacks from voting for almost a century). Giving the vote to working-class men removed the greatest direct impediment to woman suffrage. Men in power would not have considered giving the vote to women before working-class men. To do so would have seemed self-destructive to them, gaining nothing while inviting their own deposition. Full male suffrage was a precondition for considering woman suffrage. Because these events were recent, when woman suffrage became a topic for public debate, the right to vote was a much livelier and more ambiguous issue than today. (For many years, it probably aroused feelings similar to those voiced today when people debate the desirability of treating female and male soldiers exactly the same.)

The U.S. Congress debated and voted on woman suffrage repeatedly, starting in 1866, when the Senate considered removing the word *male* from the District of Columbia franchise bill (nine "yes" votes, thirty-seven "no" votes, six absent), and ending in 1919, when the constitutional amendment granting suffrage finally got the two-thirds majority needed to pass both chambers. All state constitutions had always restricted voting rights to men,[11] but the U.S. Constitution had no explicit distinctions referring to sex until the Fourteenth Amendment. While guaranteeing equal protection under law to all citizens, this amendment, a Civil War strategy, explicitly protected only *male* voting rights. This restrictive language did not reveal a rising dedication to male dominance. Instead, it showed that congressmen, for the first time, could not take men's dominance for granted. The question of women's status had become too salient. Congress could not continue to avoid the issue by assuming that women's exclusion and inferiority were obvious and universally accepted. As soon as the first mention of the word *male* as part of the Fourteenth Amendment appeared in the press, in September 1865, Susan B. Anthony and others began a barrage of petitions and visits to congressmen, ensuring that the issue was obvious to all.[12] The 1866 debate in the Senate on women's suffrage in the District of Columbia foreshadowed later debates right up to the Civil Rights Act of 1964, as the opponents of extending suffrage to the black population strategically championed woman suffrage and the supporters of extending suffrage, including the reputed supporters of woman suffrage, strategically opposed woman suffrage as an impediment to the more important goal of rights for the former slaves. Soon after that, in 1868, sympathetic legislators introduced the first general woman suffrage amendment into Congress. Two decades later, in 1887, Congress voted directly on a national woman suffrage amendment for the first time. (It lost, thirty-one to sixteen, in the Senate.) For the next three decades, every session of Congress held hearings on woman suffrage. These hearings acquired some ritual tones, as members of Congress and suffrage activists met every two years, with the participants only slightly changed, to exchange the same information and views. Still, they kept Congress well informed about the progress of woman suffrage and the woman suffrage movement across the nation.

Meanwhile, men expanded women's right to vote at the municipal and state levels. During the half-century conflict over woman suffrage, over fifty popular state referenda and several hundred state legislature votes considered the issue.[13] In 1890 Wyoming became the first state in which women enjoyed full suffrage. In 1869, while still a territory, Wyoming had granted women the right to vote by simple legislative action. It now sought to become a full member of the United States. After long debate and several sharply contested votes, Congress allowed it to retain the vote for women when it became a state. In 1893 Colorado became the first state where women won full suffrage through a popular vote (of men). After 1910, the intensity of national debate rose steadily. Before the Nineteenth Amendment won ratification in 1920, thirteen states, just over a quarter of the total, had given women suffrage through similar referenda passed by male voters. In another quarter of the states, the state legislatures had granted women the vote in presidential elections. This strategy emerged in 1913, when the Illinois legislature, one year after a popular vote had denied women general suffrage, became the first to grant women the presidential vote directly. After this strategy withstood judicial challenge, other state legislatures copied it, usually after a male popular vote had refused to confirm a woman suffrage amendment passed by the legislature. In local governments, men also extended varied municipal and special election voting rights to women.

The legislative response to woman suffrage and the response of ordinary male voters represented parallel processes. Moral passions and practical considerations each exercised influence. Both weighed the reasons for resisting suffrage against the reasons for supporting it. Woman suffrage, however, did not affect all men's interests similarly. Ultimately, woman suffrage was more a pragmatic issue for male politicians and a symbolic issue for ordinary men.

Men in government and men occupying influential positions in political parties or interest groups had significant, practical, political interests in the outcome of the suffrage issue. They recognized that suffrage gives a group a collective impact on politics that can be consequential. Yet, for ordinary people, mass democracy usually reduced the experience of voting to a symbolic act and suffrage to a symbolic issue. Ordinary men, the male electorate, thus responded to woman suffrage largely as an issue concerning their symbolic interests.

Suffrage does not really give power to individuals. It gives power to groups. The corporate character of electoral power distinguishes suffrage from the extension of legal rights that preceded it and the expansion of economic rights that followed it. For individuals, suffrage is a symbolic right and voting is a symbolic act. Only those who influence the actions of many others, for example by campaigning, personally affect the outcome of a popular ballot. As individuals, we vote to reinforce our identity as a member of the polity and to express our solidarity with others who share our assessment of the issues.[14]

With this understanding, we can separate two issues surrounding woman suffrage. First, the total impact of women's voting was a real political issue. If women were to vote differently from men, they could change the balance of political power. Second, woman suffrage was a symbolic issue concerning personal politics about gender status and the family. Voting symbolically affirmed citizenship and allegiance with like-thinking segments of the population. Symbolically, woman suffrage promised ordinary women an independent public identity comparable to that of ordinary men.

The possible political effects of woman suffrage were more salient to legislators than to ordinary men. An elected official saw his personal interests directly influenced by changing the electorate. Would it help or hinder him and his party at the polls? These concerns did not make legislators immune to the symbolic implications of the suffrage issue. Still, even as he considered the moral arguments for and against woman suffrage, the legislator was likely to think more about his constituents' biases than about his personal beliefs. Concern about such questions prompted legislators to consider, directly and selfconsciously, the predictable, short-term political effects of woman suffrage.

Ordinary men's votes were more likely to stress the symbolic aspects of the suffrage issue. A vote on suffrage was not an action that aimed directly to defend or change the conditions of a man's own life. By voting on suffrage, a man testified, mainly to himself, how he thought his world should look. His interests entered this symbolic calculus, because the predictable effect of woman suffrage was to raise women's status and affirm their individual rights.

Between the calculating interests of politicians and the symbolic beliefs of ordinary men, special-interest groups occupied a middle ground. The leaders of special interests resembled politicians because they responded to the real effects of supporting or opposing woman suffrage. Yet the crucial effects on an interest group often depended on the symbolic fit between the goal of woman suffrage and the special interests that created the group identity. When, for example, a union leadership or a church hierarchy considered its response to woman suffrage, the key issue was often how the group membership would respond to the symbolic implications of support or opposition.

These complex considerations produced diverse positions among interest groups. Southerners opposed woman suffrage because it clashed with their commitment to deny blacks the vote.[15] The liquor industry opposed woman suffrage because women were strongly associated with the temperance movement.[16] As acceptance grew near, eastern business interests opposed woman suffrage because they believed women would support further reforms to restrict economic power and protect labor. Yet xenophobes sometimes supported woman suffrage as a protection against immigrants (apparently believing that female immigrants were few or unlikely to vote). And settled men in the Western states sometimes supported woman suffrage to limit the influence of transient, wage-earning single men. A report presented at the 1907 national convention of the National American Woman Suffrage Association affirmed that in addition to the American Federation of Labor:

> Other important organizations which gave official endorsement within the year are the World's Woman's Christian Temperance Union, National Purity Conference, National Free Baptist Woman's Missionary Society, Spiritualists of the United States and Canada, Ladies of the Modern Maccabees, International Brotherhood of Bookbinders, International Brotherhood of Teamsters, Patrons of Husbandry, National Grange, and the United Mine Workers of America [and] fourteen other national organizations.[17]

In short, certain groups spied real or symbolic advantages for themselves in supporting woman suffrage. When this happened, support of woman suffrage could become part of a group's identity. This positioning of a group would prompt men in it to vote for suffrage to maintain their symbolic ties to the group.

Thus, when we ask why men came to concede the vote to women, we must distinguish several kinds of interests that came into play. For most ordinary men, giving the vote to women was a symbolic issue. Their understanding of the symbolic issue and their position on it had complex origins. They reflected the prevailing popular beliefs about manhood, women, and equality. They also represented men's real experiences of gender relations. For politicians, pragmatic concerns drove symbolic issues into the background whenever outcomes with the potential for substantial political effects became a real possibility. Similarly, those who led interest groups wanted to know if a position on woman suffrage could effect either their groups' interests or their political position within the interest group. They were prone to revise their interpretations of the symbolic politics to fit their current perception of interests.

Both the outcomes of state referenda on woman suffrage and the history of public commentary show that ordinary men moved steadily toward greater acceptance over time. Woman suffrage received considerable support among men right from the start. In the few referenda that took place before 1890, about one-third of the men voting supported woman suffrage. Thereafter the state referenda found support for woman suffrage from between two-fifths and two-thirds of the men voting. When referenda were repeated in states where they had failed, the number of men voting for woman suffrage averaged an increase of nearly 10 percent (although the support did decline in about one-quarter of the repeated referenda).[18]

Ordinary men's reaction to woman suffrage seemed ambivalent and confused over the entire history of the issue. Part of this confusion seems to have come from the obscuring overlap between gender and class inequality. Voting rights for women could be understood in two different ways. Men might emphasize their shared interests with women in their lives, or they might emphasize their competing interests. Men could see woman suffrage as an attack on role differentiation and masculine privileges within their families. Or they could see woman suffrage as extending the ability of the women and men sharing their class (or ethnic) position to act in common both with and against government. (Male unions that supported woman suffrage obviously opted for this second interpretation.) True, some men may have feared that the collective political impact of women might result in laws contrary to their interests. Certainly, this was the point of view that the liquor interests tried to stir up when they campaigned against woman suffrage. The perception that the Women's Christian Temperance Union was an organized effort of women aimed at controlling men's behavior bolstered these charges. Still, the main sources of ordinary male resistance were likely to come from vague fears. Suffrage would not give women any resources or rights that affected their relationships with their husbands. Yet some men suspected that woman suffrage augured further changes in men's and women's place in life that would turn out to be bad for men. That such changes were taking place was undeniable. (See Figure 2.1.)

The key to reducing ordinary men's resistance to woman suffrage was, therefore, not a moral conversion nor a show of force, but a practical demonstration of its limited implications. Experiments with woman suffrage showed ordinary men that women voting had little impact on people's personal lives, just as they showed politicians that they need not fear practical political costs. Women first won the vote locally. Innovative experiments occurred where special local conditions had undercut the reasons for denying women the vote and precipitating events created opportunities for woman suffrage to emerge.[19] Many states gave women votes only on special issues, particularly school taxes and school boards. By the early 1890s, at least twenty states allowed women to vote on schooling-related issues, with varied conditions. Occasionally the voting rights applied only to women who paid taxes.[20] Sometimes legislation gave women full voting rights for all local elections but not at the state level. A Kansas

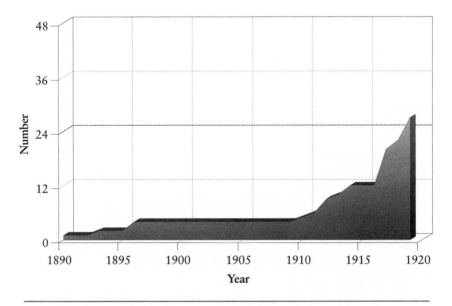

Figure 2.1. States in which women have the presidential vote, 1890–1919

experiment that gave women the municipal vote in 1887 was the most closely watched, but women got similar rights in varied places. The 1889 Senate Report from the Committee on Woman Suffrage listed twenty-two states and territories in which women had partial suffrage rights.[21] When a region granted women the vote, its political representatives at higher levels found their interests clearly aligned with supporting woman suffrage. The congressmen and high elected officials of states and territories with woman suffrage stood out. As early as 1871, for example, Governor John A. Campbell of Wyoming Territory was quoted as saying, "women have voted in the Territory, served on juries and held office. It is simple justice to say that the women . . . have conducted themselves in every respect with as much tact, sound judgment and good sense as men."[22]

A significant minority of male legislators supported woman suffrage from the beginning, and their numbers grew over time. In 1866, the first time that Congress considered woman suffrage, one-fifth of the senators present voted to allow women to vote in the District of Columbia. Deciding another aspect of women's acceptance by the state, during 1878–79 both chambers of Congress approved, by a two-to-one margin, women's appearing as lawyers before the Supreme Court. In 1882 the Select Committee on Woman Suffrage recommended passage of the woman suffrage amendment, remarking: "To deny to one-half of the citizens of the republic all participation in framing the laws by which they are to be governed, simply on account of their sex, is political despotism to those who are excluded, and 'taxation without representation' to such of them as have property liable to taxation."[23] In 1887 one-third of the U.S. senators who voted supported the woman suffrage amendment to the Constitution. In 1890 both the Senate and the House had long fights about woman suffrage in Wyoming. They debated whether the territory could retain woman suffrage when it became a state, because it would then become the first state in which women had full voting rights. Ultimately a majority in both chambers voted to accept the state's women as voters.[24]

By the time Congress passed the suffrage amendment, many of its members had simple self-interested reasons to support suffrage. Through experiment and emulation, suffrage rights for women had spread and accumulated. Men had already given women full voting rights in one-quarter of the states, the right to vote on the nation's president in half the states, and diverse special or local voting rights.

Many others seemed poised to grant women the vote. Politicians had to consider the possibility that female voters could ruin their future if they opposed suffrage.

The limited experiments with woman suffrage decisively influenced legislators by reducing their concerns about what women would do with the vote. In earlier debates over woman suffrage, legislators expressed fears about the effects of women's votes. Over time, legislators pointed more often to the results of woman suffrage experiments that showed these fears were groundless. During a congressional debate in 1915, Representative Adolph Sabath from Illinois offered this argument to sway his colleagues to accept woman suffrage: "a great many Democrats questioned the wisdom of [giving women suffrage in Illinois, but] the majority of the women demonstrated their appreciation and remained loyal to the Democratic Party which secured for them this privilege."[25]

The first places granting women suffrage—western states and some midwestern and eastern localities—saw themselves as pioneers. We cannot say with much certainty what distinguished these places. The common thread seems to have been circumstances that reduced resistance based on fear. One of these circumstances was the smaller number of women in many of these localities (especially in the West), which meant that their combined vote would carry less weight.[26] Newer political institutions also encountered less resistance from entrenched political interests. Areas in which women had become more active in public through employment, charitable work, or local cultural activities seem to have been more likely to experiment. Granting partial suffrage by limiting women to special issues or to municipal votes also restricted how much damage they could cause. To a significant degree, historical contingencies, independent of the long-term processes improving women's status, promoted experiments with women's suffrage. Local political issues and strategies sometimes made woman suffrage a viable issue.

Politicians soon realized that after it was enacted, an extension of the franchise was almost impossible to reverse. Often, some political maneuver undid an effort to give women the vote *before* it became final. A high court would declare legislative acts unconstitutional, or a governor would veto them. Once women had the vote and started using it, however, it became politically implausible to turn the clock back. It took strong support among men to give women the vote. To have taken it back, the sentiment among men would have had to reverse itself, *and* the recently enfranchised women would have had to accept the loss of their new rights. These were unlikely developments and in practice did not happen.[27] Realistically, the experiments that gave women the vote were almost assured of permanence.

With time, legislators and ordinary people increasingly viewed woman suffrage as inevitable. The woman suffrage movement played a crucial role. Its never-ending campaigns for the vote outlasted all belief that the issue would die. What died instead were its opponents. As some jurisdictions gave women the vote, the direction of change became more evident. The more inescapable woman suffrage seemed, the less willing legislators were to risk becoming martyred crusaders for opposing it. By 1910 most legislators outside the South seemed to accept that woman suffrage was inevitable.

The suffrage movement planted and nurtured the seeds that grew into women's voting rights. Women's suffrage grew in social soil fertilized by a long-expanding franchise in a climate favorable to social reform. With fertile soil and a good climate, in time something will always grow. Still, only careful cultivation guarantees a good harvest when it is needed. The suffrage movement began its work when the political climate was still harsh and the state unyielding. Replicating the experience of the groups who won the franchise before them, social changes had already given women—especially those in the middle classes—more personal liberty, legal status closer to equality, and more education. By the time the climate grew moderate, they had cleared much of the worst prejudice from popular opinions and refined their agitation techniques so that they could bring women's voting rights to bloom. Without their efforts, woman suffrage might have had to wait much longer. Still, without a promising climate, no one would have tilled the soil and nothing would have ever grown.

The question remains, why did the state ultimately assent to the demand for woman suffrage? Male legislators and male voters *granted* suffrage. They were not forced to make this concession. Undoubtedly, the suffrage movement's agitation was a nuisance to men running government. The rhetoric and activity of the suffrage proponents also must have irritated many ordinary men. Yet, if becoming a nuisance was enough to win claims from dominant groups, inequality between classes, status groups, and races would have disappeared long ago.

Declining male opposition was a key to the eventual success of woman suffrage. Resistance to woman suffrage was a complex mix of symbolic antagonism and political anxiety. These motives were played against a backdrop of rapidly changing social conditions.

Looking back from today's perspective, we might mistakenly infer that the state consistently fought to keep the vote from women. In reality, the state did not have to do anything to keep the vote from women. Or, to be more precise, the state did not have to act unless women agitating for suffrage could threaten the government's power or men (in or out of government) showed strong support for giving women the vote. Only men were in government, and only men could vote (at least initially). The issue before the state was not how to keep the vote away from women but whether (or when) to give it to them. Until legislators had strong reasons for giving women the vote, however, they needed only weak reasons to sidestep the issue.

The franchise was a constitutional issue, requiring a high level of support to win (at both the state and national levels). As only men had voting rights, this required a high level of acceptance by men. To give women the franchise, most states needed a two-thirds majority in both chambers of the state legislature and a majority popular vote. Similarly, the federal amendment needed a two-thirds majority in both houses of Congress, then affirmation by three-quarters of the state legislatures. Usually, then, substantial acceptance by men was not enough. Only overwhelming support could give women the vote. Often, even when woman suffrage suffered defeat in legislative votes or popular referenda, considerable male support was present.

The state's graceless resistance to granting woman suffrage should not lead us to infer that it had some substantial, integral reasons for its actions. A few legislators may have envisioned themselves as Knights, with fealty sworn to Men, fighting back the infidels, agreeing with U.S. Senator Garrett Davis of Kentucky, who stated in 1866: "The great God who created all the races and in every race gave to man woman, never intended that woman should take part in national government among any people." Most, however, seem to have approached the issue with less commitment and more pragmatism, spiced with odd mixtures of prejudice and confusion.

Once working-class men had received the vote, men's interests concerning woman suffrage shifted. The middle-class men who held sway in government found the inclusion of middle-class women politically less threatening than admitting working-class men. In the reforming atmosphere of Progressive politics, women even seemed a possible stabilizing force. Ordinary men's growing acceptance of woman suffrage, shown in state referenda on the issue, suggests that they did not experience voting as a resource for preserving gender advantages.

The earlier process extending legal rights to women through the Married Women's Property Acts and the process granting them suffrage had some similar underlying causes, although their outward appearance differed markedly. Suffrage repaired women's political disabilities, which did not fit the emerging social order, just as the property acts repaired women's legal disabilities that were no longer functional. The electoral government concentrated and rationalized authority as did the market economy. Each could tolerate, even reinforce, other existing systems of inequality, but this tolerance broke down if it proved too costly. Accordingly, the state abandoned women's common-law legal disabilities because they interfered with commerce and middle-class inheritance, and it conceded the vote to women because the modern political process took away both the reason and the means to keep women out.

However, economic and political progress did not create direct institutional interests in giving women the vote comparable to the interests that favored extending property rights to women. The economic and legal system *needed* women to have property rights like those of men. So it created them. Or, to be more accurate, the system needs created strong interests in change among people with political influence. In contrast, these systems had no direct need for women to participate through voting. They did not create strong interests in extending the franchise among those with power. Yet these institutions also had no need to deny women the franchise. At first many politicians did resist woman suffrage. But to a large degree this resistance reflected their prejudices, not their real interests. They initially feared that woman suffrage threatened their political interests. Experience showed, however, that this was not the case, and their opposition shriveled. Moreover, many found that they actually had interests in defending woman suffrage. As members of the state, they could benefit from the assimilation of women, who would then cease being a source of disorder and become a new potential source of support for contending political parties.

Still, because the economy had no interest in woman suffrage and the state had only marginal interests, change largely awaited political agitation that could convince politicians they would benefit (although some western states and some localities that first granted woman suffrage apparently did so with little or no agitation from women). In the face of this agitation, the state gradually abandoned women's political exclusion, finding that it had no interest in preserving men's suffrage monopoly, but it did have an interest in reducing social disorder, increasing state legitimacy, and incorporating potential political rivalries.

THE LEGAL PROSCRIPTION OF DISCRIMINATION

Government actions opposing sex discrimination have produced a third major legal transformation of women's status since World War II. Legislation, judicial decisions, and executive actions combined to create a series of policies that aimed to stop discrimination against women. These policies demanded that organizations treat women and men the same under most circumstances. They applied to hiring, promoting, educating, giving services, granting divorce, judging credit eligibility, or engaging in other activities where impersonal standards seem appropriate. Previously, bureaucratic rationality and competitive opportunism had gradually induced employers and other organizations to apply more impersonal standards. These new state policies dictated that organizations must rapidly adopt impartial procedures. The rules applied to most arenas outside the family, excepting some limited domains that could somehow justify their exclusion.

Before this, most laws aimed specifically at women tried to give them *special protection*. Shielding women from the worst rigors of jobs, aiding mothers, and guarding wives against irresponsible husbands were some goals that gained legislative and judicial support. These policies did not try to reduce the difficulties facing women's efforts to get ahead. Instead, they tried to ameliorate some unavoidable ill effects that modern societies visited on women.[28]

The policies erected against sex discrimination, however reluctantly granted, constituted a much different response by the state. By opposing institutional resistance to women's assimilation, they placed the forces of the state (or, to be precise, some of these forces some of the time) directly on women's side. Through antidiscrimination legislation, the state has eased and speeded women's assimilation by the economy. From the perspective of gender inequality, the state, though controlled entirely by men, again helped women to overcome a primary source of male gender advantage. Apparently, a conjunction of related conditions prompted the state actions proscribing discriminatory policies by organizations throughout society. The popular opposition to treating women equally in economic and political life had lost its pervasiveness and force. Women's economic assimilation had gone so far that neither employers nor the state could successfully ignore the issue. Sex discrimination by employers and institutions produced conflict, sparked disorder, and squandered resources without giving much in return. The state's actions acknowledged and completed women's advancing assimilation. Although women did not vote markedly differently from men, politicians competing for support had to consider the possible impact of their actions on the female electorate and the women who had penetrated political life. Feminist protest activity, when it occurred, highlighted all the other conditions while adding its own threats of disorder and bad publicity.

During the first half of the twentieth century, federal policies emphasized benign neglect, broken by hesitant efforts to help women when wartime production needed their labor (for example, the War Labor Board authorized equal wages for female workers in 1942).[29] During the 1960s and 1970s, policy accelerated quickly. It first defended equal pay for the same job; it then added legal remedies to punish and inhibit discrimination; it soon adopted active requirements that employers help women through affirmative action plans.

By the mid-1960s women's endeavors in arenas outside the home had extended considerably beyond that of earlier periods, more than most people realize even today. In 1964, when Lyndon Johnson was elected president, before feminist and women's liberation movements appeared, women composed more than one-third of the labor force, more than two-fifths of graduating college students, and cast almost half the votes for president. Even when their husbands were in the upper half of the male income distribution, about one-third of married women had jobs. The men who conceded the need to require equal pay for women were facing a different economic and social environment from their forebears.

The Equal Pay Act of 1963 nominally initiated the series of modern government policies prohibiting discrimination against women. The Equal Pay Act declared that "no employer . . . shall discriminate . . . between employees on the basis of sex."[30] It aimed to end the most direct, flagrant pay inequities suffered by women. It has special importance both because it laid the groundwork for women's inclusion in the Civil Rights Act and because it preceded the rise of modern feminism.

National equal pay legislation has a history in the United States reaching back to World War I. As part of the war effort in 1918, the railroads were ordered that "when they do the same class of work as men," women's pay "shall be the same as that of men."[31] The war did not have much affect on sex segregation, so most women still worked as office clerks, and wage equalization had limited impact.[32] Shortly after the war, Montana and Michigan became the first states to pass equal pay laws. Then the issue seemed to slumber.[33]

World War II brought another surge to the equal pay efforts as women joined the war production effort. Unions enrolled women and negotiated for equal pay, because they did not want their male members' wages placed in jeopardy from the competition. Unions in the United States have always favored equal pay for any group that began to threaten the jobs of their members, despite earlier disregard or disdain. The more women who held jobs, the more male unions supported equal pay. The National War Labor Board supported equal pay while resolving disputes. It also allowed employers to increase wages without the board's approval if their goal was to equalize men's and women's rates. They wanted labor to be productive and stable. Equal pay seemed a sensible support for these goals. Discriminatory pay rates commonly seemed a short-sighted effort on the part of some employers to get higher profits.

The effort to gain a national equal pay statute reflected a classic political standoff. The bill's long path to acceptance by Congress, largely unseen by the public, stretched from the end of World War II to its passage in 1963.[34] On one side was the resolute but politically weak support for the equal pay bill. The Women's Bureau, a federal agency, continuously advocated the measure, acting as the voice of women who had risen in labor, business, and politics. These women and their supporters had the advantage of absolute commitment. No matter how many setbacks they suffered, they did not give up. Still, appeals to reason and carefully nurtured, fragile political alliances were long their main resources. Against them stood a politically potent but strategically irresolute opposition. Organized employers opposed an equal pay statute, but without vigor. Only smaller firms with many female employees acted particularly concerned. Between these two sides, organized labor vacillated from support to opposition to support. With neither enough support to pass it nor enough opposition to kill it, Congress kept the bill in limbo for two decades.

While Congress held equal pay legislation in purgatory, states paved the way for its acceptance. In the two decades between World War II and the passage of the Federal Equal Pay Act, states steadily adopted equal pay laws. Between 1942 and 1962, the number of states that prohibited employers from paying women less than men rose from two to twenty-two, as shown in Figure 2.2.[35] Thus, the national equal pay law marked the culmination of a pattern of state lawmaking that had already succeeded in almost half the states. In this and other respects, the history of equal pay legislation resembles a low-key version of the woman suffrage legislation.

The effects of both the national and the state laws seem to have been more symbolic than practical. Most employers hired women for different jobs than men. While the laws generally prohibited employers from paying men and women differently if their jobs were similar, they said nothing about employers arbitrarily using women and men

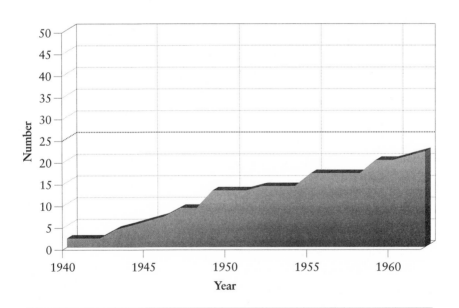

Figure 2.2. States with equal pay laws, 1940–1962

for different jobs. As a result of extensive job segregation by sex, the laws therefore applied only to a minority of jobs. Still, the laws' passage recognized women's permanent, large role in the economy and gauged the declining opposition to women's full economic assimilation. If more powerful laws had not soon followed, the equal pay laws might have acquired greater significance in the give and take of judicial interpretation.

If the Equal Pay Act was more symbolic than practical, its symbolism was potent. The Equal Pay Act declared it was not legitimate to treat women and men differently solely on the basis of sex. This was a fundamental alteration of the accepted rules governing actions within the economy. As it was, equal pay laws set the stage for conflicts over hiring and promotion discrimination. By forcing employers to pay women the same as they paid men holding the same job, it focused women's efforts on getting access to *men's* jobs.

Against this backdrop, the Civil Rights Act of 1964 became a vehicle for modernizing forces to shove aside some prejudiced debris of past discrimination. Women were added late to Title VII of the Civil Rights Act, which outlawed employment discrimination.[36] Title VII declared it "an unlawful employment practice" for employers on the basis of sex (or other social characteristics)

> (1) to fail . . . to hire . . . or otherwise to discriminate against any individual with respect to his compensation, terms, conditions or privileges of employment . . . or (2) limit, segregate, or classify his employees in any way which would . . . tend to deprive any individual of employment opportunities or otherwise adversely affect his status as an employee.[37]

Although the impetus behind the Civil Rights Act did not aim to aid women, their inclusion was symptomatic and consequential. Women's addition to the bill smacked of historical coincidence, having started, in part, as a conservative strategy to use ridicule against federal assistance to blacks.[38] They tried to make the bill *more* liberal so that it would become unpalatable to legislators in the middle of the political spectrum. Competing interpretations have disagreed about what motivated various participants in this convoluted process, but the initial political motives are not really crucial. Ultimately, women would not have stayed in the final bill unless a significant portion of Congress supported it. More important, without favorable conditions, women's inclusion in the bill would not have had the remarkable effects that followed.

The Civil Rights Act proved a deft strategy, even if unintended, for allowing the state to challenge discrimination while sidestepping direct political conflict. The act established an abstract ideal that was usually easy to defend, but it also pushed the discrimination issue into the administrative and judiciary branches. The act gave oversight to a bureaucratic body, the Equal Employment Opportunity Commission (EEOC). At first the EEOC did not consider sex discrimination a priority. However, the act gave private citizens the power to complain to the commission and to sue discriminating employers. These new rights allowed working women to take the initiative. In 1966 the EEOC's continued reluctance to condemn and pursue sex discrimination brought influential professional and business women (and some supportive men) together in the National Organization for Women (NOW). They led the legal and political assault on the commission. Political action, including demonstrations and electoral threats, made the EEOC more responsive. Legal suits forced the judiciary to decide what employment practices were legal, practical, or fair. Employees, professional groups, feminist organizations, and unions filed complaints and legal suits in all directions. Title VII of the Civil Rights Act offered women a sword of justice to use against discrimination. They picked it up and starting swinging.

Two conditions enabled the Civil Rights Act to become an influential weapon against sex discrimination. First, many women had the dedicated careers, good education, and organizing capacity that let them launch discrimination suits and become a visible political threat. Second, the judiciary, largely shielded from base concerns with political jostling, could and did choose to carry through the implications of women's economic assimilation.

Continued lobbying and protests by women's groups convinced the administration of President Lyndon Johnson that more was to be gained than lost by giving some visible support. Johnson had added teeth to the employment discrimination clauses of the Civil Rights Act by issuing an executive order (having the force of law) compelling all government agencies and contractors to take affirmative actions to end discrimination. When first issued in 1965, this order applied only to racial and religious discrimination. In 1967, after two years of prodding by women's groups, the president pursued political expediency and expanded the order to include sex. During the same years, NOW had repeatedly chastised the EEOC for failing to rule against discriminatory job advertising. After the president revised his executive order on affirmative action to include women, NOW vigorously assailed the commission, balancing public demonstrations with legal maneuvers. A suit filed by NOW in U.S. district court won judicial support for compelling the EEOC to fulfill its duties. As a result, the commission finally barred the expression of sex preferences in job advertising.[39]

After policies against employment discrimination embraced the principle that sex discrimination was unacceptable, political parties and politicians sought to ensure their standing by supporting further legislation. The resulting laws expanded the drive against inequality beyond employment, banning sex discrimination in other institutional spheres. In 1972 Title IX of the Education Amendments Act prohibited sex discrimination by an educational institution receiving federal government aid. This act placed most colleges and universities in jeopardy, and hundreds found themselves called to court on the issue. Other laws sought equal treatment for women by banks, credit agencies, police, landlords, and housing agencies. All of this legislation built on and elaborated the Civil Rights Act. It emphasized ending unequal treatment of women outside the family. Discriminatory actions that were once accepted prerogatives of employers and others with organizational authority have become illegal and risky. As a result, much of the direct, overt discrimination that was once commonplace has disappeared.

During the 1970s the judiciary reinforced legislative and executive strategies by adopting a suspicious attitude toward formerly acceptable laws and practices that discriminated by sex, although judges' decisions showed their usual resistance to sudden change.[40] To be realistic, the judiciary is primarily a conservative force in American society. It is meant to be. Precedent has great weight in judicial action because the legitimacy of law depends on consistent and predictable interpretation. Yet the judiciary sometimes seems to take a special part in allowing some social changes to occur. This possibility always exists because judicial interpretations must consider the practical demands of social life as well as the history of legislation and judicial precedent.

While most judicial decisions generated by sex-discrimination disputes were not bold or innovative, they affirmed that discrimination had become illegal and would be punished. The courts ruled against many employers and institutions who resisted suits and challenged the new laws. By reinterpreting old laws and precedents, the courts also improved women's treatment through case law. The U.S. Supreme

Court's 1973 ruling on abortion in *Roe v. Wade* has received the greatest public attention. In other cases, the Supreme Court used the equal protection clause of the Fourteenth Amendment to argue that laws could not treat the sexes differently without some reasonable and substantial grounds.[41] Usually, differential treatment was ruled acceptable only if shown necessary to achieve the goal of an otherwise legitimate law. While this position still allowed some unequal treatment, it substantially departed from the past by rejecting laws that arbitrarily treated the sexes differently.

One other crucial condition eased the introduction of policies against sex discrimination. No powerful groups nor large population segments adamantly opposed women's economic assimilation.[42] Opposition existed, but it was not potent. Some employers grumbled about government intervention and higher wages. Many ideologically conservative groups, especially religious organizations, bemoaned the disappearing "traditional" family. Some male occupations whined about losing their masculine preserves. And the usual voices that raise dire predictions when faced with change, warned of a dark future. Yet similar complaints have accompanied most social changes, including such varied events as the adoption of the motor car and the introduction of income taxes. Every significant social change causes some people discomfort even if it benefits the majority, provoking some to voice irritation and others to resist the change. The resulting social friction produces some political heat and may slow the momentum of change, but it usually does not divert it.

Notably, no group mounted a significant effort to repeal or undo government policies against sex discrimination. The depth of resistance to change is often hard to measure. Here, our best indicator may be the rapid accommodation. Universities and professional schools dismantled the barriers to women in a rush. Large corporations adopted equal pay, hiring, and promotion policies without enthusiasm, but they resisted only occasionally and halfheartedly.

One study highly critical of affirmative action, called *Invisible Victims,* describes what happened clearly, if unenthusiastically.

> Corporate and political elites appear to have yielded with minimal resistance to quotas imposed by judges or federal agencies. More than that: corporations and government agencies have initiated their own affirmative action quota procedures . . .
>
> A fusion of economic and bureaucratic interests can be seen in the contemporary acceptance of affirmative action procedures.[43]

Affirmative action policies were extraordinary in that they went beyond establishing a formal right to equal treatment. They dictated standards and practices intended to force employers actively to remedy past discrimination. While these policies may have fallen well short of imposing equal opportunity, they did prompt significant changes in hiring and promotion practices. Although the state was explicitly treating the sexes (and races) differently through affirmative action policies, these policies were consistent with the long-term trend toward reducing sex differentials. As applied to women, affirmative action laws were a temporary strategy to reduce discrimination by organizations other than the government. Although affirmative action laws distinguished by sex, they specifically sought to reduce differential (discriminatory) treatment by sex.

The backlash against affirmative action programs in recent years might seem to raise questions about the acceptance of equal opportunity. On a closer look, this pessimistic interpretation seems unwarranted. While many people have become disgruntled with the perception that women and minorities sometimes get unfair preferential treatment, opinion polls show that most people still believe that the government should ensure that such people get fair treatment.[44] Even the strongest opponents of affirmative action are generally careful to declare their support for outlawing discrimination. Thus California's Proposition 209, which asked voters to end affirmative action in 1996, did so by embracing the proscription of discrimination. From a long-term historical perspective, having conservative forces emphatically backing a direct and unambiguous law against discrimination represents a much more important change than opposition to affirmative action, always understood to be a transitional policy.

When affirmative action policies first emerged, the rejection of discrimination had not yet become a consensual value in the United States, but politicians were beginning to view sex-discrimination policy as just another issue demanding calculated political strategy, signaling considerable change in the political environment. Fifty years earlier, few politicians would have contemplated policies against sex discrimination in these terms. By the 1960s, conditions had changed.

When proposed new policies faced neither powerful opposition nor massive support, the state could treat issues affecting women's assimilation as ordinary business. As the state adopted and broadened policies against sex discrimination, neither moral fervor nor political desperation dictated its actions. Activists dedicated to moral renewal had not grasped state power. Women's advocates had not routed state officials or sent politicians scurrying for places to hide. Instead, sex discrimination had become one among many national issues that called for politicians to calculate the implications of alternative strategies. What economic effects would a policy have? What interest groups might shift their votes or support in response to a politician's position on the issue? What implications did the issue have for the ever-shifting coalitions among politicians?

Often state actors were more concerned with a proposed policy's potential effects on institutions than with women's rights. Policies seeking to reduce sex discrimination can be thought of as remedies for social injustice. They also can be considered as correctives to an incomplete application of bureaucratic rationality. From the viewpoint of organizational needs, applying the same rules to all people simplifies administration while reducing discord. Women trying to gain rights and opportunities that men already have interpret their goal as a search for *equity*. From the state's perspective, the goal is essentially one of *administrative rationality*.[45]

A look at changes that took place in factories earlier in this century may clarify this perspective. In the nineteenth century, foremen in production plants commonly had the power to hire, punish, and fire at will. As growing firms introduced an organizational hierarchy to administer their operations, the foreman's powers dwindled. He had to conform to rules denying him discretion. Hiring and firing decisions became management's prerogative, usually administered by a personnel office. The foreman lost most of his power to inflict punishments on workers. Foremen, too, were workers. Managers did not want to give them too much freedom. They could harm production or create costly conflicts with workers. The threat increased as workers' capacity for collective rebellion grew. Firms responded by introducing rule-governed standards of equity to guide workers' treatment. These standards diluted foremen's authority and diminished their discretion. Although the managers had much more sympathy and shared interests with the foremen, they found foremen's unregulated exercise of authority too costly.

From the state's managerial perspective, institutions discriminating against women sometimes have resembled foremen mishandling workers. When discriminatory organizations could arbitrarily decide, for example, who would get financial credit or how to spend educational money, they gave the state problems similar to those that foremen gave large firms. The modern state—enormous, remote, and bureaucratic—has had little to gain from preserving the right of employers, businesses, schools, government bureaucrats, the police, or others to discriminate against women. Letting organizations have this power created conflict and disorder. The vast machinery of the state and economy then worked less efficiently and less smoothly. Congressional committees that have invited representative feminists to testify have usually turned the issues into technical, administrative ones.[46] They did not invite the witnesses to question the state's goals or to supply moral education. They only admitted that the feminists might possess experience, knowledge, and skills that could help them devise effective strategies to reach their legislative goals.

Like the restrictions managers placed on foremen, the restrictions that the state placed on organizational discrimination were responses to a mixture of pressures from above and below. The history of corporations shows that they sometimes took the initiative in curbing foremen's power. They often did this to reduce functional organizational difficulties they associated with such conditions as size and distance. Corporations imposed other restrictions to defend against actions by organized labor. Similarly, although feminist protest began the process that yielded some government policies opposing discrimination, the state also launched some of its beneficial actions independently. This combination of initiatives from both above and below reflected the underlying causes promoting change.

State officials repeatedly found that unregulated, often irrational, discrimination was more trouble than it was worth. Just as businesses found it expedient to protect workers from foremen, government found it expedient to protect women from discriminatory organizations. This motive helps to explain why men in government sometimes knowingly supported policies that favored women; they sometimes gave this support although they could have opposed the policies without fear of political reprisals. Examples include the legislators who passed the Equal Pay Act of 1963 and judges who accorded legitimacy to women bringing discrimination suits. For example, the Equal Pay Act of 1963 explicitly argues that "wage differentials based on sex" lower wages, prevent optimal use of labor resources, induce labor disputes, obstruct commerce, and allow unfair competition by firms.

Under wartime conditions, the state laid motives bare when it explicitly opposed discrimination; it wanted to maximize production and minimize disruption. The federal government's first direct actions against employment discrimination occurred during World War I. These policies were repeated on a larger scale during World War II. Straightforward goals motivated these early (temporary) efforts to restrict some forms of employment discrimination. The state had an overwhelming interest in having women employed and reducing industrial strife during a war effort. To protect this interest, it prohibited employers from discriminating in ways that undermined these policies. In part, when the government launched policies against sex discrimination in the 1960s and 1970s, it was making a peacetime extension of the wartime policies. Facing similar, if less extreme, conditions, the government applied the same reasoning.

For the state, discrimination had become a more worrying practical problem because of accumulated changes in women's circumstances. Women had an increasing capacity to challenge discrimination and to hurt the political interests of those in power. Thus, policies opposed to discrimination arose from complementary forces. Because women were playing a much greater role in the economy, state officials gave women's treatment more consideration when they sought to create a dependable, productive, smooth-running economy. Because economic activity enabled more organized political activity by women, politicians also became more reluctant to risk political backlash from angry women.

Concessions to women's interests by the government and by male politicians also reflect women's rising political assimilation, made possible by the changes in the two earlier periods which gave women formal legal and political equality. By the third historical phase, women began to exhibit a new, more extensive political status. The more that women function as political actors, the more responsive the state becomes. Women's role in political and governmental activities has grown notably. Between 1960 and 1988 women's representation in the major party presidential nominating conventions rose sharply. Women went from 11 percent to 52 percent of Democratic delegates and from 15 percent to 37 percent of Republican delegates.[47] By adopting sex quotas for convention delegates, the major parties created a quasi-legal device to increase women's manifest political equality. Women's share of congressional seats has increased more slowly, going from twelve elected to the House in 1970 to fifty-one in 1996; a record nine women held Senate seats in 1996. Still, women's vote has become a major concern for national-level politicians in the last decade. And, of course, in 1984 for the first time a major party had a female candidate for the office of vice-president.

Women's presence in state and local government also grew significantly. Within a few years after gaining full formal electoral equality with men through the Nineteenth Amendment in 1920, women gained about 150 seats in state legislatures. They stayed at that level until World War II. Their numbers grew slowly through the 1940s and 1950s to around 350, then stopped rising during the 1960s. Since then, women's presence in state legislatures has grown markedly, reaching 1,539 in 1996, or about 21 percent of the total legislative seats.[48] Women also won more positions in local government. In cities with a population over 30,000, female mayors jumped from 1 percent to 17 percent between 1971 and 1991; by 1989 they made up 10.5 percent of the mayors in all municipalities over 2,500, numbering 731.[49] By 1989 women were also the chief financial officers for about one-half of the county boards and one-third of the cities in the United States.[50] Women have become mayors of major cities such as Chicago and San Francisco.

Although women are still a small minority in government posts, their political visibility has grown considerably in recent decades. Women have been experiencing a progressive assimilation into the political process similar to their assimilation into the occupational hierarchy. Women's rising political activism played an important role in the state's adoption of policies against discrimination. As women became more politically organized, few politicians wanted to invite women's opposition unnecessarily. By the late 1960s the public protests of feminist groups—marches, sit-ins, demonstrations—gained considerable attention from the news media. They made women's rights a salient political and public issue.

How much women's political activism influenced outcomes is difficult to judge. Some important government actions against discrimination, such as the Equal Pay Act of 1963, preceded the rise of modern feminism. Realistically, women's organization and campaign for rights were not threatening to state power and, through the 1970s, rarely were threatening to politicians' reelection chances (the "gender gap" in voting became a bigger issue in later years, but by then the male-dominated state had already made its major moves against sex discrimination).

People often attribute the policies against discriminations to political protests and changing popular beliefs. According to the simplest idea, and perhaps the most popular, women secured bargaining power through their collective protests. Because of women's political agitation, male-dominated government had little choice to do other than concede their claims. By the end of the 1980s this view of history had become widespread enough that the mass media often presented it as proven fact, as in these examples from *U.S. News & World Report* and *Time.*

> [T]he feminism of the '60s . . . toppled barriers to equality in employment while raising the consciousness even of those who were not politically active.[51]
>
> [F]eminism is a victim of its own resounding achievements. Its triumphs—in getting women into the workplace, in elevating their status in society and in shattering the "feminine mystique" that defined female success only in terms of being a wife and a mother—have rendered it obsolete . . . in its original form.[52]

Notwithstanding their importance, however, the effectiveness of feminism and popular beliefs depended on how strongly the modern state was committed to preserving male prerogatives. Modern feminism has unquestionably been an exceptional social movement, and popular ideas about women's roles have certainly changed dramatically.[53] Still, if the state had been committed to preserving men's ascendancy, feminist protest and changing beliefs about women in the 1960s and 1970s would have been inadequate to produce a turnabout in government policies. Similarly, no one seriously claims that American men began the 1960s fully committed to male dominance, then abandoned their biases to support egalitarian policies because they found feminist rhetoric irresistibly persuasive.

A study of efforts to gain laws benefiting women's interests suggests that a congruence between favorable state disposition, general public acceptance, and feminist agitation was key. Interestingly, its authors, Joyce Gelb and Marian Palley, had hoped to show a different result. They identify and compare several apparently outstanding feminist successes (the Equal Credit Opportunity Act of 1974, the Pregnancy Disability Act of 1978, Title IX of the Education Amendment of 1972) and several defeats (the Equal Rights Amendment, the Comprehensive

Child Development Act of 1971, and the Hyde Amendments restricting government funds for abortions and the like). Initially, they contend that "feminists can claim primary credit for a series of successes in the adoption and implementation of policies." But, they soon have to qualify this assessment. Feminists have had some remarkable successes. Yet the research found these successes limited to issues that "extend rights now enjoyed by other groups . . . to women and which appear to be relatively delineated or narrow in their implications, permitting policy makers to seek advantage with feminist groups and voters with little cost or controversy."[54] According to Gelb and Palley, the successes and failures followed a pattern that suggests several preconditions to success.[55] The issue must have broad support among the public and among pressure groups. The issue must be narrowly defined and incremental so that it does not arouse opposition or divide its supporters. The feminist supporters must show that they legitimately represent significant interests. And they must seem ready to compromise and work within the system's rules.

These prerequisites suggest that bids to change policies in favor of women prevailed only when the goals already had wide backing and avoided any serious challenge to the prevailing system of gender relations. In the successful campaigns, feminists mainly supplied information, offered rational arguments, and made restrained pleas. They stressed general norms of equity independent of gender inequality or feminist theory. Feminists won measures consistent with the direction of policy development within the state. Indeed, Congress passed the Equal Pay Act of 1963 and the Civil Rights Act of 1964, two of the most important legislative innovations benefiting women, before modern feminism began to organize.

Apparently the state was willing to oppose gender discrimination because it served no important interests that concerned the political process. Most of the opposition to antidiscrimination laws was motivated by prejudice against women and change, but a prejudice that was no longer joined to any significant interests. Some employers and occupational groups in special niches still profited from women's disadvantages. Yet so many women were already employed that continued discrimination against them had little economic value for businesses. So many middle-class men had wives or daughters pursuing careers that continued support for employment discrimination was often domestically risky. By the 1960s women were able and willing to organize politically in support of antidiscriminatory legislation. Their organizational efforts both created political interests in support of their cause and aroused a worrisome level of disorder through agitation. Thus, from the state's perspective, most discrimination against women had become a source of unrest, economic irrationality, and potential political damage with no counterbalancing interests to defend it.

Laws barring discrimination against women recognized and smoothed women's assimilation into the economy and other organizational settings. This transition was already under way, but these laws helped it proceed faster with less upheaval. The state's actions created an environment in which all organizations could start to absorb women into better positions. Organizations avoided the need for each to endure a long process in which they slowly responded to women's frustrated campaigns. The organizations were also largely sheltered from resistance by male employees.

THE POLITICAL AND LEGAL ASSIMILATION OF WOMEN

Several decades ago the British sociologist T. H. Marshall advanced a now famous proposition about the state in his innovative essay "Citizenship and Social Class." Liberal democracies, he argued, expand equality through citizenship. He proposed that the government protects economic inequality by offsetting it with citizenship rights. Marshall concerned himself with working-class men. His ideas, however, also fit the improvements in women's legal and political status surprisingly well.

Using England as his primary example, Marshall argued that liberal capitalist societies had broadened the status of citizenship (as applied to free, adult males) in three phases. These phases followed each other, roughly, in successive centuries. In the eighteenth century, the government gave working-class men formal legal equality—all men would be equal before the law. In the nineteenth century, the state extended to all men the rights to vote and to hold political office. In the twentieth century, the state assembled a patchwork of social rights to make what we now call the welfare state. The welfare state guaranteed all citizens varied social goods, sometimes called entitlements, such as education, unemployment insurance, and old-age security. Marshall considered these three enhancements of working-men's rights to be distinctive aspects of modern citizenship: civil (or legal) citizenship, political citizenship, and social citizenship.

These three phases of expanding citizenship that Marshall distinguished for working-class men resemble the sequence of improvements in women's legal and political status. In the United States, the state first acted to diminish married women's legal disabilities in the *era of separate spheres.* It removed formal political disabilities by granting women the right to vote in the *era of egalitarian illusions.* In the recent *era of assimilation,* the state forcefully combatted women's economic and social disabilities with policies against sex discrimination. The most important state actions advancing women's status broadened their citizenship.

Modern states have grown powerful by extending citizenship. These rights tied people directly to the political order. They impeded private political power exercised and sustained through ties of personal dependency. While the state embraced political inequality by extending its power over all, it eroded political distinctions among its citizens. Each phase in citizenship's growth built up new rights from many policy decisions responsive to varied state aims. In time, these rights coalesced. Initially the state purged legal inequities to fit the legal apparatus to modern commerce, to get legislative control over the judicial system, and to rationalize state bureaucracies' operations. Then, by extending suffrage the state increased its legitimacy, diminished social unrest, and disarmed hungry rising groups (by absorbing their leadership potential). While creating the welfare state, the government smoothed over the social disorder created as traditional social supports fell victim to progress. The government also diffused class conflict, enhanced its legitimacy, and increased its authority.

Over the past two centuries, state activity in the United States has developed in a comprehensible way. At first the nation's government most closely resembled a simple instrumental state representing narrow, dominant interests. Anglo-Saxon men with at least moderate property held all the power and controlled a small state apparatus. Today the government more closely resembles an executive state: autonomous, institutional, facing diversified flexible interests. The polity contains disparate groups, with complicated, overlapping interests. The state is huge and cumbersome. It often can defy powerful social groups more easily than it can discover effective strategies to reach a public goal. During the long transition from the early mechanistic state to the late executive state, the Progressive Era reforms self-consciously tried to create a trustee state. As the range of competing interests became more diverse, an anxious, declining, old middle class and a confident, ambitious, new middle class tried to shield state activities from the grip of either capitalist or working-class interests. Although the reformers' claims for a disinterested state may have been an ideological ploy, this period did create a significantly more autonomous and active state.[56]

The changing character of state activities helps to show how and why gender inequality became disembedded from the state, which represented political and legal inequality. The state expanded women's citizenship status as it incrementally disengaged from the system of gender inequality. Like working-class men, women first received legal citizenship, then political citizenship, and then civil or social citizenship. During the mid-nineteenth century, in the era of separate spheres, the state gave married women the right to own property independently. It also granted women the right to their income if anyone should agree to employ them. And it awarded to women the right to make contracts if anyone wished to join them in a contract. No one had any obligation to offer these opportunities to women. Still, these legal changes gave some women the opportunity to take jobs and enter commerce.

The suffrage legislation during the era of egalitarian illusions gave women the capacity to vote. It did not force political parties to promote women or oblige government to respect women's needs. Still, with the vote, women could influence elections and prompt the state to adjust policy more to their interests.

In the modern era of assimilation, laws against discrimination demand that opportunities and rewards be equally available to women. These laws apply to jobs and other services or positions provided by organizations. Even if equal opportunity is fully realized, laws against discrimination do not assure women they will have achievements or social positions equal to men's. Still, it prevents men and institutions from using flagrant discriminatory processes to thwart greater equality.

During each period of change, women's legal and political status transformed in ways that increased the formal equality between the sexes. Formal equality exists when governing rules or laws say or imply that groups will receive the same treatment. This condition differs from manifest equality, which occurs when groups experience the same benefits or restrictions from the law. The difference between formal and manifest inequality is important but often misunderstood. Manifest equality falls short of formal equality when the law's guardians neglect its dictates or when the law allows people with social advantages more access to its promises than it allows others. The additions to women's formal legal equality did not immediately secure them an equal increase in manifest equality. The expansion of formal equality at each stage, however, did make manifest equality increasingly plausible and probable.

Critics sometimes have questioned the importance of the legal and political assimilation of women. They have stressed that the changes in women's formal rights did not produce a rapid, dramatic change in most women's manifest status. Such criticisms have slighted the long-term practical value of legal and political rights. These rights expanded the opportunities for women and improved their bargaining positions, both individually and collectively. With each generation, more women could use these opportunities. As more women exercised these rights to become active members of the polity and market economy, women achieved a better position to gain further concessions.

Thus, over the past 150 years, the state gradually changed laws and policies to give women the right to take part in the economy and government, without ever guaranteeing them equal property, jobs, or political influence. Through these changes, the state shifted the weight of its intervention away from resistance to women's advance, tipping the scales toward supporting women's efforts to expand their opportunities and achievements.

Women's rights improved in phases that resembled the stages of citizenship rights that T. H. Marshall first identified for working-class men. This similarity seems to have resulted from two reinforcing patterns: interaction between the expansion of male and female citizenship and a parallel logic of development. In part, the rights granted men during each phase in the history of male citizenship diffused to women. Certainly, the progress of citizenship rights for working-class men influenced what rights were at issue for women. When the state granted a right to working-class men, it became salient to social critics, legislators, and women activists. Feminist ideology repeatedly strove to give middle-class women rights equal to or greater than those enjoyed by working-class men. Feminist claims stressed property and education in the mid-nineteenth century, then voting rights, and recently economic and social rights. Yet it also seems that the historical sequence of legal and political claims shows some integral relationship among the rights, leading one to another. It seems unlikely that any group could successfully claim political rights without first having legal equality. Similarly, a group's quest to protect its economic status seems much more hopeful if the group already has favorable legal and political statuses. If the citizenship rights that emerge in each phase become plausible only after people have the rights gained in the earlier phases, then a group will not get the rights in any other order without some special circumstances. Because of this inherent relationship between stages, groups usually will get citizenship rights through a similar sequence, even if the historical process giving one group expanded citizenship rights does not directly affect the process through which other groups get similar rights. This integral logic does seem to explain the sequence in which working-class men's citizenship grew. For women, the logic of the sequence was reinforced because men's earlier successes served as signposts that directed efforts to improve women's social status.

When viewed from a detached historical perspective, through its repeated extension of citizenship rights, the American state has sustained a remarkably progressive long-term record of changes affecting women's status. Over the past 150 years, it has gradually diminished the differences in its treatment of the sexes. Despite this progressive trend, the state only occasionally favored women in its policy decisions. The state commonly seemed a committed institutional defender of male privilege, because it was persistently reluctant to adopt egalitarian policies. Most legislation in each period conformed to existing expectations about women's status and rights. State decisions and policies unquestioningly assumed and accepted male dominance because it was so pervasive. Under these conditions, state officials adapted their policies to gender inequality as unthinkingly as they adapted them to human mortality or the climate. State policies reflected a routine conformity to the commonplace, a simple acceptance of ordinary differences between women and men. Usually, government officials' commitment to male dominance was irrelevant. Most did believe that conventional sex roles were appropriate, and would defend them if sex roles became a salient issue. State influence on sex roles and women's status rarely became an issue, however, unless feminist agitation challenged it. Otherwise, state support for prevailing sex roles was so ordinary that state officials and the public rarely even recognized it.

While the state's usual acceptance of sex inequality was unexceptional, the state's contribution to sex inequality's decline was truly remarkable. Realistically, we should be surprised that state actions advanced women's interests. The pervasiveness of male dominance made it implausible that the state would repeatedly reduce women's legal and political disadvantages. Yet over the long term the state granted women legal equality, political equality, and a guarantee of equal treatment by other institutions. Indeed, in each period the state made some of its early policy concessions to women while facing little or no organized effort for women's causes. Examples of this pattern included the early Married Women's Property Acts, the first states to give women the vote, and the initial antidiscrimination legislation of the 1960s. By adopting policies favoring gender equality, the state seemingly contradicted the reasonable expectation that a state will always protect the interests of dominant groups.

In fact, increasing male indifference was a primary cause of the state's willingness to alter women's legal and political status. Each significant improvement in women's rights did of course have to overcome resistance from men. But, if weighed against the possibility of a truly adamant opposition, male resistance at each stage was notably weak. When nineteenth-century state legislatures passed laws enlarging married women's legal rights, no male backlash occurred. During the half-century that women sustained the suffrage movement they were frustrated by groundless forebodings, political intransigence, and plain pigheadedness. Calculated resistance to their goals was uncommon, however. When women's suffrage rights appeared on state ballots, a significant and progressively increasing proportion of men voted favorably. Modern feminist demands met considerable derision from journalists and politicians. Nonetheless, laws and policies prohibiting discrimination against women did not prompt defenders of male interests to offer substantial resistance or even notable protest. Since the middle of the twentieth century, men answering opinion polls have consistently shown almost as much support for government policies treating women equally as have women.

When equalizing policies did incite serious opposition, the opponents were more likely to focus on safeguarding the family or market-place freedom than on stopping the spread of gender equality. Opposition linked to these goals was almost as likely to attract women as men.

While perhaps only a few men enthusiastically greeted all the changes that improved women's status, progressively fewer men faced significant real threats to their interests from these changes. Without such interests, male opposition depended on prejudice and custom. As men's interests ceased to be at issue, they, particularly powerful men, became increasingly indifferent to changes enhancing women's status. This gave the state and other institutions the freedom to reap benefits from supporting women's assimilation without fearing reprisals.

Over time, state officials were subject to fewer potential costs if new policies reduced gender inequality. They were shielded by the remoteness of the state, the obscurity of the issues, and the tentativeness of ordinary men's opposition to new policies. The state, like economic organization, was becoming increasingly remote from the system of gender inequality. This separation governed the history of legal and political concessions to women. In each case, the government had become remote enough from gender inequality that conceding the right to women had no direct implications for the structure or functioning of the state. Moreover, most decisions were about incremental changes in formal rights. As few of these policy decisions clearly implied a significant loss for men, politicians could adopt the changes without straining their commitments to male advantages. When a policy seemed more significant, as in the case of suffrage, the transition was more difficult, but led to the same end.

State interests recognized gender inequality as a fact, not a goal (although state officials' prejudices against women often belied this distinction). Most of the time, the state assumed men's dominance but did not display a committed interest in preserving it. State policies adapted to preexisting inequality may have retarded progress toward equality (this is difficult to judge), but the state took few actions *aimed* at preventing women's rising status.

Changes in the organization of the state seem to have reduced its unquestioned commitment to male interests or to the interests of any specific group. Gender inequality did not serve the institutional interests of the state. Beyond their personal prejudices, politicians' interests in preserving women's inferior status derived largely from fears of political costs that they or their party might suffer from disenchanted men. Policies and laws diminishing gender distinctions adapted state actions to emergent state interests. They reflected the organizational concentration of political power. As status inequality became disembedded from positional inequality, the prejudices that had governed decisions supporting gender inequality gave way to the practical calculations of political interest and problem solving. Once passed, legislation and policies improving women's circumstances were highly resistant to retreat.

With time, politicians had to consider the potential political costs of opposing improvements for women. Initially, while the polity excluded women, their political response was irrelevant. After women's assimilation had gone far enough to draw them into the political process in significant numbers, considerations changed. To the degree that women's political behavior seemed distinctive from that of men, politicians had to consider the possible costs of alienating women.

As the dominant pattern of state activity changed, so did the critical interests leading the state to enact polices favoring women, a disadvantaged group. Over the long run, the state's actions affecting women's status have gone from serving business, to impartial balancing of competing claims, to strategic advocacy for greater equality. During the era of separate spheres, a largely instrumental state gave women property rights because the classes controlling commerce decided this legal rationalization served their interests. During the era of egalitarian illusions, a struggling trustee state increased the state's independence from industrial class conflict by giving women political rights while it also reduced disorder and stabilized existing social patterns. During the era of assimilation, a relatively autonomous, institutional state adopted policies against sex discrimination that increased state legitimacy and gained political advantages from an active women's movement.

Class interests permeate the state policy transformations that benefited women. In each of the three phases, middle-class women benefited more than working-class or poor women. In each phase, middle-class women gained a class privilege. The Married Women's Property Acts allowed middle-class women the rights to own property and to form contracts already held by working-class men. Women's suffrage gave middle-class women (along with other women) the right to vote that working-class men had gained in the first half of the nineteenth century. As applied to women, the antidiscrimination legislation of recent decades has assured women of middle-class origins that they can enter middle-class careers. They are not condemned to the same occupations as the offspring of the working classes.

These class interests received some voice in the political debates surrounding these issues in each period, but they were never the dominant justifications used. Although isolating the importance of class interest is difficult, it seems to have influenced both middle-class women's agitation for rights and middle-class men's willingness to concede those claims. Seemingly, middle-class men's shared class interest with middle-class women, reinforced by ties of kinship, was more important than middle-class men's shared gender interest with working-class men.

Others writing about the relationship between the state and gender inequality have largely depicted the state and the men who directed it as acting consistently to protect men's advantages. In this literature, women's legal and political gains appear as victories attributable to effective organization by women or expressions of a general moral shift.

In contrast, this analysis has stressed why and how a male dominated state has progressively conceded greater legal and political equality to women over the past 150 years. Women's agitation for more rights and more participation was an important ingredient to this process. Equally important, however, were the state's development of interests distinct from and sometimes inconsistent with those of men's gender interests and the general decline of men's interests in preserving women's exclusion from these rights.

Ultimately, the logic of modern state organization has simply proved inconsistent with the needs for maintaining gender inequality. Some crucial decisions were independent of women's efforts and some were concessions to women's campaigns. Whatever the precipitating events to specific changes, the state slowly but progressively withdrew from policies that treated the sexes differently. Eventually, the accumulation of these decisions disengaged the state from the preservation of gender inequality. Since women would require years to translate new rights into political power, those wielding power could grant concessions safely, knowing their own fate did not depend on the state's concessions. After the state had largely abandoned the principle of treating men and women differently and once women had become a significant political force, the state even began to root out gender discrimination in other institutions actively.

Because gender inequality was inherently inconsistent with the logic of the modern state's development, the state repeatedly resolved policy issues in ways that favored women's status. Most men running the state were prejudiced against women and did not wish to diminish men's advantages. Yet few had such a great commitment to gender inequality that they would risk serious damage to the state, the economy, or their political status in order to defend male dominance. Each time the state improved women's rights, it was responding to other changes that were already under way, changes beyond the state's control. The state's response was partially an effort to guide and complete these externally driven events. The state repeatedly found itself caught in a whirlwind of social change that it did not initiate, often could not understand, but could not ignore.

Changes in state policies toward women ground forward like a rusty gear linked with a ratchet. Each twist forward might take time and effort, but once it happened the ratchet engaged the new position. The gear would not slip back.

Robert JACKSON 1998. Destined For Equality

HARVARD U. Press

CHAPTER THREE

EMPLOYMENT: GAINING EQUALITY FROM THE ECONOMY

For more than a century, the proportion of women earning a wage has increased with every decade. Furthermore, the proportionate increase in the number of employed women has exceeded the proportionate increase of employed men for every decade at least since 1870. This extraordinarily consistent record of growth exemplifies a powerful tide of change, swelling slowly until it builds up force, then breaking forth with great power.[1]

The juxtaposition between men's economic power and women's rising economic status seems paradoxical. Men have held virtually all control over businesses, have run schools at all levels, have controlled inheritable wealth, and have largely dominated families. Men's superior status—in the modern family and in modern society at large—has been predicated on a clear role division between the sexes. Men have held jobs and made money. Women have stayed home and raised children. Everyone, it seems, has understood that female deference to men, men's control over the family, and men's advantages in the economy were predicated on this role division. Yet women's part in the modern economy has risen steadily over the last century and ultimately uniformly across classes.

Not surprisingly, in their varied roles men have impeded women from gaining an equal stand in the economy. Employers refused women good jobs or high wages, male workers resisted women entering their occupations, husbands obstructed wives who sought jobs or careers, and fathers undermined aspiring daughters.

Nonetheless, over time, women's employment has changed from an occasional event experienced by a few to a typical, valued part of adult women's lives. One hundred fifty years ago, only some of the unmarried women from the working classes held jobs. Employers sought female workers only when they were compelled to hire cheap labor to turn a profit. People generally expected women to avoid employment, unless it was an inescapable necessity. In contrast, employers now hire women for almost all jobs. The majority of women have paying jobs. While economic need still drives many women (like men) to work, women without need also often choose to work because they want success and satisfaction.

Over the past 150 years, the employment pattern for women has changed in three ways that reduced the differences between women and men. First, the jobs open to women became more varied. Employers once hired women only for a small group of menial working-class occupations—temporary and low status. They later added low-status white-collar and marginal professional jobs. Today women work in almost every occupation and hold jobs from the lowest to the highest status. Second, the women who held jobs became more diverse. Employers first hired mainly single, working-class women. Over time, they became more flexible. Jobs became available for women with every possible marital status, childrearing status, and class background. And third, employers reduced the practice of treating women and men differently when they held the same jobs in a firm. In the past, employers paid women less than they did men holding the same job. They also gave the women far fewer opportunities to move into a better job. Now employers usually give women and men holding the same job the same pay and the same opportunities to move into better positions within the firm, although employers and others still discriminate indirectly.

While all agree that women's participation in the labor force has risen greatly over the last century, scholars still disagree about when, how, or why the economy incorporated women. Rising wages could have been decisive, slowly attracting women out of the household.[2] The economy's rising need for employees and a shortage of good alternatives to hiring women may have prompted employers to offer more jobs to women.[3] Women's growing freedom from domestic tasks may have increased the number of women free to take jobs while rising divorce may have impelled them to do so. Women's educational achievements may have made them increasingly valuable for certain kinds of jobs that became more common as the modern industrial economy developed.[4] Reduced discrimination, as exemplified by the removal of bars against women staying in jobs if they married,[5] is cited by most as a contributing factor. A general cultural acceptance of working women, often mentioned in popular accounts, probably played a role.

These disparate perspectives all have merit. Many specific, varied changes have induced women's economic assimilation. These obviously include women's actions: more women sought jobs, more women stayed in jobs, more women aspired to careers, more women gained education credentials, and more women competed for promotions. Perhaps more important, however, the transition also depended on substantial changes in men's actions: male employers sought more female workers, more husbands accepted wives' employment, male-controlled schools educated more women, more fathers (and mothers) supported daughters' educations, and male employees tolerated more women workers in their midst.

Each historical shift had its specific antecedent causes; each group's altered behavior stemmed from distinctive circumstances. The key to the long-term decline in economic inequality between the sexes, however, lies in the crucial, common causal processes that propelled the broad range of specific changes. This key has been hard to find.

Men's concession of economic opportunities to women has been decentralized and discontinuous, often appearing to be the fortuitous juxtaposition of mutually reinforcing but seemingly independent events. Events have not pushed other events in a linear fashion. Economic and political transitions have, however, driven these events in a consistent, highly deterministic but loosely coupled manner. Behind the sundry motives, identities, and circumstances that constitute the complex history of women's economic assimilation exists a continuous, consistent social process. The progressive differentiation of economic activity from familial endeavors and the migration of economic power into large, specialized organizations destined the obstacles to women's economic activity for extinction.

Modern economic organization has subverted gender inequality because modern economic interests and the interests of gender inequality are inherently inconsistent. This inconsistency does not produce new interests committed to gender equality, and new forms of economic organization do not directly attack gender inequality. Instead, economic interests and economic power become detached from general male interests in preserving gender inequality. Men's superior economic position was preserved in earlier times because men's personal economic interests generally coincided with men's collective interests in gender inequality. As the modern economy develops, this congruence ruptures. The economic interests of employers recurringly and increasingly induce them to use female labor even if women's employment erodes gender inequality. Ordinary men's interests in keeping their wives at home gradually decline, as do their resources for controlling their wives' actions.

Simply put, excluding women from jobs became more difficult, less rewarding, and less sensible for all. In particular, men lost the will, the desire, and the capacity to keep women out. As economic activities separated from family life, production and commerce increasingly concentrated in large organizations. This growing differentiation eroded the interests and practical arrangements that had allowed the status inequality between women and men to be embedded in economic positional inequality.

Women's access to high-status jobs followed a different path, depending on a political intervention. Here, women's economic and political assimilation becomes clearly linked. Surprisingly, men did not severely oppose women's access to good jobs, although they often appeared to, because the economic transition had already greatly eroded interests against women's entry to these positions. Yet, in contrast to the experience with lower-status occupations, firms had substantial interests in placing women in high-status jobs, because they did not face similar needs to expand the labor supply or reduce the wage costs. Women's prior economic and political assimilation allowed them enough leverage to prevail over the residual male and institutional resistance. Thus, while women's politically induced entry to high-status positions might appear discontinuous, it largely represents a culmination joining together women's earlier economic and political assimilation.

OPPORTUNITIES TO EARN AND ACHIEVE

American women's movement from the household into the economy is well known, but some of its historical characteristics hold unexpected surprises. Women's employment has been rising for a long time. The number of employed women has increased at a faster rate than the number of employed men every decade for the past century; more "female" jobs than "male" jobs have been added to the economy in every decade since the Great Depression. The employment rate for unmarried women—both never-married women and women whose marriages ended through divorce or widowhood—rose to over 50 percent early in the century and has been relatively stable since. The employment of married women has increased steadily since the beginning of the century, and its long-term progress shows little effect from historical events such as World War II or the baby-boom 1950s. Indeed, women's proportion of all jobs in the modern, industrial economy has risen at a remarkably steady pace since at least 1870. These characteristics of women's rising employment are important clues to the causes behind it.

From the moment of its origin in textile factories, industry used women for manual labor. The Census of Manufactures of 1850 found that over one-fifth of those employed by firms were women.[6] Many women also found employment outside industry in such occupations as agricultural labor, domestic service, and teaching. Alice Kessler-Harris has characterized women's employment just before the Civil War.

> Roughly half of all women would never undertake wage work at all. Of the remaining half, about two-thirds stopped working at marriage and one-third was somehow or other engaged in an endless effort to earn income. They began as servants or in factories and, married or not, continued to eke out minimal incomes supporting children and sometimes husbands off and on throughout their lives.[7]

This description probably fits the employment pattern of urban women more closely than that of women living elsewhere. Still, by the late nineteenth century, about one-fifth of all women in the United States worked for a wage. They held between one-fifth and one-fourth of the jobs outside agriculture. (See Figure 3.1.)

Women's overall share of all jobs rose slowly but steadily over the century since 1830, and somewhat more rapidly from the 1930s on.[8] Surprisingly, the growth rate for jobs employing women was higher than that for jobs employing men for every decade throughout the century. Because the American economy was continually growing,

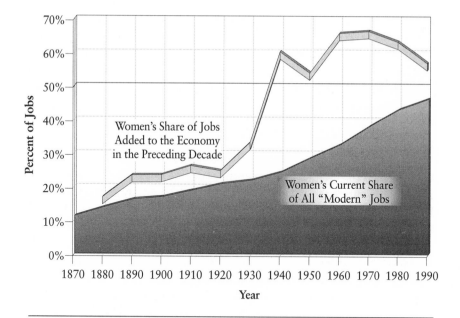

Figure 3.1. Women's share of paying jobs, 1870–1990
Sources: U.S. Bureau of the Census, *Historical Statistics of the United States,* vol. 1,
pp. 129, 132, 139–140; idem, *Statistical Abstract of the United States: 1996,* p. 428; Janet
Hooks, *Women's Occupations through Seven Decades,* pp. 34, 222, 238; U.S. Department
of Labor, *Time of Change: 1983 Handbook on Women Workers,* pp. 12, 14, 55, 56;
Employment and Earnings 36 (September 1989): 7; Alba M. Edwards, *Comparative
Occupational Statistics for the United States, 1870 to 1940,* pp. 113–129.

women's assimilation could be eased by placing them into new jobs.
Women's share of the new jobs due to economic expansion stood at
about one-quarter through World War I, then rose through the next
two decades to over one-half, and has remained over one-half since the
1930s.[9]

Taken together, the data suggest that women's part of the labor
market has risen steadily for a century, that jobs employing women
have increased continuously at a higher rate than jobs employing men,
and that during the 1920s and 1930s demand for new labor shifted
decisively toward women. Not surprisingly, once employers made this
shift, women's employment began to grow rapidly. Before 1940, the
proportion of women earning a wage increased *additively,* rising
about 2 percent each decade. After 1940, in the era of assimilation, the
proportion increased *multiplicatively,* rising each decade by a factor of

over one-fifth times the proportion ten years earlier. The changes in this rate show that the economy's great shift toward hiring female labor to allow economic expansion began between World War I and World War II and then accelerated. Since the 1930s, in *every* decade more of the new jobs added to the American economy have gone to women than to men (these were, of course, predominantly low-status jobs). Thus, since the Great Depression, American employers have depended more on women than on men to supply the labor needed to expand the economy. This dramatic transition occurred considerably earlier than many authorities and popular beliefs would suggest.[10]

Over time, as employers became more willing to hire them, working-age women left their households in a steady stream, but pools of women distinguished by marital and childrearing status joined that stream in different periods.[11] During the nineteenth century, most women earning a wage were single. In 1900 two-thirds of employed women were single. Only one out of twenty married women earned a wage. While married women in the working classes have apparently always sought jobs (often without success) when it was economically necessary, married women otherwise rarely worked for wages in the nineteenth century.[12] (A significant number of married women did earn income by taking in boarders, a strategy that circumvented the barriers of employment discrimination and household obligations.)[13] (See Figure 3.2.)

The pool of potential workers defined by unmarried women was tapped rather early, and once its limits were reached its use remained fairly steady. By World War I, about one-half of unmarried women held jobs. This proportion thereafter remained surprisingly stable, finally rising moderately in the century's last several decades. Women who had never married (the majority were young) and women who had lost or rid themselves of husbands (most of these women were older) were about equally likely to hold jobs. Both types of unmarried women had neither the restrictions nor the advantages of marriage.

Married women's entry into the work force started later and proceeded more slowly but, because most women married, ultimately had a more decisive impact (in 1950, for example, 78 percent of women aged 20–64 were married).[14] From the late nineteenth century to World War II, married women entered the modern work force in substantial numbers. The proportion of the nation's married women earning a wage tripled, going from one in twenty to one in six. (In contrast,

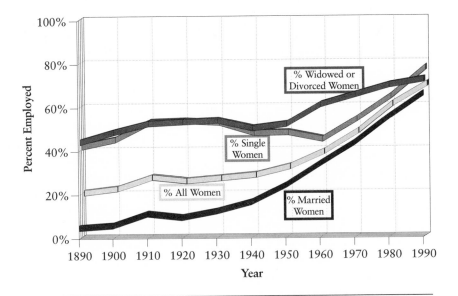

Figure 3.2. **Women's employment by marital status, 1890–1990 (women under age 65)**
Sources: U.S. Bureau of the Census, *Historical Statistics of the United States*, vol. 1,
pp. 20–21, 133; idem, *Statistical Abstract of the United States: 1996*, p. 399, tables 624,
625; idem, *Current Population Reports*, p. 3, table 1; Hooks, *Women's Occupations
through Seven Decades*, p. 34; U.S. Department of Labor, Bureau of Labor Statistics,
Handbook of Labor Statistics, 1985, pp. 7, 19, 115–122.

over 90 percent of working-age men have been in the labor force
throughout the twentieth century.)[15] As a result, the proportion of all
working women who were married went from about one-seventh to
more than one-third. Low-level, white-collar occupations accounted
for much of this gain.[16] Employers hired ever more women as secretaries, clerical workers, telephone operators, and store clerks. These jobs
had not existed before. Women also found jobs as low-status professionals. They received employment particularly as teachers but also in
other positions demanding education such as nursing and social work.
Demand for manual work from women increased mainly in the service
sector, with some jobs added in manufacturing. Growing industries
gave women more jobs, for example, as waitresses, cooks, beauticians,
and factory operatives. Urbanization also fostered women's increasing
employment.[17] Women in urban areas were more than twice as likely
to be in the labor force as women in rural farming areas and 50
percent more likely than women in rural nonfarm areas.[18] Between

1890 and 1940 the proportion of the population living in urban areas increased from 35 percent to 57 percent.[19] These numbers imply that the population shift toward cities accounted for between one-fourth and one-third of the increase in women's employment rate.

Surprisingly, the movement of married women into paid employment proceeded at a rapid pace right through the 1950s. Generally we associate this decade with the baby boom, the flight to the suburbs, and adherence to the image of the feminine mystique. Yet behind this facade of tidy domesticity, the number of married women in the labor force increased by more than one-half in just ten years. In contrast, the number of unmarried women in the labor force increased only about 11 percent and the number of men about 8 percent. By 1995, instead of the one-in-six share of 1940, over two-thirds of all married women worked for a wage. The employment of married women with preschool children went from 19 percent in 1960 (already higher than most people realize) to 64 percent by 1995.[20]

As more women took jobs, more jobs took women. Women successfully entered high-paying, prestigious positions in growing numbers, particularly after the 1950s.[21] Women went from holding less than one-sixth of all managerial or administrative jobs in 1960 to over two-fifths by 1995. After 1960 women's proportions began to increase in the high-status professions. Working women had long held jobs in professional occupations, but most worked in low-status professions such as nursing, librarian work, social work, or elementary school teaching. Between 1960 and 1995, however, women went from 9 percent to 24 percent of physicians, from 5 percent to 26 percent of lawyers, and from 29 percent to 45 percent of college teachers. Furthermore, many more women chose self-employment than ever before. As a result, in only the ten years between 1975 and 1985 women went from owning only one-twentieth of all small businesses to one-fourth.[22] Women's economic assimilation has not yet overcome all limits. So far, women hold few top positions in large corporations or other economic positions wielding great power. How much this reflects a simple historical lag and how much it represents a "glass ceiling" sustained by masculine obstacles to women's advance is not yet known. Still, women's share of high-status positions in the economy has expanded dramatically compared to their earlier absence, and it keeps growing.

Women's job opportunities improved more continuously and more gradually than their legal status. Women's employment level rose incrementally because decentralized decisions determined how many women held jobs and because the conditions that influenced those decisions changed incrementally. Hiring practices typically changed through dispersed actions of independent businesses. Usually only a few innovative businesses first tried new practices. Successful innovations then spread to other workplaces. Women's legal and political status changed intermittently and sometimes rapidly through centralized government decisions affecting everyone at once (although the judicial system often applied laws unevenly, causing the practical effects of legal change to be incremental). Economic changes were not always incremental, and legal changes were not always intermittent. Formally dramatic legal changes often changed manifest legal practices only gradually. Analogously, changes in economic practices were sometimes surprisingly rapid. Sharp shifts in economic conditions that affected everyone sometimes simultaneously prompted many employers to adopt similar policies. Wars and business cycles usually produced these responses by imposing sudden shifts in the labor supply or the demand for goods. The distinction between law and the economy became more ambiguous every time the government introduced policies regulating employers' hiring practices as state policy shifted more and more toward continuous surveillance and control of the economy. Still, allowing for these qualifications, women's economic status usually changed more gradually than their legal and political status.

Indeed, women's share of modern jobs, which excludes work in agriculture or in private household service, has risen remarkably smoothly for more than a century, increasing incrementally every decade (see Figure 3.1). The focus on modern occupations is important, because the critical issue is how women became assimilated into the modern economy of industry, commerce, and government bureaucracy. Other studies have largely ignored this distinction, so that their depiction of trends has been influenced by the changing size and changing employment rates in premodern economic activities. The steadiness of women's rising participation in the modern sector of the economy is striking. It belies many people's beliefs that women's growing economic role happened recently or through bursts associated with historical events. This is strong evidence that a consistent, enduring process within the economy was propelling women's assimilation.

WHY EMPLOYERS RECRUITED WOMEN

Every year over the past 150 years, more employers chose to hire women, and every year more women sought jobs. Why did employers and women change their behavior?

Three evolving conditions directly nurtured employers' willingness to hire women.[23] First, economic growth and historical events altered the balance between demand and the labor supply. Occasional, sometimes prolonged, shortages of male workers prompted employers to hire women in some labor markets. Second, certain occupations composed largely of female employees grew faster than most occupations that mainly hired men. Employers hired women for some new occupations that soon became known as "female jobs." When the unfolding economy rapidly expanded these occupations, the demand for women accelerated. Third, employers judged women's worth as workers higher than they had in the past. Compared with the past (and, possibly, with men) women seemed more productive, more dependable, or more vulnerable to discipline and exploitation. Expecting more for their money than they had in the past, employers recruited more women.

Industrialized, capitalist economies breed growth and capital accumulation. As the economy expands, it must recruit ever more wage workers. This growth advances unevenly and unpredictably. The pace depends on state policies, international relations, natural resources, technical innovations, and cultural conditions. The growth continues while unused resources and unsaturated markets remain to attract it. To keep expanding, the economy pulls ever larger proportions of the productive population into wage labor. In the United States, those employed in the modern economy—defined here as all paid labor except that in agriculture and domestic service—amounted to about two-fifths of the working-age population (including both sexes) toward the end of the nineteenth century, about three-fifths in 1950, and about three-quarters in the 1990s, so the proportion nearly doubled over the century.[24] This growth creates unanticipated new occupations which service new production processes and new organizational forms. As new labor needs arise, employers must recruit suitable workers as best they can. Eventually, these include women.

In the twentieth century, employers found that the sources of labor that had fed earlier growth were not unlimited. The nineteenth-century economy had grown by recruiting its workers from immigrants and transplanted farm folk. With each passing decade, the expanding economy and the maturing political order reduced these traditional pools.

The dramatic curtailment of immigration after World War I cut off the only practical, unlimited source of labor for an expanding economy.[25] In earlier years, unlimited immigration had been possible, even prudent, in the United States and other colonized areas. Large tracts of unsettled land and explosive economic growth had created a demand for labor, particularly unskilled labor, that greatly exceeded the population's natural growth. The surrounding oceans insulated the United States from international conflicts. But by the early twentieth century the American frontier had almost disappeared, and World War I plunged the United States irreversibly into international rivalries. The material interests (mainly employers of unskilled urban labor) and ideological motives favoring open immigration had receded. Free immigration's ouster only awaited the proper political climate.

During one of America's periodic flirtations with xenophobia, Congress closed the gates to most prospective immigrants. World War I increased discomfort with the numerous immigrants from southern and eastern Europe. In the decade before the war, about one million immigrants arrived annually in the United States. This influx fell off drastically during the war but started to rise again afterward. The government acted when diverse special interests and political philosophies allied against immigrants. Conservative politicians and writers opposed immigration because they felt they must preserve the American people's racial integrity. Organized labor opposed immigration because it felt that immigrants weakened unions by competing for jobs. Some employers did believe high immigration was in their interest, yet most foresaw no immediate difficulties, because the high immigration before World War I had left a surplus of labor. A nation of immigrants had become afraid of immigrants. So ended industry's dependence on immigrant labor to fuel growth.

At first, the existing stockpile of immigrant children deferred the squeeze of the labor supply; later, people who immigrated illegally partially offset the effects of immigration quotas. Still, the quotas had a huge numerical impact. During the first two decades of the twentieth century, immigrants accounted for about one-half of the population's total growth. In contrast, between 1930 and 1950 this proportion shrank to about 5 percent. While about one-fourth of the adult male population was foreign-born in 1900, the immigrant portion dropped to about one-tenth by 1950.[26]

Workers from rural areas could not take up the slack. People did migrate steadily toward urban areas, but over the long term this migration depleted the rural population's capacity to contribute. The number of rural Americans today is the same as in 1900, while the urban population has increased more than fivefold.[27] Industry and commerce have invariably shifted populations toward urban centers. The modern economy has thrived on market density and has created a powerful centripetal pull by offering jobs, goods, and culture. The rural population was stable because it sent its excess youth to the urban areas. When urban areas and the paid labor force grew rapidly in comparison, the rural migrants filled an ever smaller proportion of new jobs.

Not only were new workers harder to find, but the men who did take jobs did not put in as many hours as in the past. As productivity rose, labor organization expanded, and government assimilated the working classes as voters, the work week gradually shrank about one-third, from sixty hours in the mid-nineteenth century to forty hours in the mid-twentieth.[28] This decline forced employers to hire considerably more workers to get the same labor. If employers wanted to avoid investing more capital per employee, then they had to introduce a second shift. If they were unwilling or unable to do that, they still had to increase their work force to produce as much as before (or, if we take rising productivity into account, to sustain the rate of increase in production).

Through these processes, economic and political expansion disrupted the flow of labor in the social environment, draining some pools of male workers, diverting others away from employment. The repeated threat of a labor drought sent employers scurrying to tap new sources. To manage without more workers, the economy had to slow its growth or use technology that increased workers' productivity. The multitude of firms, competing to survive and thrive, found curbing growth as impractical as it was disagreeable. Employers could and did try to reduce their labor needs by adopting production techniques that used more capital and less labor. Usually this strategy reached inherent technical and economic limits.[29] For a while, introducing more or better technology could increase labor productivity. Yet, no matter how much a firm was ready to invest, technical knowledge allowed only fractional increases in short-term productivity. Technological strategies soon started to increase total production costs. Because short-term considerations have usually guided business, investing capital ordinarily offered little help for labor shortages. As the old sources of labor dried up, either employers had to find workers elsewhere or they had to cut expansion.

Thus, the economy generated pressure to find more workers. This pressure was especially strong during economic upswings and in any industry expanding into new markets. During the twentieth century, employers brought blacks into the economy as one response to this problem, drawing on one remaining stagnant rural reservoir. Still, racial hostility and educational disadvantages restricted the jobs that employers offered blacks. Women were the other logical choice for new recruits.

Employers, when worrying about hiring, implicitly saw the population as pools of potential workers.[30] Demographic characteristics—sex, age, race, nationality, education, and the like—defined these pools. Young, single, white men with a high school education and middle-aged, married, college-educated white women were examples of two distinctive pools. Employers preferred hiring from some pools over others, according to the worth they attributed to a typical member of each labor pool. Generally, employers favored prospective workers who seemed easy to recruit, properly skilled, compliant, stable, unlikely to cause problems with the existing work force, and willing to work for low wages. Specific characteristics of the job, firm, and industry dictated the weight an employer gave to each of these criteria.

These implicit cognitive maps dividing the population by demographic features were arbitrary and crude. Yet the idea behind them was the same as that motivating insurance companies' formal actuarial categories.[31] More informally, people have used these distinctions to categorize the anonymous mass of society into the similar and dissimilar, the familiar and unknown, or friends and foes. Social science teaches us that people usually have differed more within these categories than between them. Still, these categories have had both predictive and symbolic power, so people have used them.

The labor supply dictated employers' strategies for hiring from the labor pools. When labor was abundant, employers could be choosy. If possible, they used routine strategies to hire new employees, without consciously calculating the alternatives. They hired new workers the same way they had hired the old. As workers became hard to find, employers had to take what they could get. When faced with hiring difficulties, employers tried new labor pools. Employers recruited workers first from the pools that seemed better bets. Then, as the economy grew and these pools dwindled, employers shifted their recruiting toward the best pools still left. As the objects of this process, potential employees' choices resembled those of fish. Once employers fished their pool, they could rise to the bait or ignore it, but they could not affect where employers sought their prey.

One obvious female social characteristic caused many employers to value women less than men as employees: the degree of family obligations. Given the dominant sexual division of labor, getting married and having children altered both women's and men's lives. However, while men became more committed to jobs, women became less dedicated to earning money. A wife and children obligated a man to earn an income. Family men impressed employers as good workers. In contrast, a husband and children compelled a woman to care for a household.[32] So men seemed preferable for a wide range of jobs.

Women's marital and childrearing status distinguished groups who seemed easier or harder to hire and control. Employers' expectations followed prevalent cultural beliefs about domestic obligations and suitable social roles. They generally preferred women who were not wives and not mothers, because they expected women to be easier to recruit and more dependable when they were not burdened by a family at home. Childless, unmarried women had the least domestic responsibility. To get them to seek and accept jobs demanded less inducement, they seemed least likely to leave work unpredictably, and popular cultural beliefs did not much oppose such women taking jobs. In contrast, married women with young children had extensive domestic responsibilities, probably needed strong inducements before they would take full-time jobs, were vulnerable to domestic crises that would draw them away from their jobs, and faced strong popular beliefs that mothers should stay home with their children. Married women who had no young children at home were in between: harder to hire than the unmarried and easier than those with young children.

In the nineteenth century, most working women were single. In the first half of the twentieth century, employers had started to hire married women with no children or with only older children. By 1970 these were as likely as unmarried women to hold jobs. Women with young children were the last to join, their employment becoming increasingly common over the second half of the twentieth century.

This historical pattern fits the theory that employers' needs set the pace at which each demographic pool of women entered the labor force. Over time, various conditions upset the balance between the available labor supply and the number of new employees needed to sustain growth. These conditions included declining foreign immigration, declining rural immigration, a shortened age span spent in the labor force, and shortened hours of labor. Employers substituted pools of female labor for male labor, first hiring the women with fewest family obligations.[33]

Employers did not wait until all men had jobs before hiring any women. Firms in some industries have employed women since the early nineteenth century. Straightforward competitive pressure to reduce wage costs forced the hand of some employers. For menial work and for jobs in highly competitive industries, a low wage rate was a crucial criterion. If employers discounted other criteria, such as experience, skills, or dependability, they could get workers more cheaply. This concern explains some of employers' interest in women. The more that a low wage rate overshadowed other considerations for an employer, including bigotry, the more willing he became to disregard a worker's sex (or age or ethnicity). The employer most wanted to hire those who would accept the lowest wage.

Employers also had to contend with the difficulty of hiring men for jobs that had become female identified, even if most employers did not face a general shortage of male labor. Employers and workers associated some jobs exclusively with women and others with men. This custom resulted in independent markets for female and male labor.

Occupational segregation was clearly defined by the distinctive occupations in the modern economy that typically employed women. Jobs in farming and domestic service largely represented the old economic order, which has only a marginal relationship to women's rising employment. In 1870 only one-fourth of the women earning a wage held jobs in the modern economy. (See Figure 3.3.) By 1940 three-fourths of all wage-earning women had jobs in the modern sector. In 1870 women holding jobs in the "modern" part of the economy were most often seamstresses (private and in factories), operatives in textile mills, or teachers.[34] By 1910 women in the modern sector mainly

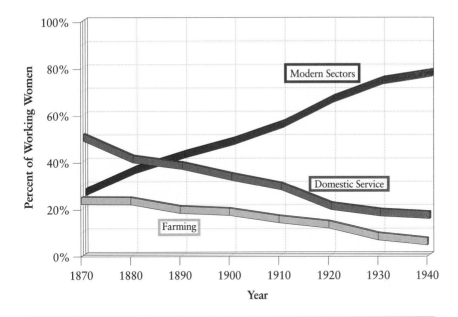

Figure 3.3. Working women's shift into modern jobs, 1870–1940
Sources: Edwards, *Comparative Occupational Statistics*, pp. 122–130; Hooks, *Women's Occupations through Seven Decades*, pp. 207–251.

held jobs as office secretaries and clerks; retail clerks; teachers; operatives in textile, clothing, cigar, and shoe factories; telephone operators; nurses; and, in personal service, as waitresses, boardinghouse keepers, and laundresses. (See Figure 3.4.)

Although some occupations hired both sexes, they largely worked at different jobs. During the first half of the twentieth century, the female-oriented occupations in this short list yielded women three-quarters of their jobs in modern occupations. These same occupations embraced only one-fifth of men's modern jobs. The remaining, male-oriented occupations provided four-fifths of men's modern jobs, but only one-fourth of women's jobs in modern occupations. More detailed studies suggest that the degree of occupational segregation was stable for the first half of the twentieth century, and that about two-thirds of women would have had to change occupations for the sexes to hold similar jobs.[35]

Varied impulses of employers, male workers, and women seem all to have led toward job segregation.[36] Sometimes employers may have

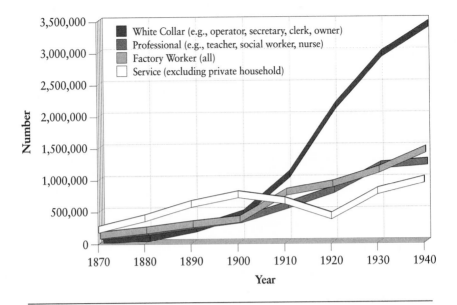

Figure 3.4. Women's jobs in the "modern" economy, 1870–1940
Sources: Edwards, *Comparative Occupational Statistics,* pp. 122–130; Hooks, *Women's Occupations through Seven Decades,* pp. 207–251.

acted out cultural assumptions in attributing distinctive capacities and roles to the sexes. Some employers engaged in statistical discrimination, often unknowingly. They tried to use rational techniques to judge prospective employees while still relying on popular stereotypes. Sometimes male workers have tried to exclude women from better jobs, perhaps with the help of employers hoping to divide and conquer. Sometimes women seem to have chosen jobs differently from men because of their extensive domestic responsibilities and lower need for economic success. Sometimes women seem to have pursued different interests and different ideas about appropriate jobs because they were socialized to conform to different stereotypes from men. Probably economic sex segregation has been broad and durable because all these causes have supported it.[37]

New occupations played an important role in defining the boundaries of occupational segregation, because they gave employers the best chance to adapt to the changing availability of competing labor pools. When recruiting for a new occupation, employers were more likely to calculatedly assess their alternatives.[38] Employers also ran less risk that male workers would oppose women getting jobs. None had a claim to protect.

People did not decide which occupations to create or how much occupations should grow. Economic, technical, and organizational imperatives guided the creation and growth of occupations. For example, the expanding economy multiplied large-scale organizations, recordkeeping, merchandising, and social services. These advances rapidly bred demand for typists, sales clerks, waitresses, and school teachers. The rise and expansion of new occupations were usually unforeseen by employers and often recognized only in hindsight.

When employers tried to fill jobs in new occupations, they were in a good position to hire women if this strategy seemed profitable. With no entrenched labor force, employers could hire more freely. For example, employers discovered that women with some education and few job prospects made a good choice for clerks and teachers. Men qualified for the same jobs—having enough education and a proper demeanor to interact with clients—demanded higher salaries and greater opportunities to advance. As Graham Lowe says in his study of women's movement into clerical work, "Employers were pragmatic enough to recognize the clear advantages of women's higher average education, traditionally lower pay and greater availability for menial tasks."[39] Rapid growth of these occupations, declining immigration, and wartime labor shortages added to the reasons for hiring women. Employers hired women because they seemed to offer the best balance between costs and productivity.[40]

By itself, the newness of an occupation did not explain which sex filled it. Instead, new occupations *sometimes* offered employers an opportunity to use female labor advantageously without any opposition from an entrenched male labor force. Men flooded some new occupations that grew from old male occupations. Some employers filled new jobs with men because it made practical or economic sense. Still, some went to women, some that went to women were expanding at a rapid rate, and these new occupations were critical to women's entry into the labor force.

Although no one sought it, segregating occupations by sex gradually turned an *opportunity* to use female labor into a *necessity*. At first new occupations gave employers more freedom to hire women (or any other group). But once an occupation's sexual identity had solidified, employers found it hard to recruit workers of the opposite sex.[41] As

Valerie Oppenheimer observed, after a "job has acquired a traditional sex label . . . employers will tend to follow this tradition unless some special problem arises. If, in addition, skills are required, then the employer is probably more firmly committed to the utilization of the labour of one sex. It is hard, for example, for an employer to find a qualified male secretary, even if he should desire one."[42] They found it particularly difficult to recruit men for "women's" jobs.

This effect of occupational segregation helps explain women's increased employment. Two interacting conditions brought ambiguity into the relationship between inequality and occupational segregation. First, once an occupation became "women's work" or "men's work," employers found it hard to hire anyone of the other sex. Second, the economic fate of occupations was largely unpredictable and uncontrollable. Both women's and men's occupations swelled and shrank in rhythm with business cycles. But the long-term growth of women's occupations was nearly detached from the growth of men's. It was also faster. Together, these conditions meant that the rigidity introduced into the labor market by sex segregation partially sheltered women from men's opposition. After an occupation became identified with women, men had far less leverage to control access to the occupation. If the occupation grew, men could not easily deny women access to the expanded opportunities. Occupational segregation was not primarily a boon to women, but it did provide one mechanism that enabled women's economic assimilation. Women experienced segregation mainly as a disadvantage. In particular, the barriers against women's entry to high-status occupations restricted their advance for many decades. Still, occupational segregation had an unanticipated, long-term, secondary effect of accelerating women's movement into jobs.[43]

In addition to labor shortages and the sex segregation of occupations, a third factor seems likely to have induced employers to hire more women: a rising assessment of women's worth as workers. This reassessment would prompt employers to adjust their rankings of labor pools. Standard economic theories have long supposed that employers would hire more women if they could make more money by hiring women than by hiring men.[44]

Unfortunately, we cannot easily ascertain how and when employers' might have changed their assessments of women as potential employees. We cannot use rises in women's employment as a guide, because they depend on all the other factors we have discussed. We do know that women's value, as measured by *human capital,* did rise. Women's rising education gave employers good reason to raise their expectations about women's general productivity. To employers, education credentials showed that a person both accepted disciplined work and had greater knowledge. Educated women seemed worth more even for jobs that did not directly need their education.

Women's declining domestic responsibilities also probably did make them more reliable. If so, employers who hired them would be more likely to hire other women. The economy also indirectly raised women's apparent worth by creating more jobs that needed the characteristics usually associated with women. For example, employers may have preferred women for retail clerks because of their social skills, especially with female customers.[45] Similarly, restaurant employers could have believed women fit the job of serving customers better than men. (Alternatively, however, employers voicing such sentiments may have been manipulating popular prejudices to legitimate exploiting cheap female labor.)

Employers' strategies for hiring women as clerks, secretaries, or for other new office jobs at the turn of the century illustrate the alternative calculations about women's worth. According to Elyce Rotella's study of clerical work, employers mainly hired women for new jobs created by technological change (such as the typewriter) or production changes.[46] These changes produced a high demand for workers with skills obtained through education, skills not specific to any firm. Women proved ideal. These same women were not desirable for the old-style clerical positions that really were entry points to management, she argues. Both employers and the women expected the women to stay on the job only a short time. When employers wanted a few permanent clerks with considerable important knowledge about the firm, the wage savings made possible by hiring women were offset by the costs and inconvenience due to turnover. As firm-specific skills became unimportant and the number of modern clerical positions rose rapidly, women became attractive. Women's value to employers increased both because women were different (as a result of more schooling) and because employers' labor needs changed (they had less need for permanence).

Seeing women employed profitably in their firms or competitors' firms probably struck employers as the most persuasive evidence that they should hire women. Observing women work well for their wages could dispel employers' doubts about women's value. In a competitive economy that gave women some opportunities and a fair amount of liberty, experience could correct a mistaken undervaluation of women. While we lack direct evidence that employers' assessment of female workers rose, the circumstantial evidence supports this idea.

Three mutually reinforcing economic processes—the demand for labor rising faster than the supply of male labor, the sex segregation of jobs, and the rising value of female labor—had integral inducements for employers to offer more jobs to women. To thrive in an expanding economy, employers had to find ever more workers. As men became difficult to recruit, employers turned to women. Occupations became sex segregated as ordinary men tried to protect their labor markets and employers tried to exploit women for higher profits. Occupational segregation magnified labor recruitment problems by artificially separating the efforts to hire women and men. Segregation banned women from some occupations but awarded them others. Social progress also increased women's worth to employers; it made them easier to recruit, and it raised their productivity through education. Over time, then, employers faced increasing labor needs that men could not meet, while women seemed to become—if anything—more dependable and knowledgeable potential employees. These circumstances gave employers good reason to use more women, especially in rapidly expanding new occupations.

WHY MORE WOMEN SOUGHT JOBS

Two contrasting scenarios could represent women's rising employment. In one, women were always at least as prepared to take jobs as were men, and the pace of women's assimilation depended entirely on how many jobs firms were willing to give them. In another, firms were always indifferent to the employees' sex, and women's increasing presence in the labor market depended entirely on how many women were prepared to take jobs. The true process probably lay somewhere between these two scenarios. Employers' willingness to hire women probably depended partly on women's availability, partly on their apparent value, and partly on the dynamics of prejudice. Women's efforts to get jobs probably depended partly on the likelihood of getting a job, partly on the monetary and nonpecuniary rewards, and partly on the constraints of prejudice and circumstance. The supply of female labor and the demand for female labor influenced each other, as well as each being subject to other historical pressures.

Apparently, several conditions prompted fewer women than men to seek jobs in the past. Households needed considerable domestic labor. Cultural expectations held men responsible for providing family incomes and sanctioned those who voluntarily neglected this duty. Women had no similar external motivation for seeking employment, except perhaps in some poor subcultures. The jobs available to women also were less attractive than the jobs available to men, and there were fewer of them. Moreover, husbands commonly opposed any employment aspirations of their wives unless economic need dictated acceptance.

The evidence available, though crude, suggests that such circumstances limited the women who were available to hire. In the 1890s, for example, the Department of Labor surveyed hundreds of employers across the country, asking, among other things, if women's employment was increasing and why employers sometimes preferred women workers. Some employers said they preferred women but also said that female employment was not increasing. They offered varied explanations. These included: "very often women who are better adapted and cheaper [than men] are unreliable," "women can be employed only in certain occupations," "very scarce, and hard to find suitable women," and "women in many instances can not be depended on."[47] Fifty years later, it still took great effort to recruit women for jobs, even under the patriotic pressures created by World War II. Women's rapidly increased employment during World War II was a milestone showing women's potential economic role. Yet it took an extraordinary campaign to get women into these jobs. Once the war was over, most apparently wanted to leave employment.[48] Claudia Goldin assessed the years before World War II with a careful analysis of retrospective employment data collected by the Women's Bureau in 1939. In the years just after World War I, between 80 and 90 percent of all employed single women quit work immediately after getting married.[49] This number seems considerably higher than we would expect from employers' rules ("marriage bars") that women could not stay in their jobs after marrying, suggesting that women were voluntarily leaving jobs when they married. Evidence amassed by Goldin also showed an enduring division in the twentieth century between two lifestyles. A growing minority of married women held jobs much of their lives while a shrinking majority rarely took jobs. Again, this finding suggests the majority were not competing for the available jobs.[50]

Unemployment data also suggest that fewer women than men wanted jobs. Female unemployment rates often exceeded male unemployment rates, but the differences were small. For example, women held jobs about one-third as often as men did in the first half of the twentieth century. Similarly, the number of unemployed women was usually about one-third that of unemployed men.[51]

The data we have, therefore, suggest that women's interest in finding jobs was less than that of men. None of these data are decisive, but they are consistent. Unemployment data could be misleading because they neglect those who give up or never try to find jobs. Some women must have stayed outside the labor force because prospects seemed so dismal—these women would have responded if employers had stopped discriminating against them. Others, however, would not. They took jobs only when circumstances forced them to do so.[52]

After a careful study of women employed by industry in the first three decades of the twentieth century, Leslie Tentler's assessment is telling.

> Employment followed schooling, generally terminated with marriage, and continued—if at all—intermittently and casually during the long years as wife and mother. Paid work was not the primary focus of most women's lives.
>
> For most women, the work experience failed to alter significantly their role in and their dependence on the family, for nearly all women's jobs offered less security and status than did life as a working-class wife and mother . . . generally only severe poverty induced a married woman to return to work.[53]

As they had less financial need and higher standards for acceptable jobs, middle-class women were even more prone to reject employment as a goal.

Suggesting many women did not want jobs does not mean they were different from men. Just the opposite. Many men holding jobs did so because they had no choice (or thought they had no choice). Economic need and social expectations forced them to work. Without similar pressures, women were unlikely to take jobs at the same rate as men, even if employers completely ignored sex while hiring. By 1970, over one-half of the women working in blue-collar jobs still said they would stop working if they did not need the income.[54] Neither women nor men showed much enthusiasm about becoming wage earners. Realistically, most jobs in the American industrial economy did not have enough intrinsic rewards to attract either women or men who could live adequately without a job. In the nineteenth century, agitators and reformers often expressed popular feelings by referring to lifelong employment as the horrible burden of *wage slavery*.

Most men sought jobs not because they were intrinsically attractive, but because they could not see any other choice. By eroding the opportunities for self-employment, the industrial economy gradually forced men to depend on the market. Working-class men became wage laborers. Middle-class men became salaried staff. By 1890, only one-third of all gainfully employed people were self-employed. Among managerial and professional ranks, the bulk of the middle class, two-thirds were still self-employed. These numbers kept declining. (See Figure 3.5.) By the start of the 1960s, less than one-third of the middle class ranks were entrepreneurs or independent professionals.

The movement of married women, in particular, into the economy followed the erosion of self-employment as a viable alternative for men. When men could be self-employed, families could operate as business enterprises. The need for a wife to take a job outside the family enterprise signaled a failing. Once men became dependent on paid employment, women could contribute to the family's income production only by taking a job.

Without material need or social expectations to motivate them, women were not likely to compete for bad jobs that would only increase their burdens. Cultural expectations relieved women of the responsibility for income while proclaiming their domestic obligations. Family organization sheltered most women from an economic need to earn an income. In the past, when a family needed substantial labor at home and only men could get good jobs, a wife often could take a job only by sacrificing the family's standard of living.[55] Without economic need or cultural pressure, only the lure of a good job would have drawn most women into the economy. In the nineteenth and early twentieth centuries, good or permanent job prospects were so hard to find that most women could no more reasonably seek careers than embark in search of the Holy Grail.

While exclusion from good jobs kept all women responsible for

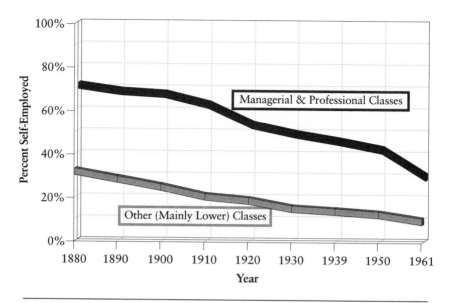

Figure 3.5. Self-employment, by status, 1880–1960
Sources: Spurgeon Bell, *Productivity, Wages, and National Income,* p. 10; John E. Bregger, *Self-Employment in the United States, 1948–62,* p. 40. Business and Professional are mostly men whether self-employed or not; the remainder of the gainfully employed, however, includes considerable women workers (men were 80 percent of all the self-employed in the 1950s). Data for 1950 were estimated by simple linear interpolation from 1948 and 1955.

household work, domestic duties impeded most women from using any opportunities that did arise. Because *most* women did not get paying jobs, *all* women had responsibility for household work. This standard erected a cultural barrier of role expectations and practical obstacles of commitments of time and effort. The doubts about women's employment influenced nineteenth-century cultural expectations of manhood and womanhood, embodied in the new roles of the *breadwinner* and the *homemaker.* After the difficulty of getting good jobs left women caring for their households, their domestic obligations usually frustrated any future job aspirations.

Because of these circumstances, the married women who did get jobs usually fitted one of three special categories with offsetting conditions. First, some women were in families so hard up that they severely needed any wages that the wife could earn. Family hardship probably motivated most employed married women through the middle of the twentieth century. Second, some women were in families so well off that they could easily replace the wife's lost household labor time with servants, commercial services, and commodities. Before World War II, however, few affluent women sought employment. Apparently, most affluent women used their surplus time for voluntary services or leisure; or they plunged into domestic activity despite their affluence. Still, a good proportion of the few married women in the more desirable white-collar jobs probably came from affluent, middle-class families. Third, some couples cared so much about egalitarian relations that they felt the wife had to seek a job even if the material quality of their lives worsened. This possibility would include couples in which the wife was adamant about holding a job and the husband merely acquiesced in her doing so. People in this category probably accelerated the rise in women's employment after World War II.

After World War II, women's rapidly rising employment had little relationship to their husband's income. (See Figure 3.6.) Married women with high-income husbands and those with low-income husbands seemed to flow into paid work with similar force. We can assume that women were often economically needy if their husbands' income was in the bottom quarter of wage earners. In 1940 just over one-fifth of these needy women held jobs. By 1990 this rate had almost quadrupled, so that over three-fourths had jobs. Compare privileged women, whose husbands had incomes in the top quarter. In the same forty years, these advantaged women's employment rate increased even faster than that of needy women. Before World War II, fewer than one-tenth of the women with affluent husbands had jobs. By 1990 71 percent of the women in these advantaged families were employed. The wives of men with intermediate incomes showed a similar record. The progress of the most affluent wives into employment has lagged about a decade behind that of other wives. Except for this historically minor difference, the primary trend of wives joining the work force has been overwhelmingly independent of husband's economic status.

This pattern contradicts the common belief that an increasing economic need for wives' income, propelled by inflation, prompted the increase in women's employment. The inflation explanation implies that women with poorer husbands should have moved into the work force much faster than women with more affluent husbands. Instead, the historical pattern implies that a set of conditions common to all

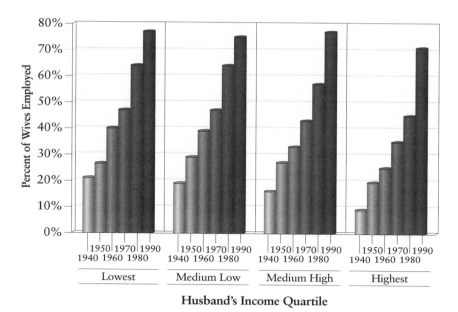

Figure 3.6. Married women's labor force participation, by husband's income, 1940–1990
Sources: U.S. Bureau of the Census, *Sixteenth Census of the United States: 1940,*
Population: The Labor Force (Sample Statistics), "Employment and Family Characteristics
of Women," pp. 132–137; idem, *Current Population Reports, Consumer Income,* nos. 9
(March 1952) and 12 (June 1953); idem, *Census of the Population: 1970,* Subject Reports,
Employment Status and Work Experience; Paul Ryscavage, "More Wives in the Labor
Force Have Husbands with 'Above-average' Incomes"; and a new analysis of data from the
Panel Study of Income Dynamics for 1980 and 1990 (the PSID is described in Martha S.
Hill, *The Panel Study of Income Dynamics*). Because these data are defined differently for
the various years, the estimates for the decades are not strictly comparable. Data for 1940
cover women 18–64 with husbands present for couples in nonfarm areas in which
husbands had no income other than wages or salaries (other income was not reported).
Data for 1960 and 1977 include married women 16–55 and those over 55 with children
under age 18 (older women's husbands have usually retired). Data for 1951–52 average
estimates for the two years and include all married women by husband's total income. Data
for 1970 include married women 16–64 whose husbands earned some income. Data for
1980 and 1990 are based on couples with a husband aged 20–64.

classes pushed or pulled women into jobs. While working-class
women more often claim they work only because they must and middle-class women assert they would work even if they did not need the
money, this difference also occurs among men and reflects the better work experiences available to the middle class. The consistent pattern of rising employment across classes points us toward all women's

increasing dissatisfactions with declining household responsibilities, women's higher personal aspirations sparked by greater education, and the increasing availability of jobs.

Women were being pushed and pulled from the household into the economy. The same market economy that once fostered women's domestic responsibility later turned about and undermined women's domesticity.[56] Economic changes reduced the proportion of women's lives devoted to children by precipitating a decline in mortality and fertility. Economic growth also lowered the need to produce services and goods within the household. People could substitute goods bought from a store for those formerly produced in the home. As families had less household work to do, women's domestic responsibilities could neither justify nor guide a sexual division of labor.

Since early in the nineteenth century, women of each successive generation have borne fewer children. (Women were also living longer, but because much of the change was due to lower death rates for the young and the old, its influence on the lives of women during their productive adult years is unclear.) Except during the two peculiar decades following World War II, the birth rate has consistently declined for two centuries. By the end of the 1930s, women aged fifteen to forty-four were having only *one-third* as many children as their counterparts had a century before. During the postwar years, one generation defied this trend, resulting in the baby boom of the 1950s, but in the 1960s the decline resumed with renewed force. These demographic shifts diminished both the length and intensity of childrearing.

Declining fertility had a direct, inherent relation to the reorganization of family life in a wage-labor economy.[57] Improved contraception, an incidental effect of economic development, eased people's efforts to reduce family size, but the motives came from elsewhere. Family size declined as children stopped acting as permanent economic supports for their parents. Children offered less practical value when they would not someday contribute to the family enterprise and were unlikely to care for their parents in old age. People also had greater confidence in their children's survival as a result of improvements in food, sewage treatment, cleanliness, and medical care. As love objects, companions, and symbolic links to the myth of an immortal family line, children remained attractive. Still, the movement of production out of the family so changed its organization—including the trade-off between burdens and benefits of children—that declining fertility followed.

Women's need to be with their children was also reduced by two nineteenth-century inventions. The development of effective substitutes for breast milk meant that someone other than the mother (or a substitute lactating woman) could care for infants. The development of universal education turned schools into a vast child-care apparatus. They also greatly relieved families of the need to teach their children. So people not only had fewer children; those they had required less investment of labor.

Concurrently, the expanding industrial economy made other forms of domestic labor redundant, as households consumed prepared commodities, relied more on commercial services, and used efficient machinery to speed the remaining chores.[58] Goods once produced at home—such as yarn, clothing, and food—became available in the marketplace. Services such as laundries and restaurants shrank other domestic chores. Labor-saving devices, such as sewing machines, washing and drying machines, and vacuum cleaners, became readily available. Therefore, the time necessary to maintain a household declined progressively.

Relocating productive activities outside the household did not cause a sudden surge of women into jobs or create a new ideal of the leisured housewife. As the labor necessary to maintain a household gradually declined, women who remained at home continued to spend about the same time doing household tasks. Only after the necessary household labor had declined appreciably were women markedly freer to hold jobs. Then, the economy could only gradually absorb this new source of labor.

Significant changes in tasks, time, and effort needed to support a household probably took a generation or two. Several studies have shown that women did not surge into employment as an immediate response to changes in domestic labor needs.[59] When labor-saving devices or goods became commercially available, households did not buy and apply them with immediate enthusiasm, women did not find a rapid drop in the time spent on household duties, and women did not all dash into the labor market. When women gained access to devices and services, and when they had fewer children, they *could* uphold a household standard with less labor. Still, no single device was so time saving that it alone could dramatically reduce household labor time. Moreover, each new product and service improved and diffused gradually. Most machines and services meant to reduce domestic labor also were not efficient when they first appeared. The pace of change varied with each appliance or service. As labor-saving devices became available, households adopted them gradually and unevenly. More affluent families would adopt them first. As they became cheaper and popular culture began to portray them as necessities, they diffused.

As the need for domestic work fell, full-time housewives started to look redundant, resembling workers whose duties shrank as a factory automated. In a firm, management would have cut workers to keep up profits. Families eventually had to face similar choices. Compared with that of women in the mid-nineteenth century, modern women's domestic productivity seemed meager. Relying on commercial goods and machines, women could accomplish the modern equivalent of traditional household tasks using much less time and effort, with the exception of caring for young, preschool children. What could women do in these new circumstances?

One choice was to create more household work. The decrease in the time needed to maintain a household did not automatically reduce the time women spent doing domestic work. Research has shown that American women who did not hold jobs claimed to be spending as much time on domestic chores in the mid-1960s as they had fifty years earlier.[60] Still, the labor *necessary* to maintain a household had declined a lot. Giving support to this interpretation, research has shown that couples have devoted much less time to household work when the wife has held a job.[61] The research on time use in the 1960s also showed that full-time housewives spent even more time than employed women did on housework over the weekends. Housewives did this excess work even though they had already done much more housework than women with paid jobs.[62] This evidence strongly supports the idea that full-time housewives were commonly putting in more time than they needed to keep their households in a reasonable condition. Three conditions seem to explain this anomaly. Some new tasks emerged—for example, shopping and chauffeuring children— that expanded the range of activities demanding effort. In addition, women increased their work load by raising household standards. For example, clothing had to be washed more often and children had to be given more attention. Apparently, women also purposely extended the time they labored. This added more significance and legitimacy to the only responsibility allowed them. They were working just as long, but not as hard.[63] As women did not get paid for domestic work, the time they spent was the clearest yardstick to measure their effort. They needed to keep this time large enough to convince both themselves and their families that they were making a worthwhile contribution. Some women became obsessive consumers and domestic managers who strove for perfect houses, children, and husbands. In the 1960s Betty Friedan effectively exposed a new truth: suburban housewives were hopelessly pursuing the illusions of a *feminine mystique* through the creation of more household work but suffering from an overwhelming, debilitating malaise.[64] Housewifery had rewards, but it could not give women the full-time fulfilling life that popular culture implied.

Others did choose to seek a life outside the domestic sphere. Spurred by economic need, large numbers of working-class women held jobs by the 1950s. Responding to different motives, a considerable number of middle-class women were trying to pursue careers by the 1960s. Employment had many drawbacks for middle-class women, but it also offered them independence and fulfillment. The rapid response of middle-class women to feminism's rallying call in the 1960s and 1970s demonstrated decisively their desire to seek realization through careers. Falling domestic labor responsibilities also promoted women's employment indirectly by letting them compete for better jobs. As women's household responsibilities declined, they could consider a wider range of jobs. When domestic responsibilities ruled women's lives, they often felt restricted to temporary jobs and were ill placed to compete for promotions. They compiled checkered work histories that denied them opportunities to get ahead in the economy. Research has suggested that men commonly have more continuous employment, and this continuity advantage seems responsible for much of men's superior occupational status and wages.[65] As women's domestic responsibilities declined, more women could hold jobs for long periods, increasing their competitiveness with men.[66]

Rising divorce rates (themselves probably partly the result of women's increased employment) also prompted more women to seek jobs.[67] Divorced women needed jobs more and did not have to contend with a resisting husband. Even male workers and employers were less likely to resist the idea of divorced women's getting a job, seeing them as needing an income more legitimately than married women.

The decline of necessary household labor also reduced husbands' interest in resisting wives who were seeking jobs, because men found their wives' domesticity less valuable. The value of wives' domestic productivity is one of several considerations affecting husbands' interests in their wives' taking or avoiding jobs. Consider an analogy. Many people might like to have a servant, yet few care to pay a servant unless they feel they are getting benefits worth the cost of the servant's labor. As household labor lost importance, a housewife came to mean something different to her husband. Her persona was gradually transformed from a valuable attendant to an encumbering responsibility.

Although it is difficult to substantiate that rising real wage rates had a decisive historical influence on women's employment rates, they seem likely to have increased the sense that women's household contributions had diminishing value. As a result of the long-term increase in economic productivity, "real" wage rates also had a long-term increasing trend throughout most of the past two centuries, although they fluctuated with the business cycle. This increased the value of both sexes' employment, even if it did little to alter the differential between them. A higher real wage implies a higher opportunity cost to those who forgo employment. Economists have suggested that the "pull" of this rising real wage was the primary cause of women's rising employment.[68] What we know about women's entry into jobs suggests that this formulation somewhat misinterprets the process. Women largely took jobs either because they and their families badly needed their added earnings or because they wanted the freedom, status, and identity conferred by employment. We would expect a rising real wage rate to influence actions based on either of these motives, but not to rule the actions.

The long-term increase in women's desire for jobs influenced the rise in women holding jobs.[69] Even if women's increased availability did not influence employers' hiring objectives, a rising demand for female labor still depended on the presence of women who were ready to respond. Moreover, the growing number of women seeking jobs did affect employers' behavior in two ways. First, it made women a more salient and practical choice as a permanent source of labor for a firm or occupation. Second, by enabling greater economic expansion, the rising female labor supply accelerated the rising demand for women. The total demand for labor usually was not the issue. Instead, what mattered was how much employers drew from diverse pools of labor to fill that demand. Varied motives prompted employers to consider new sources of labor. The most common reasons were difficulties filling jobs using customary hiring strategies or a plan to cut labor costs. As women's domestic obligations shrank and more sought jobs, they better fitted what employers wanted. As more women sought jobs, more employers could envision hiring women as a sound strategy.

The processes that assimilated women into the economy recall how the enclosure acts in England produced a labor force for the early factories. The capitalist transformation of agriculture left many rural dwellers without either land or employment. This transformation turned the rural population into a ready-made work force for labor-hungry factories. Later, industrialization similarly "enclosed" women's traditional productive activities in the household by absorbing them into the economy. This process was quieter, less self-conscious, and less extreme than the enclosure movement. Still, it had the same result.

RATIONALIZATION VERSUS DISCRIMINATION

A long-standing debate about discrimination has bedeviled efforts to explain women's employment in terms of interests. One side argues that overwhelming evidence shows that employers consistently discriminated against women in hiring and promotions. The other side argues that competitive market processes severely limit the amount of discrimination that can persist in the economy. In truth, employers' reasons for discriminating against women mixed rational calculation and prejudiced beliefs. To grasp employers' actions, we must reconcile two opposing, influential positions that treat these alternatives as mutually exclusive.

Some adherents of neoclassical economics have claimed that prejudiced discrimination is practically impossible because self-interested competition forestalls it. They believe that a calculating concern with profits was unavoidable in a competitive market economy. According to this perspective, if employers consistently acted rationally, women must have received less pay and poorer jobs than men because they really were less motivated, less trained, and less dependable employees.

Opposing interpretations have claimed that only bigotry can explain employers' self-evident refusal to hire or promote women. Proponents of this view believe that women with the ability and motives to become good employees were consistently rebuffed. The accounts stressing employers' discrimination imply that many employers consistently championed male ascendancy and believed in male superiority.

Both sides stand on sound empirical foundations. Historical experience shows that any known opportunity to make significant profits will attract some enterprising businessmen, even if they must violate laws and ethics. An abstract identification with male gender advantages could do little to impede a lust for money. Yet experience has also shown that ambitious women were consistently and emphatically obstructed by discrimination. Women were denied jobs, refused promotions, paid poorly, and generally treated badly by employers.

To make sense of these apparent inconsistencies, the proper question is *not:* did employers act rationally or did they irrationally discriminate against women? Instead we need to figure out how employers could both rationally pursue their interests and discriminate against women.

Economists have long recognized that employment discrimination—expressing employers' prejudices against women, racial minorities, older workers, and others—seems to contradict the expectations of economic theory. Economic theories usually assume that rational calculation and self-interest will guide people's economic behavior. This assumption implies that employers will always hire cheaper labor if they can increase profits. Discrimination seemingly defies this premise of modern economic theory. In response, economists have sometimes proposed that employers may indulge a *taste for discrimination* by accepting lower profits to avoid certain types of workers.[70] Treating prejudice as a consumer preference places bigotry on the same footing as enjoying ice cream, fast cars, risky investments, or health insurance: all appetites are equally irrational, but rational economic processes can control how much we get to fulfill them. Still, treating employers as consumers of labor does not explain discrimination, because *it is the absence of employers willing to exploit a lower-status group, not the presence of bigoted employers, that preserves discrimination, and thus needs explanation.*

The circumstances and motives causing employers to discriminate against women were varied. Distinguishing among these will help us to understand the opposite: why employers would start to hire or promote women.

- *Indirect or prior discrimination.* Employers without any explicit discriminatory bias in their hiring strategy often still hired only men. This outcome was unavoidable when every available person who fit the job-related criteria was male (no matter why this was true). In its pure form, this process implied *no* direct discrimination by the employer. Women did not compete successfully for the jobs because of past discrimination. Women lacked the skills, experience, or availability needed for jobs because of inequality and discrimination outside the firm. A contractor wanting to hire skilled plumbers, for example, would have been wasting his time seeking female plumbers. This discriminatory effect appeared mainly in hiring, but it could also occur in promotions when they depended on experience or opportunities external to the firm.

- *Statistical discrimination.* Employers sometimes mainly hired men because they believed men much more often met their needs than women did. In its pure form, employers who practiced statistical discrimination[71] were indifferent to employees' gender. They recruited consistently from a group they judged a dependable source because they considered that an effective strategy. In simple terms, statistical discrimination implied that the men available were not so consistently preferable to women as in indirect discrimination, yet employers believed that too few women were potentially good employees to merit the effort of recruiting them. Note that employers usually discriminated statistically only when hiring new employees.

- *Extorted discrimination.* Employers sometimes refrained from hiring or promoting women because they feared costly male retribution. They discovered, or at least believed, that they would incur added costs because their male employees or men in other firms or husbands would resist women's employment.[72] In its pure form, employers who practiced extorted discrimination were indifferent to employees' gender, but responsive to masculine racketeering.

- *Prejudiced discrimination.* Employers sometimes hired and promoted men because they believed that only men should have good jobs and that women should stay at home. This ideologically induced strategy typically increased costs. Consistent with Gary

Becker's analysis, it implies that employers willingly paid higher wages to ensure that women stayed home where they *belonged*. (In contrast, the preceding forms of discrimination were consistent with employers' efforts to curtail costs.)

All four forms of discrimination were widespread and persisted for two reasons. First, the widespread inequality between women and men meant that all forms of discrimination were pervasive and mutually reinforcing. Second, a small amount of prejudiced discrimination by employers could go a long way to sustain a much larger pattern of economic discrimination against women. This second point is terribly important. Most employers' decisions that favored men were economically reasonable decisions derived from indirect, statistical, or extorted discrimination. In the limited circumstances when women did offer themselves as serious job competitors with men, employers incurred little cost by refusing women good jobs. Therefore, employers could indulge the typically low costs of prejudiced discrimination, and these acts effectively reinforced the other obstacles preventing women's economic advancement.

At any time, few employers faced a realistic opportunity to increase profits significantly by employing or promoting more women. As Kenneth Arrow's analysis of discrimination has stressed, women offered employers few economic advantages and potentially high costs when in the short run only a few could be added to an established male work force.[73] Several circumstances limited the possibilities for profit. The general effects of inequality made women less experienced or trained, less likely to be seeking jobs, and less likely to succeed in positions mainly held by men. Because inequality caused jobs to become sex segregated, women were usually not applying for jobs in male occupations, increasing the effort and cost required to replace men with women. Also, within the short time frame that influenced thoughts about hiring policies, employers usually expected to hire only a small proportion of their work force (to replace others or to expand). Realistically, then, employers wondering if they should change strategies and begin hiring cheaper female labor would usually see that only a few jobs were at stake and that even finding women for them was a risky business. As a result of these circumstances, employers who did not hire or did not promote women usually were not sacrificing an opportunity to boost profits significantly by altering their policies toward women.

Therefore, employers usually could indulge prejudiced discrimination against women *at little cost*. From most employers' perspective, the cost of prejudiced discrimination was the value of forgone opportunities they experienced, not the profit potential theoretically available through broad employment of women in their firms. Employers only occasionally had to decide if they would pass over women for promotions or hiring. On those occasions, employers commonly saw little economic incentive for choosing women.

Though only narrowly exercised, employers' prejudiced discrimination against women was effective because it guarded the ports of entry by which women would gain access to better jobs. This resembles the way legal or social sanctions punishing a few people who violate our norms restrain the actions of many. Typically, a few ambitious, determined, or desperate women led the way into an occupation, industry, or firm. By blocking the first women who would lead the way, prejudiced employers blocked all those who would follow as well. Discrimination also had a self-enhancing effect that was particularly consequential for higher-status jobs. The existence of widespread discrimination against women, for any reason, diminished women's effectiveness and potential as employees. This made women poor risks for high-status jobs, giving even unprejudiced employers pragmatic interests in not advancing women.

The processes sustaining discrimination against women suggest a bizarre mutation of Adam Smith's "invisible hand," which produced a collective good from individuals' pursuits of private self-interests. Here we see something different. As many employers occasionally indulged their prejudices with slightly irrational hiring, together they produced economically irrational discrimination on an extensive scale.

Over time, because hiring women increasingly coincided with employers' interests, more women did get jobs. When women's labor offered a substantial opportunity to raise profits, at least in some industries and occupations, practicality ultimately prevailed over prejudice. Labor shortages, women's lower wages, or the threat of legal battles could make hiring women a profitable strategy. Firms that seized the opportunities for higher profits by hiring women gained an advantage. Others would find it more difficult to expand and to endure until they copied the strategy of hiring women.

Women's rising employment did not end discrimination, however, but changed its form. Employers usually hired women for different jobs than men. Occupational segregation allowed women to find jobs but denied them entry to "men's" jobs. Occupational segregation between "women's jobs" and "men's jobs" allowed employers a moderately rational balance between preserving discrimination and exploiting women's cheaper labor for profits. Segregation, both within firms and between firms, avoided resistance from threatened male workers without fighting against extorted discrimination. Segregation within firms allowed employers to exhibit prejudiced discrimination without forgoing the benefits of women's cheaper labor. Distinguishing between "women's jobs" and "men's jobs" had allowed employers to hire women without adopting completely impersonal employment practices. Women's and men's labor markets remained distinct. Instead of the separate spheres of employment and household that had divided men and women in the nineteenth century, the economy had created separate spheres of "men's jobs" and "women's jobs." This artificial division of labor in the economy proved even less durable than the earlier division of labor between economy and household.

The displacement of prejudiced discrimination in favor of impartial pursuit of economic interests was furthered by rationalization, another process integral to the development of the modern economy. Rationalization was a dominant theme in the work of the great social theorist Max Weber.[74] He considered rationalization a fundamental principal of modern society. According to Weber, rationalization permeated and transformed most institutions, revealing itself in such diverse arenas as the law, economic activity, political domination, and even musical composition. Organizations rationalize by adopting rules and procedures for decision making. In firms, rationalized processes stress practical calculations of the costs, benefits, and risks associated with alternative actions or strategies.

Generally, effective rationalization meant a firm was more responsive to organizational interests. Rationalization in the economy reduced the importance of employers' prejudices and increased the importance of interests for employment practices. Rational administration inherently opposed procedures that did not well serve the pursuit of profit. When discrimination against women was economically unsound, it was inconsistent with the rationalization of business practices.

Two primary processes motivated rationalization in the economy.

The first was competition. Because firms following rational practices usually had a higher likelihood of success, the marketplace impartially weeded out more irrational firms and let the more rational ones grow and propagate. Competition between firms favored the rationalization of employment practices in a simple, indirect, but brutal manner. If firms chose strategies lowering labor costs, they could expand their sales through effective price cutting. This pressure toward rationalization mattered most in highly competitive industries.

The growth of large, complex organizations was the second process that propelled rationalization in the economy. When firms grew large, those at the top found that controlling their organizations was inherently difficult.[75] As Weber's work implies, large organizations, consisting of positions filled through employment contracts, had an inherent tendency toward rationalization. In large organizations with diverse activities, control became a political problem, requiring intervening levels of authority. To control these intervening levels of authority and to stabilize practices against an unpredictable turnover of personnel, organizations adopted rule-based governance. Rules could be, and often were, irrational, of course. Still, the logic of a rule-based control system stressed rational interests over prejudice. Also, competition (between firms, organizations, divisions within organizations, and managers aspiring for promotions) punished those whose irrational rules significantly limited effectiveness.

As firms rationalized, they increasingly applied impersonal standards. A systematic, calculating approach to decisions always clashed with the use of particularistic criteria and personal biases. Organizations used rules and standard procedures to regulate the hiring and promotion decisions (and other actions) occurring at intermediate ranks. These rules also increasingly restricted the exercise of simple prejudice unless the rules embodied prejudice. As impersonal standards prevailed, economically unsound discrimination became easier to abandon.

This intensified rationality did not everywhere lead to greater employment of women. Some industries, regions, and firms experienced less rationalization. The circumstances of some rationalized firms promised no benefits if they hired more women, especially for high-status positions. Still, if hiring or promoting women offered a predictable opportunity to increase profits, rationalized firms usually would hire women.

Rationalization did not lead firms to embrace egalitarian philosophies or to champion promoting women into good jobs. A rationalized firm simply became increasingly indifferent to the sex of its lower employees. It still needed an incentive to change its practices. When and only when firms perceived worthwhile economic incentives did they make serious efforts to hire or promote women.

Employers' interests in abandoning discrimination rose as changing conditions altered their interpretations of self-interest and the opportunities to increase profits. Indirect discrimination occurred through general unequal treatment of women external to any specific firm. Indirect discrimination necessarily declined as the other forms of discrimination and other aspects of gender inequality it represented declined. Statistical discrimination against women gave way when employers believed more women were worth hiring. Shortages of male labor, greater availability of female labor, increased value of female labor, and occupational segregation shifted employers' interests toward hiring women. The amount of discrimination "extorted" from employers depended on the costs they expected from men's resistance to women's employment weighed against the opportunities to increase profits by hiring women. Such discrimination declined when the costs of male resistance fell or the value of hiring women rose. Therefore, the same conditions that reduced statistical discrimination by increasing the profit incentives for hiring women also worked against extorted discrimination. In the long run, male workers, businessmen, and husbands resisted women's employment less, reducing the pressure on employers to engage in extorted discrimination. Once conditions made external statistical and extorted discrimination inconsistent with their interests, employers either abandoned discrimination or pursued it because of prejudice.

The conditions that eroded prejudiced discrimination were also similar, though less well-defined. Employers responded to the tradeoffs between discrimination's costs and their commitments to a prejudiced view of the world. When employers had good opportunities to make money by hiring women, prejudiced discrimination became costly. Employers did not lightly endure significant costs they could avoid. Over time, the costs of discrimination rose.

As more women were hired and promoted, the success of these women validated the rationalization process on two levels. Workers and employers saw that women were capable. This result ratified the opinions of those who supported rational standards and eased the fears of those who did not. To the degree that women's productivity surpassed their costs, companies that employed these women experienced apparent economic benefits. These outcomes reinforced the rationalization process and further fueled the advancement of women.

The debate over seemingly irrational discrimination has persisted because both sides have somewhat confused the issues. In particular, the time frame is crucial. Economists who claim that competition will discipline employers so as to prevent sustained discrimination sometimes neglect the constrained conditions within which employers make decisions. In the real world of short-term strategies, employers could long engage in discrimination against women (and others) without incurring significant costs. Given the difficulties of attracting female applicants and identifying good female workers, the resistance of the male work force, the cultural lenses through which people were evaluated, the detrimental effect of past discrimination on the experience of female labor, and the marginal hiring that most employers would do in a short period, employers usually found that discrimination against women came cheaply if it cost anything. However, those who reject the economic analysis have largely overlooked the same processes. For the economists are right to argue that market forces are powerful and that economically irrational discrimination is unstable. In the long run, market forces do induce employers to use female labor where it will enhance profits. Economists have sometimes erred by suggesting that market forces will have the instantaneous effects in real life that they obtain in theory. Those rejecting the economic account have made the same error, inferring that if it could be shown that market forces did not prevent prejudiced discrimination in the short run, it could be inferred that they were not effective.

Thus, two essential points allow us to resolve the debate over discrimination. First, much discrimination that might appear to be economically irrational on the surface is really rational or at least not very costly to employers. Second, the market forces that economic theory suggests should clash with discrimination are influential, but their effects take generations to play themselves out.

Even as economic conditions swung employers' interests firmly on the side of hiring women, however, occupational segregation allowed high levels of discrimination against women. In pure economic terms, the prospects of completely integrating women into the economy rather than restricting them to low-status occupations did not promise any significant opportunities to increase profits. To put it differently, if we restrict ourselves solely to the effects of people's job performances, substituting the more skilled, talented, and experienced women for less valuable men in high-status jobs would have been economically rational. Yet even if we consider a complete transformation rather than the incremental changes within employers' power, no evidence suggests that productivity would have been significantly affected. Production simply was not that sensitive to the quality of personnel available to fill high-status jobs (partially because job allocation processes were too crude to reflect such a change in potential). Something else had to happen.

SMASHING THE BARRIERS BEFORE HIGH-STATUS JOBS

Women's gradual movement into the economy seemed unable to extend above the middle rungs of the occupational ladder. After World War II, women took new jobs at a continuously rising rate, accelerating their century-long movement into the economy. Yet they still rarely got positions with authority or high rewards. High-status jobs seemed insulated from the effects of the long-term processes that induced employers to hire women for lower-status jobs.

From the 1960s onward, political actions, not gradual economic or structural changes, finally let women penetrate high-status occupations, for example as professionals or managers.[76] The state enacted policies against discrimination and allowed women legislative and judicial redress of discriminatory practices. Through political organization and collective action, women used these channels to arrest employment discrimination by making it too costly. Women's organizations sometimes also used direct action against employers with sit-ins, picketing, or strikes, tactics also designed to discourage discrimination by making it too expensive.

Why did women move into high-status occupations through a political process rather than smoothly completing the long-term process that had gradually brought women into the economy for over a century? Essentially, the processes that had great impact on low-status occupations and low-status positions in firms had only weak impact on high-status jobs. The circumstances of high-status jobs subdued each of the economic processes favoring women's assimilation.

Labor shortages, which created significant pressure for women's assimilation in lower-status jobs, were not an issue for high-ranking jobs. A surplus of aspirants shielded high-status jobs from this influence. Men who wanted to be managers or professionals were never hard to find. Men continuously scrambled over each other to get positions that would give them wealth, authority, and status. This competition for good jobs generally forestalled labor shortages.

Employers still sometimes faced job-specific shortages because they needed talents or skills that were scarce (at least temporarily). Yet even when employers found men difficult to get for some high-status jobs, they rarely considered recruiting women. However hard appropriate men might be to find, women with the appropriate skills and likelihood of continued service were even rarer. Discrimination's pervasive effects made it difficult to disregard when trying to rapidly alleviate a shortage of people to fill high-status positions. Discriminatory practices usually excluded women from professional programs and from jobs with low-level authority. Denied access to the positions that gave men the requisite experience, women could not compete successfully for most high-status positions, even if employers had not considered sex when hiring for them. Therefore, even when employers felt hard pressed to find men who could fill high-status positions, women did not seem to offer a better alternative. Exceptions occurred when some employers needed to keep salaries low and when many employers faced labor shortages because of a war or rapid business expansion. These exceptions probably did precipitate much of women's limited movement into professional and managerial positions before the 1960s.

Women's willingness to work for less had little effect, because firms usually paid less attention to simple profit-and-cost calculations when filling high-status positions. Large firms paid their higher-status personnel for loyalty and commitment. When filling high-status jobs, firms and professions preferred people who seemed more reliable and predictable with more leadership potential, even if they cost more. Compatibility and familiarity outweighed impersonal standards in making these judgments. They did try to weed out those who lacked the necessary skills and drive, but this usually still left them considerable choice. If cost was not an issue, a firm could almost always find some man preferable to the best female candidate.

Usually the gateways to independent professions also could disregard simple profit calculations when deciding whom to admit or support. These gateways included professional colleges, hospitals, law firms, and the like. Many men vied for these positions. Neither difficulties in filling positions nor potential cost savings were likely to make women a more appealing alternative.

The impracticality of sex segregation retarded another potential mechanism for women's assimilation into high-status positions. Recall that much of women's gradual assimilation into low-status positions relied on sex segregation of occupations or jobs. This strategy was difficult to pursue in the case of managerial or professional jobs.[77] The relationships between positions made the rigid boundaries of occupational segregation impractical except in special circumstances. Managerial jobs were organized into hierarchical pyramids, with a high degree of short-range lateral and vertical interaction. Promotions usually widened the range of a manager's influence. Professions, unless embedded in a managerial hierarchy, showed a contrasting pattern of minimal formal distinctions between practitioners. Both of these patterns required dispersed mobility and interaction between positions that conflicted with the segmentation needed for occupational segregation by sex.

Still, before the 1960s, most of women's limited movement into managerial and professional positions occurred where segregation was possible. Women's employment in less prestigious professions such as nursing, elementary school teaching, and social work is well known. Women seem to have held managerial or supervisory positions mainly when their subordinates were women, as in the cases of head nurses, managers of secretarial pools, supervisors of female factory workers, and managers of female retail clerks. These were positions in which employers were much more likely to perceive women as having the right skills and experience. Employers also faced the least opposition from male employees, because no man was in line to be promoted to these positions, and few men would be subject to the woman's supervision. These specialized positions that opened some moderately high-status jobs to women were limited. They could not become female identified and then show a burst of growth as happened with some of the lower-status female occupations. Management activities and promotion patterns linked high-status positions in ways that impeded incipient sex segregation.

The closer men were to the top of their organization's authority structure, the less chance there was that superiors could apply a disinterested administrative rationality to their positions. Personal relationships and intermingled interests diminished enthusiasm about impersonal standards. Men with authority were much more likely to apply organizational rationality to positions well below them than to those occupied by their close associates. The same was true for independent professionals.

Also, as a person ascended the authority ladder, promotions depended on judgments vulnerable to cultural belief and personal biases. No clear-cut test allowed firms to judge a person's reliability or leadership ability. As the judgments were inherently subjective, those in authority would rely on projections of their experiences and the accepted beliefs in their milieu. When men held all authority positions, their experience and their preconceptions associated women with a pattern of deference, not leadership. These expectations gave the men in authority a cultural or ideological predisposition against promoting women.

The same authority positions whose occupants usually promoted rationalization became obstacles when rationalization threatened their self-interests. This resistance does not mean that people with power opposed all applications of rational procedures to their tier. They probably accepted many changes that increased efficiency, though sometimes begrudgingly. Still, they had little incentive to subject themselves to the same rational procedures they used to gain effective control over subordinates.

Power and rationalization processes pushed and pulled with what some would call a dialectic tension. The power concentrated in modern organizations fostered rationalization, which later came to threaten the organization of power. As firms, markets, and the state grew and became more complex, they increasingly needed to control and integrate activities within their boundaries. Rationalized procedures and organization gradually superseded other forms because they proved more successful. Yet ultimate control of institutional power often resided in positions whose rationale escaped rational standards, and people gained those positions through processes insulated from rational procedures. This disjunction created an organizational tension. Although rationalization was unleashed originally to serve power, it had the potential to challenge the stability of irrational power.

At the upper echelons, the effects of rationalization were also mitigated because discrimination could be a rational strategy in a discriminatory society. Discrimination has a powerful self-reinforcing effect on high-status positions. No matter how irrational its origin, once widespread discrimination exists, employers' rational interests can become attached to further discrimination.

Discrimination against women lowered their effectiveness and therefore their value to employers. As a result, even employers who were not prejudiced were unlikely to hire or promote women into high-status jobs. The presence of widespread discrimination objectively reduced women's capacity to perform and made them risky choices for any employer.

Even if men did not wish to treat women differently from men, a widespread belief that discrimination against women was effective would make discrimination effective. For example, a company manager filling an important position would be likely to promote a man over a woman whom he thought better qualified, if he feared that contacts in other companies or other important men in his own company would respond so poorly to the woman that she would fail, to his own disadvantage and the company's. This subtle process deserves more attention than it has received. To the degree that employers and managers *believed* that discrimination against women was active, they had sound reasons to expect women to do worse than men with similar abilities. This belief made it rational to favor men for high-status positions where the belief suggested women's effectiveness would suffer. If this belief was widespread, then rational behavior by employers would commonly reinforce it so that reality matched the belief, even if employers generally had no prejudice. Unlike many inaccurate beliefs about causal processes in the economy, experiments ignoring this belief were not likely to produce success. Why? Because, if employers acted in a reasonably calculating way, the validity or effectiveness of this belief was a direct function of its pervasiveness. If people believed it, it became true.

Because so much indirect, statistical, and extorted discrimination kept women from high-status jobs, employers usually had no reason to contemplate prejudiced discrimination. Yet this social environment also increased the likelihood that employers would display prejudiced discrimination in the unusual circumstances when women appeared as good alternatives to men.

Overall, the powerful processes that had induced women's gradual economic assimilation simply placed too little pressure on high-status jobs to have a substantial effect. Competition for good jobs prevented pressures from male labor shortages. High-status jobs stressed loyalty, predictability, and minimizing risks more than productivity, so pressures to lower wage costs were weak. Sex segregation of occupations became less practical in higher-status positions, lessening the likelihood that special niches would develop for women. Rationalization's effects were also muted by the greater influence of positional power, self-interest, and personal ties in higher-status occupations.

While economic processes did not directly lead to women's assimilation into high-status jobs, they set the stage for this outcome. Rational administration and the enhancement of organizational interests greatly diminished the interests and power rationally committed to women's exclusion, although they did not break down women's exclusion from high-status positions. By extensively assimilating women to lower-status positions, the general economic processes created the social interests and organizational potential to rebel effectively against the barriers to women's advancement. The combination of bureaucratic rationalization, irrational barriers to women's advancement, and an increasingly dense female work force produced an inherently unstable social combination. This could not last.

Because high-status positions excluded women for so long, the men running organizations or occupying high-status positions might seem to have resisted women's entry much more forcefully than men at lower levels. The resistance may have been higher than for many low-status jobs, but we should not exaggerate the difference. Resistance to women's entry existed at all levels from the men who worked at that level. High-status jobs differed from low-status jobs not because they resisted women with peculiar intensity but because high-status jobs offered much less opportunity to profit from hiring women and because the resistance of high-status men was more effective.

While high-status jobs were largely insulated from the pressures that opened lower-status jobs to women, they were not invulnerable or even particularly well protected if pressures appeared. Economic changes did not offer employers the same incentives to assimilate women into high-status jobs as they did for low-status ones. But economic changes created conditions that made continued exclusion of women from most high-status jobs problematic. Most important, the dominance of bureaucratic organization induced considerable indifference to the gender of most high-status employees.

By the 1960s, most large bureaucratic organizations were ill pre-pared to determinedly oppose women entering high-status positions, because discrimination served no organizational interest. The re-sponse of top corporate executives was critical when women agitated for, and government policy demanded, an end to sex discrimination. Top executives had ultimate control over employment policy. These men's prejudice toward women varied widely. Yet usually neither their organizational nor personal interests conflicted with women's becom-ing managers in their firm. Their interests did prompt them to resist hiring or promoting employees who might create organizational havoc, damage authority relations, or seriously diminish their com-petitive position. But they had little reason to fear such consequences from allowing women to enter the higher ranks on an equal basis with men. Under these conditions, top executives responded ambivalently to the prospect of women's entering higher organizational positions. Some consistently opposed women because bigotry ruled their behav-ior. Yet many strongly resisted only when they feared measures might force them to hire or promote women over men who were truly better qualified. Many might have preferred keeping an all-male manage-ment, but this was not a burning issue among executives at the top of corporate hierarchies. To them, most managers were simply more em-ployees.

Bureaucratization had less impact on the professions, but showed a similar pattern.[78] By the 1960s, most basic professional training oc-curred in large colleges and universities. These schools were the initial gatekeepers for the professions. While personal prejudice against women appeared common in professional schools, they too were bu-reaucratic structures. Their interests coincided with discrimination against women only so long as external discrimination denied women the chance for professional success. If women could have successful careers, then a professional school had nothing to gain by preferen-tially selecting inferior men who would have less successful careers. Women's access to desirable professional positions (after completing school) was influenced by the same processes as managerial positions. By 1961, 88 percent of the Americans classified by the census as pro-fessional or technical workers were *not* self-employed.[79] Many worked in large bureaucratic settings that responded to the same rationaliza-tion forces as any other organization.

In some sense, the economy had created a transition problem.

Women's partial economic assimilation and the dominance of bureaucratic organization were inconsistent with continued discrimination against women for high-status jobs. Economic rationality and the balance of interests favored women's full assimilation. Yet the structure of opportunities and incentives facing individual employers did not push them to question and defy the pattern of discrimination that kept women out. Agitation by women and government intervention, rather than profit opportunities, prompted businesses to assimilate women into high-status jobs.

The economic system had reached a point where women's partial assimilation provoked enough widespread resentment to give rise to the modern women's movement. By the 1960s enough women had careers in business or as professionals that they could organize as a visible political force. Because of lifelong discrimination, most of these women had stunted careers. Also, because of the discrimination, these women who survived the pressures against them tended to be tough and committed. Colleges and universities, responding to organizational processes similar to those in the economy, were giving degrees to about 200,000 women each year. Partial assimilation gave a lot of women enormous resentment over transparent injustices they suffered from discrimination and the resources needed to organize against it.

The state took women's side on this issue. From the perspective of the state's abstract interests, most economic discrimination against women was an irrational policy. It produced social unrest, an inefficient allocation of resources, and political conflicts without giving much in return. Without an autonomous state interest in preserving women's economic disabilities, state officials had an interest in sustaining discrimination only if influential political forces backed discriminatory legislation. By adopting policies intended to enforce women's assimilation into high-status positions, the state championed rationalized promotion processes. They rationalized selection by barring the use of an irrelevant criterion—sex. Businesses and other institutions found it hard to adopt nondiscriminatory policies independently. Yet the rules that the state forced employers to adopt could only improve the quality of personnel over the long term. This imposition of rationality was not a new role for the state. Theorists with varied perspectives largely agree that the capitalist state has repeatedly had to save business from itself.

Contrary to Adam Smith's hopes, capitalist firms and markets have had a bad habit of creating turmoil and crises that they could not resolve. Left to themselves, they produced trusts, cycles of boom and bust, vast labor unrest, and political discord. Competition, self-interest, and short-term priorities prevented businessmen from solving these problems. The state stepped into the breach. Some representatives of business interests always opposed these state efforts. Their motives mixed ignorant intransigence with strategic efforts to protect their interests. They feared that the state policies might go so far that they threatened the collective interests of corporate business. Businesses' inability to complete the rational assimilation of women differed somewhat from these other economic or political problems. Still, the state's role in solving the problem was similar.

THE ECONOMIC ASSIMILATION OF WOMEN

In practice, a group of related changes increases the potential for women's rising employment, without any one of those changes directly requiring women's assimilation. An unfulfilled demand for labor arises unevenly over time in various industries, occupations, and regions. Similarly, changing circumstances increase the likelihood that women will find employment practical or desirable without deciding concretely how various women will respond to these circumstances. Growth in the latent female labor supply (the increasing numbers of women who would be willing to take jobs, if they were offered) creates an opportunity for competitive capitalist expansion. The less advantage that businesses take of this opportunity, the greater the opportunity becomes, as low wages and desperation for jobs open female labor to exploitation for profiteering. While nothing forces any employer to use female labor, competitive pressures and a thirst for profit make it highly unlikely that all employers will continuously refuse to exploit an attractive, expanding source of good, cheap labor. Whether or not women's employment realizes the potential improvement offered by any specific opportunity depends on a variety of other variable, historically specific conditions.

The argument here is not that, to be viable, capitalist economies inherently require female labor, but instead that economic expansion combined with economic rationalization has an inherent tendency to create a demand for female labor. Equally, this analysis does not suggest that women's household labor necessarily declines over time, but instead that modern economic and familial organization do have an inherent tendency to reduce the amount of domestic labor necessary to sustain households, and the lower that amount, the easier it is for women to hold jobs. The analysis does not suggest that men ever consistently promote women's employment, but instead men's interests in opposing women's employment have an inherent tendency to decline in modern economies, ultimately reducing men's willingness and capacity to obstruct the rising demand for and supply of female labor.

As the modern economy developed centralized production, wage employment, and large-scale, bureaucratic organization, the distribution of economic power and interests slowly dissociated from gender inequality. As a result, gender inequality was gradually disembedded from economic inequality. Economic expansion generated a rising demand for employees, eroded the need for household labor, and induced a bureaucratic indifference to economically irrelevant criteria such as gender. As these evolving conditions drew women into the labor force, they also transformed working women into a latent interest group whose organized voice carried weight.

Industrial expansion drew ever more women into jobs no matter what anyone understood or thought. Economic expansion needed continuous additions to the labor force, and the old sources of new male recruits had to run dry eventually. Industrial expansion, and related demographic changes, also dramatically reduced the work needed in the home. Women's increasing availability for employment complemented employers' increasing need for a new source of workers. Moreover, women's economic marginality allowed employers to hire them for less. These conditions opening jobs to women had accelerated effects when they caused some rapidly expanding occupations to become known as "women's work."[80]

The long-term movement of women into the labor force followed some consistent patterns. Once we exclude the premodern occupations of household help and agricultural labor, the proportion of women among all those working in modern occupations has risen with remarkable uniformity since 1870. Over the past half-century, women's movement into employment did accelerate somewhat, but this acceleration began well before World War II, the event often believed to have changed the long-term pattern. Similarly, the movement of married women into the labor force between 1940 and 1990 was consistent and surprisingly independent of their husbands' income. Women with lower-income husbands moved into employment at a higher rate early in this period, but women with higher-income husbands caught up later. The data show a marked regularity in women's economic assimilation both over time and across classes.

Processes inherent to the development of an industrial market economy led to economic assimilation by increasing both the demand for women employees and the supply of women seeking jobs. The economy has persistently absorbed more of the productive activity in society, as it commercialized, industrialized, and bureaucratized wherever possible, gradually reducing the need for women's domestic labor. To fuel this expansion, the economy has drawn an ever-growing proportion of the population into its system. This expansionist tendency gradually increased employers' interest in female labor. As firms became larger and more bureaucratically organized, their owners and managers assessed hiring and promotional policies differently. They increasingly stressed costs and benefits over cultural patterns of gender inequality. If employers found they needed to hire women to avoid losing profits to a shortage of male labor or they faced an opportunity to enhance profits significantly by exploiting female labor, they would hire women unless some countervailing force offset these interests. Over time, as firms and industries depended more on female labor, employed women gained leverage against employers and male workers. By applying this leverage, they could force employers to treat them more as they treated men. Women's ability to use the leverage they gained from extensive assimilation into low-status jobs was especially important to gaining them access to high-status jobs.

High-status jobs were partly insulated from the economic processes that brought women into low-status jobs. While bureaucratic rationalization reduced the potential for a committed resistance to women's entry, neither a labor shortage nor competitive pressure on wages pressured employers to hire women. Before the 1960s, women's economic assimilation occurred mainly through low-status jobs. Small numbers of women had gradually begun to enter professional and managerial occupations, but the big influx waited until the 1970s. When women's economic assimilation progressed far enough, they created pressures in the economy and political order. When combined with rationalized interests of those controlling employment, these pressures became great enough to break through the weakened resistance that remained.

The reasons why the economy has absorbed and elevated women are, paradoxically, both more complex and simpler than most people expect. Most accounts seeking to explain women's rising employment stress one process that influenced women's employment, especially shortages of male labor, a rising female wage rate, reduced household work, greater education, and fewer children. Realistically, these economic processes all contributed to the transformation. Even more processes that have not received sufficient attention, such as rationalization and occupational segregation, also contributed to women's rising employment. Yet, while women's economic assimilation happened only through the complex combined effects of these varied processes, a simpler explanation also exists at a higher level of abstraction.

All the processes that stimulated women's employment reflected a growing inconsistency between the interests produced by modern economic organization and the requirements for preserving gender inequality. This inconsistency created an ever-increasing pressure to disembed gender inequality from economic inequality. The economic resources committed to male advantages declined as the opportunities to profit by women's employment expanded. The rate at which various specific economic processes helped to advance women's status depended on historical contingencies independent of the long-term causal pressures. Under different historical conditions, the timing and importance of the individual processes would have differed. Yet the overall pattern of women's rising employment would still have grown out of the same range of economic influences, all traceable to the inconsistencies between modern economic organization and gender inequality.

CHAPTER FOUR

INSTITUTIONAL INDIVIDUALISM

Modern economic and political organization fostered individualism, which stressed what people know and do over birth and status. Grades in schools, standardized entrance exams, rules governing promotions, no-fault divorce laws, and a belief that jobs should go to the most qualified applicants are all signs of individualism. Individualism applied impartial standards to people's performance, skills, and effort. As it permeated other social institutions, such as the educational system and the family, individualism subverted gender inequality, contributing to its decline, even as the institutions continued to discriminate against women.

Again, a paradox. Men have dominated these institutions, so we would reasonably expect they would consistently support gender inequality. Nonetheless, they adopted practices and ideas that effectively helped to undermine gender inequality. These institutions have been justifiably criticized for sustaining gender inequality by treating women differently from men. Yet these same institutions helped erode inequality over the long term, although few expected or intended this. Three institutional contexts that illustrate this paradoxical relationship to gender inequality are the modern educational system, the family, and, a context that cuts across institutions, the prevailing ideology about fair and effective ways to select people for jobs and other positions.

In each of these contexts, institutional individualism—individualism embedded in an institution's practices and ideals—generated interests, expectations, perceptions, and social conditions that favored increasing gender equality, although the men guiding all institutions believed they were preserving "traditional" distinctions between women and men. Modern schools steadily eroded differences between what women and men learned, although they were committed to maintaining distinctions. Similarly, meritocratic ideas made discrimination appear increasingly impractical and unjust, although the ideas were intended to legitimate existing inequality and rationalize organizational power. The modern family also produced individualistic parental and spousal interests that had a poor fit with gender inequality, although men clung to their role as head of the household.

As with economic and political shifts, the changes were diffuse, uneven, and gradual. The long-term causal processes created an expanding potential for actions benefiting women rather than directly improving women's status. Historical conditions decided the specific changes, when they occurred, and who induced them, as people adapted to spreading institutional individualism, each according to their circumstances. Over the long term, however, institutional individualism consistently degraded sex distinctions crucial to gender inequality's persistence, elevating actions, expectations, and ideals that ignored gender.

Institutional individualism emerged in the transition to modern society, and the concept of individual was created in the effort to understand that transition. Because it refers to important, pervasive, and complex phenomena, the term *individualism* has been used in many ways. Steven Lukes has shown that various thinkers have used *individualism* to refer to the right or the ability to withdraw to a realm outside civic control, the ideal of free citizens who grant legitimate sovereignty to a representative government, the ideal of free property owners and laborers who constitute an economy (either concretely in history or abstractly in theory), the belief that people may achieve legitimate moral judgments through critical thinking rather than through applying prescriptive rules, and other, sometimes more abstract, ideas.[1] In intellectual discourse and as an idea in popular culture, individualism largely refers to a set of beliefs. In contrast, here we are concerned with individualism as it exists in the pattern of institutional practices and ordinary people's lives, reflecting early social theorists' interpretations of the transition toward individualism as a defining characteristic of modern societies. These theorists emphasized divergent causal processes and used different terminology, but all stressed aspects of individualism. Each sought to understand what made modern societies different from earlier societies. From their ideas emerges a sound theoretical conception of individualism.

The term *individualism* apparently first appeared in English in *Democracy in America,* a classic study by Alexis de Tocqueville, a Frenchman who visited America in the 1830s. This influential work tried to identify what distinguished the Americans' new democratic culture from backward aristocratic regimes in France and other European states. Tocqueville primarily identified individualism with a personal independence that gave people's self-interests precedence over their obligations to other segments of the community. Tocqueville considered individualism a singular product of democratic political organization. He contrasted it with aristocratic society in which everyone's identity derived from group membership. There, a strict hierarchy of relations connected everyone from the lowest peasant to the king. The lack of formal status groups and higher social mobility of democratic societies eradicated these connections, leaving everyone as an individual.

Other nineteenth-century theorists identified similar individualistic characteristics distinguishing modern society from those that preceded it, although their portraits varied in accordance with the historical and intellectual currents surrounding them. In Great Britain, Henry Sumner Maine claimed that *contract* had displaced *status* as freely bargained relations and individual obligation supplanted fixed ranks and family dependency. In Germany, Ferdinand Tönnies contended that *Gesellschaft* was displacing *Gemeinschaft* as the impersonal, contractual, secular relations of the modern economy superseded the intimate, constant, morally saturated bonds in families or small communities. In France, Emile Durkheim contrasted modern societies with primitive societies. In modern societies, Durkheim proposed, *organic solidarity* had replaced *mechanical solidarity,* so that people were conditionally linked through varied roles as a result of a high division of labor rather than unconditionally linked by sharing a common identity as a result of a low division of labor. Others expressed similar ideas about the individualistic transformation of social life.[2] In the twentieth century, these diverse theoretical oppositions were consolidated by the influential American sociologist Talcott Parsons, representing each with what he called a *pattern variable.*[3] Each pattern variable defined a continuum, with modern and premodern societies at opposite ends. Modern society produced a new bundle of orientations that guided social action in a much more individualistic way than premodern societies.

These theorists believed the transition to modern society dramatically transformed human relationships, resulting in individualism. They each tried to characterize the differences between modern contractual, bureaucratic relationships and premodern ties characterized by kinship, fealty, and bondage. They associated enduring, multistranded, ascribed relationships with families and communities of the past. In the future, which they associated with modern economic and political life, they foresaw ever more temporary, limited purpose, voluntaristic (elective) relationships. Or, individualism.

Individualism, therefore, can be conceived as a characteristic of social practices, organizational rules, and relationships. This *institutional individualism* exists insofar as the relations between an institution and people are direct, consensual, and functionally circumscribed. Direct social relations are unmediated by any intervening personalities such as husbands, families, lineages, guilds, communities, or organized castes. For example, universal suffrage gives all citizens a direct relationship to the state. Consensual social relations operate within rules that proscribe coercion (except as a response to illegitimate actions violating the rules) and respect self-determination. For example, people are formally free to quit any job (unless bound by a contract freely signed). The rules, activities, and considerations legitimately active in a functionally circumscribed relationship are limited to its defined role in people's lives. For example, a bank's lending decisions are formally limited to the prospective borrower's economic circumstances and detached or isolated from such considerations as kinship ties or ethnicity. Practical considerations, conflicting claims of overlapping relationships, and the simple pursuit of power commonly restrict the attainment of institutional individualism.

Institutionalized individualism has arisen gradually out of modern political and economic organization, largely over the last two centuries. As it unfolded, individualism reinforced economic and political interests' disengagement from gender inequality, helping pave the way for women's rising status. This individualism diffused to other institutional contexts as they adapted to the transformation of political and economic organization.

In the political realm, modern citizenship's expansion was an inherently individuating process. As the state granted legal, political, and social citizenship rights, it broke apart ties of personal dependency. Earlier, people lacking these rights from the state had to depend on others to represent them, to defend their interests, and to provide them security. Mainly, families served these purposes. This dependency gave men, who controlled familial resources, a strong upper hand. Citizenship rights severed many of these dependencies, substituting direct relations between women and the state for relations mediated by men. The state also bolstered individualism in other ways. It tied its legitimacy to the claim that it represented all the people; it subjected all people to more shared standards as it gradually extended the scope of government activities; and it applied bureaucratic principles in its ever-expanding activities.

In the economic realm, expanding employment had a similar individuating influence. Paid employment necessarily displaced self-employment as economic production moved from families into firms. Separation of jobs from families exposed both sexes to more economic individualism, but the change affected women and men differently. Earlier, when families organized most economic activities, men controlled households while most women were directly dependent on a husband or father. The modern economy forced all people, male and female, to rely more on jobs for income. Men experienced this trend as a decline in economic independence. Women had the opposite experience. As jobs became available to them, women became more economically independent, because they became less dependent on individual men. Modern economic practices also promoted individualism in other ways. They stressed impersonal market criteria; they increased the role of temporary economic relationships between people; and they expanded anonymous, bureaucratic authority in large firms.

Because other societal institutions were highly integrated with and dependent on economic and political processes, they too became, to greater or lesser degrees, individualistic. In particular, modern education, meritocratic ideology, and companionable marriage all exhibited more institutional individualism. Modern schools placed children in a formal, bureaucratic setting to prepare them for the world beyond their family boundaries. Meritocratic ideas and practices promoted abstract standards, idealizing their justice and effectiveness. The modern family became loosely bound by sentimental ties that encouraged autonomy. What we want to understand is just how these tendencies toward institutional individualism were induced by the reorganization of economic and political processes, and how these individualistic tendencies slowly created institutional support for gender inequality's decline.

MODERN EDUCATION'S IMPLICIT CHALLENGE TO GENDER INEQUALITY

The educational system favored equality between the sexes sooner and more fully than did the men who ran it, the parents whose children were in it, or the society it served. Its aid to women's rising status is still often underestimated. In recent years, studies have shown that women long had less access to schooling and that what education they could get was different and inferior, reflecting and helping perpetuate gender inequality. Nonetheless, modern education has been a powerful and largely unintended force eroding the foundations of gender inequality. While women have had fewer educational opportunities than men until recently, the educational system incorporated women early, quickly, and soon began to lessen the gap between the sexes. Educators and parents did plan to educate women differently from men, but the core subjects and skills were largely taught in the same way. Somewhat better schools were available for males, but most education was coeducational and largely equivalent in quality. Unavoidable individualistic tendencies in modern education defied people's efforts to make it fit and sustain traditional gender roles.

Infused with individualism, the modern educational system is a defining invention of modern life that signaled a fundamental realignment of society's primary institutions. Indeed, by separating people from their families, the organization of modern education may have contributed more to individualism than all the new ideas arising from science, philosophy, or reforming religions. Modern education wedged itself between the private world of the family and the public world of the economy and the political order. The modern economy and government produced the needs and the resources that led to the extensive expansion of education. Before this, people learned their work skills from their parents or by working with others who had the skills. As the family economy disappeared, the state, industry, and families needed a school system to prepare young people for their adult roles.

Families felt the need for schools most directly, as with each passing year fewer parents worked at home or had the skills their children needed. Families relied on schools to watch over their children, to instill morality, and to prepare them for their adult roles. Businesses turned to schools to instill skills and discipline, hoping to ensure an adequate supply of productive employees. The government relied on schools to generate loyalty and consent to its rule. Schools thus arose as a functional response to the needs of both the public realm—the economy and the state—and the private realm—the family. Organized bureaucratically with meritocratic standards and rational procedures, modern education increasingly linked private institutions to public institutions and older generations to younger ones.

The division between schools and households marked the emergence of modern social organization, much like the more commonly cited division between work worlds and households. When viewed from afar, using a long-term historical perspective, what could be stranger or more dramatic than modern education? People send all their school-age children into the arms and ideas of strangers, for a duration almost equaling the work week, from a very young age until they are young adults. Most have little influence over which school their children attend, and even less influence over who teaches their children or what they are taught. Schools teach children how to think, how to succeed, what is true, what is right, and what is wrong. By the time children reach the age when they can assimilate moral ideals, they spend most of the work week away at school even if their mothers stay at home. "Traditionalists" arguing that working mothers plunge their children into moral deprivation have been blind to historical realities. Women's modern employment has *not produced* significant changes in childrearing. Instead, women's employment, in part, has been *produced by* the changes in childrearing that have moved so much of children's upbringing outside the household.

The egalitarian bias of the educational system developed in fits and starts through a complex process lasting two centuries. The changing treatment of women was intermingled with the perpetual expansion and transformation of schooling. Primary schooling became standard during the late nineteenth century, high school became standard during the first half of the twentieth century, and college education has now become a middle-class standard. At each level of education, private schools for boys helped start the process, but state-controlled, coeducational public schools soon developed to serve the majority.[4] Girls' schooling first caught up with boys' at the lowest level. The equalizing process repeated itself at each successive level. Not only were women gradually given similar amounts of education; the education at each level also moved toward a similar curriculum and quality of education for girls and boys. For this to occur, the parents' and girls' demand for female schooling had to rise, schools' and colleges' willingness to educate females had to increase, and male resistance to women's improved education had to fall. This powerful equalizing trend in education reflected the power of institutional individualism both in education and in the surrounding social environment.

The American commitment to public education and coeducation exceeded that of most other industrializing countries, although similar developments were widespread. Exactly why the United States was a leader is not certain. Probably the greater purity of capitalism and representative government in America rendered the inducements to modern education more intense and the limiting conditions less problematic than in other industrializing nations. The most comprehensive historical account, David Tyack and Elisabeth Hansot's *Learning Together: A History of Coeducation in American Schools,* offers some evidence about what people involved in these developments thought they were doing.[5] These illustrate general concern for the higher costs of separate education, some school administrators' interests in teaching girls in order to sustain enrollments, and some middle-class families' commitment to educating daughters. Costs and enrollments were also issues in countries less open to coeducation, however, so some other causes must have also made a difference. The early extension of suffrage to working-class men was probably one influence. Once the working class had membership in the polity, government provision of public education was difficult to avoid. Middle-class politicians and administrators probably valued issues of cost and control higher when designing education for the working classes than they did when setting goals for their own children's education. No illusions that working-class girls were being prepared to become ladies guided their decisions. The early development of public education, cross-class conflicts, and the absence of any competing educational traditions probably all contributed to the coeducational bias.

Secondary schools first revealed an egalitarian potential for women in American education. Just one of fifteen young people completed high school in 1900; receiving a high school degree at the beginning of the twentieth century was about as common as receiving a master of arts degree today. When high school education was still a privilege enjoyed by only a few, we might particularly expect that the privilege would be reserved for men. Yet in the decades preceding World War I, for every two men who earned high school degrees, three women graduated. Later this gap narrowed, until women received only 10 percent more than men by the beginning of World War II.[6] Where secondary education remained sex segregated, these numbers probably masked inferior schooling for girls, but as coeducation became widespread, girls and boys gained similar (though not equal) educational opportunities.

Apparently, more women than men received secondary education because schooling had a different relation to women's roles than it did to men's. High school education had considerable practical value for young women, whereas it served mainly as a path to college for young men. At the end of the nineteenth century, a high proportion (according to official statistics, as many as 90 percent) of all men who finished high school also finished college.[7] In contrast, only 15 percent of women completing high school received higher degrees. Instead, women's high school degrees let them enter several expanding occupations, including teaching, sales work, library work, nursing, and clerical work. The hope of becoming a school teacher, in particular, probably spurred many women to get their high school degrees.[8] More than half a million women were teaching in public elementary and secondary schools by 1920.[9] No similar spur to high school education existed for men. High school degrees did not yet play the same role in men's occupational pursuits. Boys not aiming for college probably left school for a job more often than girls, because they could find work more easily than girls could and were more likely to face demands that they contribute income to their families. Nonetheless, while these considerations may explain why proportionately more women than men completed secondary school, this differential favoring women shows the educational system operating almost at odds with gender inequality.

In contrast to their edge in receiving high school degrees, women gained only limited access to college in the nineteenth century and did not attend with the same regularity as men until the end of the twentieth century. Even affluent women had much less chance to go to college than men. (See Figure 4.1.)[10]

Nonetheless, for a society that generally treated the sexes so differ-

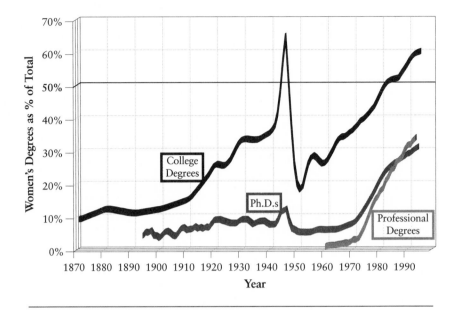

Figure 4.1. **Women's share of higher education, 1870–1994**
Sources: U.S. Bureau of the Census, *Historical Statistics of the United States,* vol. 1,
pp. 379–380, 385–386; U.S. Department of Education, *The Condition of Education: 1984,*
pp. 58, 88, 98; idem, *Digest of Education Statistics, 1996,* pp. 253, 281. Data include both
public and private institutions. College degrees = bachelor's or first professional degrees.
To lessen data peculiarities of particular years, before comparisons the data were converted
to three-year running averages centered on the reference year.

ently, women's access to college also progressed at a remarkable rate. By the Civil War, only a few private and public colleges admitted women, and all kept the female students in a separate and secondary status. In response to the resistance of private male colleges, some affluent supporters of women's education founded women's colleges, with Vassar (1865), Smith (1875), Wellesley (1875), Bryn Mawr (1885), and Mount Holyoke (1888) leading the way. During this same period, public universities throughout the Midwest and West adopted coeducation and increasingly admitted women to the same program of studies as men. By the end of the nineteenth century most public universities admitted women, although most also still restricted their number. In 1890, 20 percent of all colleges were women's colleges and 43 percent were coeducational, although many of women's degrees were from inferior "normal schools" or teachers' colleges.[11] By 1900, over two-thirds of the women attending college were at coeducational schools. By the end of the nineteenth century, women received one-fourth as many college degrees as did men. This proportion rose to one-half by the conclusion of World War I, to three-quarters by the beginning of World War II, and to equality by the 1980s.

In a culture ruled by sexual inequality and distinctive sex roles, it was not surprising that women went to college less often then men. It was surprising that women's educational opportunities steadily increased, seemingly defying the logic of their inferior status. (See Figure 4.2.) Comparing the college-graduation rates of women and men over time shows that women have been little more than a decade behind men since the mid-1920s (except for a few years in the 1950s that reflected postwar effects).

Given the much lower employment rates of middle-class women in relation to men and powerful cultural beliefs about sex differences, this outcome is remarkable. Because the overall rates for obtaining college degrees rose rapidly over the twentieth century, the ten or so years that women's progress lagged behind men's sustained a signifi-

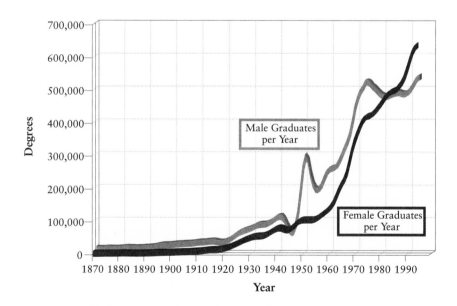

Figure 4.2. College degrees, by gender, 1870–1994
Sources: See Figure 4.1.

cant difference in their concurrent college attendance rates until recently (see Figure 4.1). From a historical perspective, however, the temporal lag was more telling than the difference at any particular point in time. The brevity of this temporal lag was exceptional. Women's access to higher education fell short of men's access, but, being only a decade behind, women's treatment by the higher-education system was more egalitarian than their access to good jobs, organizational authority, or political influence.

The reason that women attended college in ever-increasing numbers was that several individualistic trends in modern society converged. Economic success and status increasingly depended on personal credentials and skills. Families treated daughters and sons more alike. And schools were increasingly indifferent to the gender of their students.

The pioneering women who first attended college came predominantly from affluent middle-class families. Barbara Solomon explored the social origins of these women in her study of women's higher education.[12] Extremely wealthy people did not perceive education as a means to advancement and continued to tutor their daughters at home. Working-class families could not afford to send children of either sex to college. Only middle-class families regularly had both the means and the belief in the value of higher education. This was especially true of socially mobile families. Women attending college often had fathers who had climbed the social ladder to their middle-class status. Consistent with this portrait, Susan Ware found that the majority of women who became prominent in Washington during the New Deal had attended college, but those who had not usually had upper-class or working-class backgrounds.[13]

In the late nineteenth century, college degrees, not family lineage, were becoming the tickets to travel the track to success. Middle-class people in business and the professions were the first in line. For them, economic activities decisively defined status, and college gave practical advantages of credentials and useful knowledge.

Parents' increasing support for their daughters' college education was part of a more general shift toward equal treatment of daughters and sons. Since early in the nineteenth century, middle-class families also increasingly bequeathed to daughters significant, sometimes equal, shares of the family wealth.[14] The wish to give property to daughters was one source of support for the Married Woman's Property Acts. As college education became a bridge that ever more men traversed on their way to prosperity, colleges became advantageous places for young women seeking competitive advantages in the marriage market.[15] A college education gave a woman status and marked her as a worthy marital prospect for a young man with aspirations. It also put her in the right place at the right time to find a husband. Whether or not parents saw a good marriage as the highest goal they could hope their daughters might achieve, they believed higher education was inherently valuable. It functioned as a practical safety device if death or divorce left a woman to fend for herself. College education became a means to endow a daughter. In a society in which women still had little hope for positions in commerce or public institutions, higher education was something special that parents could give their daughters.

In the twentieth century, daughters of wealthy and working-class families also took advantage of expanding opportunities to attend college. The brighter and more ambitious daughters of the upper class probably talked their families into college for its merits. Over time, other wealthy families came to believe that college improved their daughters' marital prospects. As financial assistance programs became more common, working-class families also began to send some of their daughters to college. They were pursuing social mobility strategies like those common among middle-class families of the nineteenth century.

These patterns accelerated during the twentieth century. Both parents and daughters became more concerned about education, especially in the managerial and professional middle classes. A college education was becoming more decisive for career success. More middle-class women took jobs. More found their husbands either through their college experience or through a job that followed college. And more divorced and returned to jobs. As a result, young middle-class women who did not go to college seemed increasingly disadvantaged by comparison with those who did.

Women striving for access to these educational opportunities, particularly college education, initially had to force the issue by agitating and accumulating supporters among reformers. As colleges grew, however, they became more bureaucratic. Regardless of college administrators' prejudices, their interests became indifferent to the sex of students, even prompting some to recruit female students eagerly. As these conditions advanced, colleges, particularly public universities, increasingly accepted women. Colleges' willingness to accommodate the rising aspirations of young women and their parents probably developed similarly to employers' willingness to hire women. Higher education had its ideologues and moral leaders—both supporting and opposing women's education. Like employers, many had prejudices against women. Also like employers, however, pragmatic goals often guided educators, administrators, and trustees, who wanted to enhance their personal and institutional statuses. If those who were making policy in colleges believed that female students presented a valuable opportunity, some would be ready to suppress their biases to get a step up. The need for schooling outside the family made education an industry. It socialized the young to standardized specifications, preparing them to be useful, conforming adults. As organizations needing a market for their product (education), colleges had straightforward interests met by accepting female students. Most public universities enrolled only men when they began in the nineteenth century, but they admitted women more rapidly and flexibly than private colleges. By 1900, 70 percent of women enrolled in college were in coeducational colleges.[16] Prompted by funds available through federal land-grant policies, midwestern and western states inaugurated many public universities. These new institutions were responsible to their state legislatures rather than to a controlling network of wealthy alumni.

Often, some faculty members, administrators, trustees, or students initially resisted women's entry, but this fluttering resistance was usually more consistent with generalized anxiety and bewilderment than with entrenched opposition. Commonly, women were first accepted on a separate track or were first admitted to a normal-school program to prepare primary and secondary teachers. Once these experiments showed that no dangers lurked behind the female invasion, the public colleges adopted coeducational policies (with rules to protect the young women's moral standards that all concerned seemed to expect and support).

When the issue of coeducation in colleges became a public controversy during the 1870s and 1880s, educators claimed that their experience showed higher education for women had been almost universally successful. A letter written by James Angell, president of the University of Michigan, in 1884 is a typical assessment:

> Most of the evils feared by those who opposed the admission of women have not been encountered . . . We made no solitary modification of our

rules or requirements. The women did not become hoydenish; they did not fail in their studies; they did not break down in health; they have graduated in all departments; they have not been inferior in scholarship to the men; the careers of our women graduates have been, on the whole, very satisfactory.[17]

By 1900 the state universities were open to women everywhere except in four southern states.[18]

Reflecting the circumstances of three key masculine roles, male students, fathers, and college officials might have found it in their interest to oppose women's college education. None did. Prejudice still motivated men to resist women's education, but an absence of consistent self-interest robbed the opposition of sustaining force. Students had temporary, isolated, and dependent roles. They were students only a few years, they did not share a future fate, and they lacked ties to male students in other schools. Therefore, male students had no real interests in opposing female students, no practical means to repel them, and often enjoyed the availability of female companions (although bigotry sometimes prompted young men to taunt, ridicule, and shun female students, especially the pioneers). Fathers had less reason to fear or oppose their daughters' advance than they did the advance of women in their own generation. A father had always expected to lose authority over his daughters when they married. He had little interest in trying to preserve control. Usually, a father could expect to gain more than he lost if his daughters bettered themselves. Similarly, college administrators and faculty generally could expect to profit if admitting women increased enrollments. The administrators did voice fears that female students might unsettle the male students, alienate male alumni, or perform poorly. Only the fears about male alumni proved valid, and those largely concerned the older, private eastern colleges which had no need to attract more students (and which did hold out much longer against women).

To some degree, curricular segregation by sex reduced the motives for opposition in higher education, much as occupational segregation reduced opposition to women's taking jobs. To the degree that women and men pursued distinctive educational programs, the competition between them was reduced. However, while this eased women's assimilation, it also threatened to isolate them in lower-status programs.

As colleges shifted toward a model in which students chose a major that was expected to relate to their future occupation, women's and men's disciplinary choices came to reflect the occupations available. Disciplinary segregation reflected the sex segregation of occupations. In the nineteenth century, colleges generally did not offer practical or business-oriented preparation; they followed a "classical" model. From the late nineteenth through the early twentieth centuries, colleges dramatically revised their curricula by introducing many practical studies and moving toward an elective system giving students wide-ranging choices. When engineering and agricultural training emerged, they became male bastions. As coeducational colleges widened their acceptance, perhaps two-thirds of female students studied education to prepare for teaching as a possible occupation. Coeducational colleges introduced "home economics" just for women early in the twentieth century; these programs, however, also aimed largely to prepare teachers, not to help women become good wives and mothers.

The differences between "feminine" and "masculine" college curricula should not be exaggerated. Often, much of the basic curriculum followed by women was not very different from the "masculine" curriculum. In most colleges, women were largely absent from engineering, agriculture, professional programs, and graduate programs.[19] Because such programs were conduits to exclusive male occupations, they faced only occasional challenges by unusual women, and this fact made it easier for them to resist women. Women were also sparse in undergraduate science and math programs. Still, women had fairly routine access to most other undergraduate specialties.

The uneven pattern of women's assimilation by higher education crudely resembles the pattern of women's assimilation by the economy. While women's general access to college education was high, until the 1960s they received only about one-tenth of the doctorates granted in the United States and even fewer professional degrees, less than one in twenty-five, which were mainly in law, medicine, or dentistry. (See Figure 4.3.)

Conditions in doctoral and professional programs reflected those of high-status jobs, including insulation from the processes motivating women's assimilation to lower-status programs. An excess of potential students and the closer links between education and professional activity prevented the development of interests favoring women's entry (as occurred elsewhere in the educational system). So long as these occupations remained male monopolies, they gave a loose rein to many men's personal bigotry about women. The direct discrimination result-

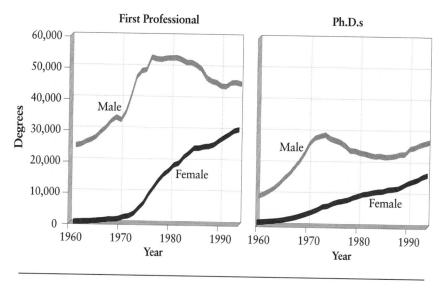

Figure 4.3. Advanced degrees, by gender, 1960–1994
Sources: See Figure 4.1.

ing from this bigotry, however, would still have left significant opportunities for women in programs guided by men less prejudiced or more motivated by other goals. A secondary effect of prejudiced discrimination cut off such opportunities. Everyone administering these academic programs had to contend with the reality that occupational discrimination against women made them poorer bets to succeed. With an excess supply of young men competing for entry and advancement, few could convince themselves or others that it was in their interests to admit more women.

Since the 1960s, the remaining barriers troubling women's access to professional programs, graduate schools, elite private schools, and male-dominated disciplines have fallen to more or less the same processes that have given women entry to high-status jobs. As a direct offshoot of the activities surrounding women's political and economic assimilation, the state has intervened through antidiscrimination and affirmative action policies, and organized women's groups have engaged in direct political agitation. Simultaneously, women's assimilation into high-status occupations removed the essential support for their exclusion. Programs competing to raise enrollments or to improve their academic standing suddenly found women an opportunity rather than a burden. When private male colleges such as Yale and Dartmouth opened their doors to women, they were responding, in part, to practical issues about enrollments and getting the best students. Those who admitted young women not only immediately doubled the pool of good candidates; they also increased their attractiveness to young male students. Most doctoral programs and professional programs already admitted women. Other than some men's prejudiced wish to avoid contact with women in their professional world, men in these arenas had little to fear from women's entry. Few college administrators wanted to jeopardize government funding or risk lawsuits for the dubious goal of discriminating against women in admissions, financial aid, or other activities. Under a legal prohibition against discrimination and the scrutiny of activist women (and nervous college administrators), most of these programs quickly removed overtly discriminatory policies. Programs in higher education also reduced residual discriminatory practices, such as teaching and advising practices, that reinforced unequal role stereotypes.

Bureaucratic rationalization of admissions and grading processes had largely prepared the ground for eliminating residual discrimination against women. By the 1960s standardized examinations such as the Scholastic Aptitude Test were standard for college admission. Graduate and professional programs used more advanced and specialized standardized tests.[20] For schools with thousands of applicants and programs with hundreds, facing records from diverse colleges that defied direct comparisons, standardized procedures and standardized tests were godsends. Similarly, the need to give grades in classes that could have hundreds of students induced considerable use of tests easy to score and standard grading scales. In this institutional environment, the removal of residual barriers to women seemed an obvious completion of the rationalized practices already in place.

Once schools opened their doors, women's presence unleashed an added individualist impulse that reinforced and accelerated the decline of gender inequality. Schools exposed women and men to a much more egalitarian experience than would fit their adult roles, preparing women to take part in the worlds of business and politics as they prepared men.

Schools and colleges, with rare exceptions, did not aim to change women's status or the relations between the sexes.[21] Most educators shared popular beliefs about the differences between women and men.

They believed that the education they offered fitted popular mores. Somehow, they were wrong.

Unquestionably, teachers treated male and female students somewhat differently, reinforcing the expectations that male students would eventually hold jobs and compete for success while female students would stress marriage and households in their futures. However, so did parents, peers, churches, the media, and almost everyone else. How much effect teachers added to this general cultural orientation is difficult to know. While they sustained stereotype expectations about gender roles, they largely taught girls and boys the same material and exposed them to the same standards. We have some reasons to expect that school teachers would reinforce sex-role expectations less than other people would. Female teachers, who dominated the lower grades, gave all children a model of employed women that contradicted stereotypes of female domesticity. Female teachers, who were employed women, seem less likely to have shared popular expectations about women's roles. Teachers also generally favored quiet, studious children over noisy, unruly ones, thereby generally rewarding conformity to female stereotypes more than male ones. For these reasons, school teachers were likely to treat boys and girls more similarly than were their parents or others.

Undoubtedly politicians and vocal interest groups affected what was taught and how it was taught through their control over funding. Their efforts could influence how much time each subject received and even the textbooks used in lower schools. Yet even these actions depended on educators' advice and had limited effects on the organization and primary aims of education. Most of these efforts were concerned with the education of all children and did not produce significant differences in the education offered girls and boys.

Even as schools consciously tried to provide distinctive educations for women and men, they largely failed. Early in the twentieth century, public schools added vocational courses to their curricula, home economics for girls and mechanics for boys. These courses remained sex segregated until the 1970s. While often cited for their obvious differentiation by sex, these courses were never more than a minor part of the curriculum. They, and similarly segregated physical education courses, may have effectively reinforced the distinction between male and female identities (although adolescents never seemed to need reminding), but they had little impact on the schools' main educational activities. Colleges experimented with distinctive curricula for men and women when they first admitted women to coeducational programs, but most soon dropped this strategy because it had little value. At all levels, girls and boys faced a similar core curriculum, and they commonly took these courses together.

Schools had organizational needs and limits that directed or overcame everyone's goals. The effects of these constraints made the content of modern education considerably different from the learning experiences children used to have. Like government bureaucracies and large capitalist enterprises, most schools and colleges had all the defining characteristics associated with bureaucratic organization. In addition, schooling produced knowledge, an exceptional commodity. Education's focus on learning gave a privileged place to expert knowledge and rational assessment, key elements of bureaucratic organization. The organization of modern education impelled schools to stress standardization. Every college and school had to adapt to the definitions of acceptable curricula accepted by other schools. Shared standards first became common because schools competed for students and financial support. As credentials became more important, the state and educational organizations systemized the process. The state imposed requirements that schools had to meet to gain financial support and legal recognition for degrees and to avoid taxes. Professional organizations demanded conformity to normative standards as accreditation processes spread.

Additionally, schools could not easily adapt to variations among students. Running a college with 15,000 students or a high school with 2,000 students is like running a town in which most people are temporary migrants. Such schools have had to regulate courses, curricula, and evaluations through rules and standards, or chaos would have overwhelmed the enterprise. The history of American public schools in the nineteenth century shows that the administrators of growing urban school systems recognized their organizational imperatives. They consciously experimented with standardized methods to meet these needs.[22]

The educational system treated women and men differently, but it long treated them much more similarly than other institutions. Outside the classroom, women and men consistently occupied distinctive social roles. Inside the classroom, they pursued the same goal. Bolstered by the inherently abstract precepts of modern science, schools and colleges adapted to organizational pressures for standardization. Teachers, like businessmen, were prone to prevailing prejudices, and few were morally or intellectually committed to gender equality. Still, because many teachers in the lower grades were women and because many observed female and male students competing directly, more teachers than businessmen were likely to recognize and to value women's potential. More important, however, the educational process—presenting standardized material and applying standardized assessment procedures—created a common learning environment for much of the educational experience.

The educational experience helped unleash women's aspirations while eroding people's belief in the ideas that had once made women's exclusion from the world outside their families seem fair and beneficial. The first generations of women attending college furthered both political and economic change. From these women came many of the agitators who sustained and expanded the women's suffrage movement. For example, the reference work *Notable American Women: 1607–1950* includes biographies of eighty-one women who had some significant involvement with the suffrage movement. More than 40 percent of these women attended some college (at a time when less than 1 percent of adult women had a college degree), and most of the rest graduated from a secondary academy or had private tutors.[23] College-educated women also made the early inroads into white-collar careers, for example as social workers, educators, or librarians.

The women's movement that erupted in the 1960s and 1970s owes much of its origins and fervor to higher education. Almost 2.5 million American women received college degrees in the two decades following World War II. These educated women were mainly between their early twenties and mid-forties in 1965. They provided most of the leaders and followers who began the modern women's movement in the 1960s. Some had long experience of employment discrimination. Others were still immersed in college. Women holding middle-class jobs formed an older, more conservative wing of the women's movement. Women recently graduated or still in college formed a younger, more radical wing.

College-educated women had limited hope for sailing a smooth course between the Scylla and Charybdis of bad jobs and confining domesticity. Their increasing college education made affluent women more tempting to employers for varied white-collar jobs. Yet most educated women who joined the labor force garnered more resentment than promotions. Too many barriers still prevented fair treatment and advancement. Equally, many educated women who had forgone employment to raise children must have harbored their own resentments, part of a bitter legacy for their daughters. Many young women graduating from college in the 1960s were daughters of these frustrated women and had good reasons to avoid repeating their mothers' experiences.

By admitting women, the higher education system unintentionally inflated the pressure against other social institutions that discriminated against women. Colleges have received and deserved much criticism because they often succumbed to gender bias. They typically favored male students, they discriminated against female professors, and their curricula were riddled with the bigoted assumptions of sexual prejudice. Still, they moved toward gender equality faster than most other societal institutions and played a leading role in women's rising status.

Propelled by the modern economic and political orders, the educational system fostered individualism. As schools and colleges grew, educational credentials supplanted family trees as the master keys giving access to high-status positions. Educational credentials became a primary means of legitimating authority in organizations, required even of those with property.[24] This change ultimately favored women's advancement.

MERITOCRATIC NORMS

Arguably, the most important ideas benefiting women's status were ideas embedded in the dominant ideology. The economic, political, and educational systems each fostered meritocratic ideas. Meritocratic ideas comprise the assumptions, beliefs, and arguments suggesting that advancement and rewards are and should be based on people's skills and achievements. What you do, not who you are, decides what you get. These ideas are the moral embodiment of institutional individualism. They are also logically and practically inconsistent with the practice of status inequality.

That ideas and practices produced by the those controlling the primary institutions in society should largely contradict a primary form of social inequality seems paradoxical. It has become a commonplace assumption that the dominant ideology in a society reflects the interests and understandings of the dominant groups. Meritocratic ideas fit this expectation. They did not arise from the system of sex inequality or from a reaction against it. They grew from the new economic and social order that developed in the nineteenth century. Yet they inherently clashed with gender inequality.

The word *meritocracy* was born in a book of satiric science fiction written by British sociologist Michael Young and published in 1957.[25] The term quickly entered the popular lexicon and won a special place in the social sciences. Its meaning broadened, however, from the book's concern with a ruling class chosen by merit (an aristocracy by achievement) to mean a system in which able and talented people are rewarded and advanced.

In modern American culture, meritocratic practices and ideology are so pervasive that their predominant influence is self-evident. While it is difficult to trace the spread of meritocratic conventions, some practices institutionalized during the past 200 years clearly illustrate the change. In business, the adoption of rule-governed promotional practices signaled the victory of meritocratic standards. Often accompanied by the creation of personnel departments, promotion standards considered such criteria as seniority, job performance evaluations, examinations, and credentials. Since the early twentieth century, when these were being championed from diverse sources, they spread steadily throughout the economy, instilling in all the expectation that expertise and experience were the legitimate criteria for promotions. The government civil service systems begun around the turn of the century were a self-conscious and highly public effort to instill meritocratic standards by the state. The American military's use of tests and their efforts, often faulty, to apply meritocratic standards became particularly well known during World War II. The accumulation of various entitlements from the first pension programs to the expansion of the welfare state from the Great Depression onward embraced meritocratic standards in a quiet way. The educational system's adoption of grades, a standardized means of comparatively evaluating students' performances, signaled their meritocratic leanings in the nineteenth century. The spread of standardized tests and particularly of college admissions examinations in the twentieth century accompanied a complete embracing of meritocratic standards. In universities, the gradual shift toward highly competitive hiring and tenure-review practices, stressing strict evaluation of scholarly accomplishments, erected one bridge between the meritocratic procedures in education and those in the economy.

By exhorting those controlling opportunities and rewards to treat everyone equally and impartially, meritocratic ideas conflicted with sex inequality in two ways, making it harder, both practically and morally, to justify refusing women the opportunities granted men. As pragmatic guides, meritocratic ideas promoted a belief that organizations became more effective if they hired and advanced people who did jobs best. They altered how people framed organizational interests in ways that made gender seem increasingly irrelevant. As moral guides, meritocratic ideas promoted a belief that personal merit should decide who wins good things in life. They altered how people judged the allocation of positions and rewards in ways that made discrimination against able women seem increasingly unfair.

Those who fostered meritocratic ideas within the evolving organizational contexts did not intend to influence beliefs about sex inequality or to benefit any lower-status group. On the pragmatic plane, they used merit as a tool for rational, efficient administration. On the ideological plane, they advocated meritocratic norms to legitimate their authority. Yet, once unleashed, meritocratic beliefs took on a life of their own, leaping over their original boundaries. Rather than being a tool wielded by administrators, they became imperatives limiting their actions. Rather than legitimating authority, they questioned inequality. Under the strong, critical light of meritocratic standards, the justifications for restricting women's opportunities seemed unconvincing facades.

The rise of meritocratic ideas did not eliminate the ideological defense of gender inequality, but it transformed and weakened it. Ideas legitimating gender inequality had to explain why women should take most responsibility for children and caring for the home, why women should not hold positions with status and power, and why women should defer to male authority. To survive, the rhetoric legitimating sex inequality had to adapt to meritocratic premises. Rather than simply declaring that the gods willed women and men to do different things, the ideology legitimating inequality in a meritocratic environment had to say something about women's and men's abilities and aspirations. A revised rhetoric suggested that women and men had different roles because they had different skills and desires. Women were not being denied positions they deserved. Either they did not want men's positions, or they were not as good as men. For example, some ideas claimed that women were better at mothering and enjoyed it more than did men while men were better at the impersonal or mechanical activities of employment. Such ideas implied that a sexual division of labor was both practical and fair.

While this perversion of meritocratic ideas could be a powerful tool for justifying the common difference in women's and men's roles, it foundered when it tried to justify aspiring women's exclusion from good positions. Once merit became a criterion, legitimating arguments became vulnerable to pervasive evidence that many women had merit but were still rejected. This Achilles' heel impaired every effort to legitimate status inequality through meritocratic ideals.

The significance of meritocratic ideas to gender inequality's decline rested in part on two special characteristics. Unlike many other ideas that would favor more egalitarian practices, meritocratic ideas achieved almost universal acceptance. In this overwhelmingly capitalist nation, the idea that opportunities should go to those who were most talented and who made the greatest effort gained near reverence. Of course, talent and effort were open to dispute. Every time women sought to improve their circumstances, they made meritocratic arguments. Every time, those opposing them largely accepted the validity of meritocratic criteria but challenged women's suitability. However, once merit was reduced to specified talents, achievements, or efforts, it was often possible to assess empirically in ways that were hard to control through ideology. Of course, gender bias could be integrated into what purported to be the most impartial tests, standards, or means of assessment. Still, in most arenas even the most biased means of judging merit were hard pressed to show that most men were better than most women. Moreover, some men with economic or political power fully accepted meritocratic standards as a pragmatic guide to effective action, committing themselves to a perceptual framework that could challenge their prejudices.

The predominance of meritocratic principles in modern society is irrefutable. The contradiction between those principles and discrimination against women based on status inequality and prejudice is self-evident. The paradox to explain is why and how the major structures of social power created the ideological doctrines and practices challenging exclusionary status rights of those in power.

Businessmen adopted meritocratic ideas with considerable enthusiasm, believing them an ideal fit to their ideological, social, and practical circumstances. Initially, private property's inviolability within capitalism ignored merit. Capital produced more capital. Wealthy men begot wealthy sons. Those owning the capital could do as they wished with it. Nonetheless, merit-based claims crept into businessmen's beliefs. Appeals to the role of merit arose from businessmen's efforts to elevate their social status and to control their employees. The dogma legitimating the modern economy built on a claim for unfettered liberty to use and transfer privately owned capital. Successful businessmen needed to justify their accumulation of wealth through the market. They sought recognition for their accomplishments from others with status. They also wanted secure, stable control over their employees. Over time, businessmen found that principles of merit seemed to help solve all these needs.

As parvenus in a market economy, the rising class of businessmen naturally favored ideas that associated success with merit. A successful class lacking an honored status, rising businessmen tried to translate their economic achievements into claims of moral worth. Meritocratic ideas supplied businessmen with just what they needed to stake a claim for acceptance in society's higher circles when old wealth still regarded them as upstarts. In their clearest ideological formulation, these claims coalesced to defend a perspective known as social Darwinism in the second half of the nineteenth century.[26] Society, according to this world view, was a competitive struggle in which people's fates were determined objectively and fairly. If one man had more talent and drive than another, then he would gain more power, status, and privileges. The competitive struggle was an impartial judge, and its decisions were inherently fair.

Social Darwinism's contribution to critical or subversive thought is easily overlooked. When it was directed at lower-status groups, it was largely used to defend the status quo. According to social Darwinism, all people had to bear individual responsibility for their fate. Since social selection processes accurately and consistently rewarded the deserving, those with less money, particularly those in businessmen's employ, should accept their circumstances without rancor or dispute. If they railed against their fate, they were denying the truth that they were inferior. In particular, social Darwinists argued that women's inferior status revealed their inferior abilities. However these ideas were used, they always implied that rewards *should* equal a person's abilities, effort, and contribution. Social Darwinists abused science and truth by claiming that the social order always did award merit where deserved. Still, their moral claims implied that the distribution of rewards could be fair if, and only if, merit decided who got more and who got less. Having hinged their authority and the validity of their policies on the rule of merit, social Darwinists found they could not dictate how others evaluated worthiness. More than this, many of those who influenced the allocation of positions and rewards truly believed the meritocratic assumptions and were placed in a quandary if evidence seriously challenged the accommodation they had between their prejudices and their meritocratic principles.

Social Darwinism was an upstart's ideology, and its idealization of merit served every successive wave of upstarts. The moral standard promoted by social Darwinism was a profound belief in the justice of rewarding merit. Ultimately, social Darwinism withered, poisoned by the false claim that the most successful people were also always the most deserving. Yet its moral ideal, tying rewards to merit, flourished.

Businessmen's affinity for meritocratic ideas reflected not only their common acquisition of social status through economic success, but also the practical and political strategies induced by their common administrative goals. In the first half of the twentieth century, as businesses grew larger, they adopted rational hiring and promotion practices. They sought to impose administrative rationality. They aimed to reduce conflict, lessen disorder, and increase control over workers. Capitalists won tangible profits by using these rational standards to boost their employees' productivity.[27]

With hundreds, even thousands, of employees, an employer could hope to retain control only by installing a system of rules. These rules had to govern the relations between supervisors and subordinates. The rules also had to define the relationships between rewards, sanctions, and actions. Rules governing hiring and promotion sought to protect employers' interests. The rules generally balanced two criteria: merit and seniority. Employers relied on seniority, which rewarded loyalty and experience, to resolve choices when the candidates were equivalent from the employers' perspective. Seniority was a safe criterion for positions that had little discretion and little impact on the quality of work done in other positions. Employers stressed merit much more when filling higher-status positions in which a poor employee could prove costly. By asserting merit's role in deciding promotions, employers and others running organizations promoted competition among aspiring employees, each of whom sought to show that he (rarely she) could further the organization's interests better than others could.

These administrative innovations promoted meritocratic ideas even when they embraced discriminatory practices, which were ubiquitous. The rules governing promotions and job evaluation systems introduced by employers commonly incorporated gender biases, both flagrant and subtle. For example, they openly assumed that the existing segregation between male and female jobs was natural, good, and unavoidable. Less obviously, but potentially more problematically, they assumed that skills associated with male jobs were inherently more difficult and more valuable. These assumptions meant that promotion procedures were normally discriminatory. Even when biased, however, such practices established the legitimacy of meritocratic principles and opened their own discriminatory assumptions to criticism.

Businessmen promoted meritocratic ideals both through their ideological claims for legitimacy and status and through their practical strategies for bureaucratic control. Although market capitalism sustains economic inequality while expanding material wealth, it breeds an ideological commitment to meritocratic standards. Successful people and dominant classes must try to legitimate their ascendancy. In market capitalism, the competition for success is so pervasive that appeals to meritocratic ideals are almost unavoidable when businessmen justify themselves. Large, complex organizations also induce businessmen to adopt strategies for control that have similar, possibly more important, influence. To meet this goal, organizations commonly have to rely on merit in allocating positions and rewards.

The state's contribution to ideals of merit paralleled the influence of business. The government was concerned with legitimacy and control. By extending citizenship status, the state added weight to the idea that all people should be judged by the same standards. By intruding more into people's lives through government bureaucracies following rationalized and legalistic principles, the state reinforced the idea that uniform rules should guide institutional behavior.

Like other modern states, the U.S. government promoted meritocratic ideals by extending citizenship. The government enlarged citizenship and extended it to more people to satisfy the needs of business, to preserve its own legitimacy, and to ease the discontent of potentially disruptive subordinate groups. The men who designed the American system of government did not want universal equality; they envisioned a nation of independent property owners and businessmen. In successive phases, however, the logic of modern political organization induced the state to extend to other groups legal equality, the right to vote, and guarantees of social welfare. By giving citizenship rights to more people and enlarging the scope of citizenship, the state directly promoted the individualistic tendencies of modern society. As they became full citizens, wage-earning men, women, and minorities gained individualistic legal, political, economic, and social rights.

As the state enacted policies enhancing citizenship, it also created an ideal that implicitly promoted merit. This ideal of citizenship grew by reducing civil inequalities and by spreading rights and opportunities more equally among people. As citizenship evolved, the culture presented to the public mind ever more colorful images of individual rights. The symbols accumulated over time, as generations of Americans reread key passages from the Declaration of Independence, the U.S. Constitution, Lincoln's Gettysburg Address, and the twentieth-century Pledge of Allegiance. These sacred texts evoked the goals of liberty, justice, and equality. Individualistic symbols were central to the doctrines legitimating the American state. People often disregarded the contradictions between these ideas and discriminatory practices, but their disregard did not abolish the contradictions' effects. Expanding citizenship rights made it progressively tougher to convince most people that the nation's historic ideals justified castelike inequality.

As it grew, the state produced large bureaucracies to administer its programs. These organizations created and applied what Max Weber long ago termed rational-legal principles.[28] Law defined the organization's mission, for example to promote commerce or education. Bureaucratic officials then elaborated its mission through rules. These rules governed each state organization's relations to those that it regulated, helped, or otherwise affected. As bureaucratic government activities grew more extensive, increased exposure to bureaucratic rules swayed people to believe that universal standards should govern opportunities and rights.

Civil service systems embodied rules that served as prototypes. In the United States, governments at all levels established merit procedures during the Progressive Era to stop political influence over hiring and firing in government agencies. These civil service systems employed ever more people over time. They wielded power through the law's force and the state's moral influence. In harmony with citizenship and bureaucratic rationalization, civil service systems added the state's considerable authority to the growing importance of ideas promoting meritocratic expectations.[29]

The government's influence on people's lives grew steadily. People had contact with government rules and government officials ever more often—when they paid taxes, when their jobs became subject to laws about overtime or minimum wages, when they received a traffic ticket, when their children attended school, when they served on a jury, when they served in the military, and when they collected benefits for the unemployed, the elderly, or the poor. As the state expanded its activity and its powers, it extended its application of rational-legal principles. Even as people learned to disdain bureaucratic rules and behavior, they also came to expect that people working in and representing state bureaucracies were bound by those rules.

The state fostered meritocratic ideals both through its extension of citizenship rights and through the expansion of government bureaucracies. The modern state promoted ideals of merit because it instituted rule-bound relations that applied to the whole populace. These replaced the casual, personal, or family relations of property-owning men. The state grew in parallel to the economy. As that wage economy grew, the state assimilated ever more people into the polity by widening citizenship rights. People gained a sense of membership and entitlement that enlarged as government activities grew. The ideas of membership and entitlement made violations of meritocratic principles ever harder to defend.

The educational system directly influenced people's ideas about merit only when they were young, but it potentially had a more intense influence than either the economic order or the political order. Schools followed merit equally as a practical strategy and as an ideal. Meritocratic standards gave teachers (and schools) an expertise they could hold over parents and children. They also served both to motivate and to control children. Meritocratic standards combined with standardized curricula allowed educators to avoid chaos.[30] Once schools grouped children together, teachers displaced tutors. Soon educators faced a need to organize schooling so they could teach many pupils effectively. As the state became involved in education, especially through the creation of public schools, pressure increased to give education a common content across schools. In response, in the nineteenth and early twentieth centuries, educators gradually standardized what students were taught, defined standards for adequate scholastic performance, and adopted standardized grading schemes to label varying performances.[31]

The meritocratic aspects of modern education met opposition from the prevailing cultural biases of sex-role stereotypes. While education had a general meritocratic orientation, educators consciously and unconsciously treated boys and girls differently. As diligent substitutes for parents, schools selectively reinforced children's conformity to these stereotypes. Educational materials portrayed *good* men and women faithfully following the stereotypes. In the mid-twentieth century, for example, secondary school images depicted boys seeking to be star athletes while girls hoped to become popular cheerleaders. In the background, however, girls and boys still vied to prove themselves in never-ending competitions over the same grades in the same classes. Indeed, we can wonder if the stress on male high school athletics did not, in part, develop to compensate for boys' inability to dominate scholastic activity.

Schools encouraged meritocratic beliefs as they used standardized grades applied by impartial criteria. Usually, teachers applied standard criteria to rank students' work. Better work got better grades. Grades won advancement. These methods for evaluating school work instilled meritocratic ideals in both sexes. These effects were all heightened when boys and girls went to school together, so the general acceptance of coeducation in America increased education's meritocratic impact.[32] Even when teachers' biases corrupted their assessments, so that they applied different criteria to girls and boys, they could not hide two fundamental truths from children. First, many girls could equal or surpass boys in competitions decided by academic prowess. Second, schools' reliance on grades, tests, and formal standards conferred legitimacy on meritocratic judgments.

Schools, particularly coeducational schools, put the idea of male intellectual superiority to the test. It failed. In schools, girls and boys' experiences vividly belied beliefs in unequal intellectual potentials. Contradicting myths, girls did as well as boys. Often girls did better. These experiences did not prevent people from claiming that men were smarter or better at mental tasks. As these claims gradually became more inconsistent with people's experience, however, they became more vulnerable to challenge. The more that selection processes in firms and other organizations emphasized schooling, the more that women's educational achievements challenged the legitimacy of discrimination.

The meritocratic ideals developed in the economic, political, and educational systems did not supplant the ideas linked with women's inferior status (or other forms of inequality) but grew up inexorably alongside them. Meritocratic norms did not cause privileged people to reject their self-interested beliefs and justifications for inequality. They did not end people's efforts to evade meritocratic standards that would penalize them. Nor did they cause the economic, political, and educational systems to dedicate themselves to realizing a meritocracy. Many people, particularly men, argued that women were inherently less able than men. All women, they suggested, were less intelligent, less rational, poorer leaders, and less dependable than all men. Meritocratic ideals did not sap men's motives to pursue and justify their self-interests. Nor did they turn men's interests upside down.

Nonetheless, meritocratic standards (bolstered by rationalization and egalitarianism) *did* increasingly influence ideology. They helped shift men's and women's interests by altering both the practical and moral terrain. One hundred fifty years ago, most people found women's dependent status obvious, natural, and unexceptional. People candidly affirmed women's inherent inferiority to men. They openly, casually declared women's rightful place in the home. They spoke of men's patriarchal control as we might discuss parents' authority over young children.[33] Discrimination against women was not hidden, defended, or even given much thought. The rise of meritocratic principles helped change all this. Meritocratic ideals gave women ideological symbols to which they could attach their discontent arising from discrimination and unequal opportunity. Meritocratic ideals also weakened men's belief that discriminating against women was just. Weakening that belief lessened the likelihood that men's actions would consistently, unthinkingly reinforce women's secondary status.

Meritocratic doctrines came from institutions whose leaders explicitly embraced male dominance but unwittingly set loose ideas that contradicted status inequality. Following their inherent developmental logic, the educational, economic, and political systems marched doggedly down a road toward meritocratic ideals. The men who led this advance commonly used corrupted interpretations of merit to justify continued discrimination against women. Yet meritocratic norms were weapons that could easily fall into the hands of the enemy. Like scientific processes, meritocratic processes have empirical tests that prejudiced practitioners found hard to deny continuously. At this meritocratic road's end, ideas useful for building a case for keeping women in their place were hard to find.

FROM THE AUTHORITARIAN FAMILY TO THE INDIVIDUALISTIC FAMILY

The family may be the last place where most people would look for signs of individualism or for sources of women's rising status. Often, social practices and relationships seem defined as individualistic to the degree that they are unlike family relationships. Over the past century, most critics of women's lower status have cited the family as one cause, sometimes as the principal cause. Unquestionably, women largely experienced gender inequality through their family roles. Nonetheless, over time the family has become more individualistic and, through this transition, more conducive to gender equality.

The family as we understand it today, bound mainly by sentiment and governed by mutual consent, is a recent historical creation. We now think of the family as a private place of intimate relations, in contrast to public domains, with their formal distant relations, such as economic arenas where we hold jobs or buy goods.[34] The economic and political changes that permeated society were the root causes of the family's altered role in social organization.[35] While the family has shown considerable capacity to adapt to a changing social environment, it has little capacity to induce changes in that social environment, and it has not been an engine of change in the manner of the economic or political orders. The family has been limited to a small group of people associated by current and past reproduction patterns, by personal intimacy, or by common residence and communal sharing.[36] With its limited scope, the family could not independently generate a path of cumulative change. Yet, as the family adapted to the powerful forces transforming society, its increasing individualism made it, too, an instrument of change.

Although individualism is often conceived as arising in opposition to the family, both theorists and the popular press have long recognized an individualistic transformation of the family institution. Sometimes this shift is characterized in negative terms, as in studies exploring the specter of the "decline of the family."[37] This negative perspective focuses on the family's *loss* of functions, activities, and usefulness. It portrays the modern family as a partial remnant of some richer, earlier institution. Alternatively, the family's transformation is sometimes characterized as a positive development. Characteristically, those adopting this viewpoint suggest that the family has become more egalitarian, more democratic, or more companionate. Whether they view the changes through optimistic or pessimistic lenses, most commentators believe that the modern family is more specialized, that it exercises less control over people's lives, and that individual interests have become more important at the expense of family interests.

Individualism embodies abstract relational characteristics distinguishing modern economic and political institutions from their predecessors. *Institutional* individualism occurs insofar as people's relationships to the institutions impinging on their lives are unmediated, consensual, and functionally circumscribed. While the family has not come to look like a formal organization, it has become more individualistic in each of these ways.

Family relations have become more direct, as they are less likely to be mediated by relations to a wider kin group or the surrounding community. In an effort to symbolize this change, Talcott Parsons characterized the modern family as "isolated." With some justice, other authors widely criticized this terminology for overlooking the continued importance of extended kinship and community ties. Parsons was correct, however, to suggest that the relations between spouses and children in modern families had become increasingly private, in both practice and ideals.[38] The family gradually became less extensive and less enduring as the unpredictable relationships between two spouses and their children defined its boundaries and existence.

Family relations have become functionally more circumscribed to stress concerns directly relevant to people's more limited family roles. Husbands and wives commonly both have jobs and often have separate memberships in other activities. Even children have parts of their lives at school, in organizations, or with friends that are private. Parents and siblings usually intrude little on these private aspects of a child's life. In the midst of these complex connections between people and the outside world, family relationships and familial interactions concentrate on the activities and concerns recognized as directly and intrinsically relevant to the family. The important ones include sustaining sentimental feelings between kin, rearing children, operating a joint household, and controlling joint assets. Family relations have remained more diffuse than typical organizational relationships, but they have been increasingly focused on concerns identified with the family.

While family membership has not achieved the voluntary or contractual character of membership in formal organizations, it has become progressively less confining and less compulsory than it was 200 years ago. Husbands and wives can divorce their spouses and now regularly do. Children can seek their fortunes as adults without relying on their parents. Once they leave their parents' home, children can easily limit or end their relationships with parents or siblings. They often do. Aging parents can find means of support and care without relying on their adult children, and often have to do so. People need not remain in the families to which they are born or into which they marry. Similarly, people cannot count on others to remain within their families. These changes have occurred gradually, with each generation experiencing more freedom from family ties than the last.

As family relationships have become more discretionary, more consensual, and more narrowly defined, the modern family has become more individualistic without becoming a formal organization. The family has not succumbed to unlimited individualism. Throughout all these changes, permanent family ties have remained a common expectation. Even more important, however much familial individualism has grown, families continue to treat their members according to their membership, not according to their achievements. Still, the modern family is much more individualistic than was the family of two centuries ago.

As part of this individualistic trend, the family has lost importance in the shaping of individual interests. Families have lost their centrality to people's lives and to social structure. Families were once the units from which societies were built; they were at the center of most people's lives, every day, all day. Now people spend much of their time outside families and conceive their long-term goals as individuals, not as part of a family. Society is built from individuals and organizations, with families being only one of many important social organizations.

This individualist restructuring of family life has reduced men's motives and their capacity to obstruct their wives or to favor their sons over their daughters. Families cannot guarantee their children occupational or organizational success (unless they own the organization and perhaps not even then). Each organization has mechanisms, usually standardized practices, by which it recruits and promotes people. To gain entry, a person must have the required credentials (usually appropriate education and experience). Anyone wanting to get ahead must advance through the stages demanded by the organization. The separation of kinship from employment made industrial labor markets possible. Both Karl Marx and Max Weber, though analyzing the rise of modern societies from divergent perspectives, emphasized the importance of this separation. Wealthy, prestigious families can do a lot to improve their children's chances for success. They can furnish education, ensure economic security, and exercise influence through personal networks. Still, they can neither guarantee nor prevent a child's success. Because families do not control the resources for earning a living, a man can neither pass such resources onto his sons nor deny his wife access to them.

Equally important, men have less reason to want control in modern families. In the past, the family controlled the means to gain an income. This family capital conferred status on present and future generations. Authority within the family then had considerable worth and meaning. Everyone in the family worked at the enterprise; all depended on its productivity. Running such a family gave real scope to the one in charge. In contrast, most income in modern families comes from external employment. Children leave once they become adults. Through these changes, the scope of family authority has dwindled steadily.

Perhaps this shrinking family authority explains William Goode's observation that men have resented their loss of *centrality* more than anything else, when confronted with women's self-assertion in modern families.[39] Men had been used to being the center of family life, to their well-being, their preferences, and their interests being given priority within the family. This centrality was a residue from an earlier age. Even though the circumstances supporting male family authority had dissipated, families still deferred to the man who was husband and father, and they showed him special regard. This centrality was precarious, however, and it came under direct attack by modern feminism. Still, to a surprising degree, the upsurge of women after the

1960s did not wrest family authority from American men, because they had already largely lost it.[40] Men still wanted to be central, and they still had more resources than women, but families were a weakening restraint on women's aspirations.

Unlike those in the past, families in the twentieth century were not inescapable prisons. Women seeking to better their status found that their husbands' opposition represented increasingly fewer resources and declining resolve. Rising divorce rates and less restrictive divorce laws both reflected and fueled growing familial individualism. The practical availability of divorce affects all marriages, not just the unhappy ones. When it is easier for women to leave a bad marriage, the balance of marital power is more nearly equal, and the standards governing acceptable behavior by husbands are higher.

As leaving a husband becomes both legally and practically easier for women, they become less dependent on men and more equal to them. In a male-dominated society, marriage can easily become an instrument of women's subjugation. If women can choose to leave bad marriages, they have an escape from some of inequality's worst circumstances. More divorce means less dependency. Of course, marriage can also give women security and protection. Divorce allows men to abandon women just as much as it allows women to abandon men (although the acceptable grounds for abandonment may differ). It is hard to say precisely what alternatives must be available to women for easy divorce to benefit them. Theoretically, women should benefit from divorce when marital inequality within families exceeds sex inequality outside families. We can safely say that the better the alternatives appear, the more women seek divorce. We do know that women have shown the value of divorce by their willingness to pursue it when the alternatives were still bleak.

The divorce rate has risen almost continuously for the last 150 years, roughly doubling every half-century, then leveling off during the last two decades.[41] Divorce ended one in twenty marriages by the end of the Civil War era. Around the turn of the century, early in the period of egalitarian illusions, divorce ended about one in eight marriages. In the 1930s about one in four marriages ceased with divorce. As many as half of all people marrying today will eventually leave those marriages through divorce. Today's divorce rates also mean that somewhere between one-third and one-half of all children will experience the end of their parents' marriage while still living at home.

Many changes in divorce law over the past 150 years made the rising divorce rate possible.[42] In the early nineteenth century, the law only marginally tolerated divorce, regarding it as an extreme measure suited only to circumstances so extraordinary they warranted an act by the state legislature to end a marriage. During the nineteenth century, the states created a standard judicial process for divorce. They shifted jurisdiction over divorce from the state legislature to the judiciary and made it a legally recognized alternative, although it remained morally objectionable. Most states recognized a variety of grounds for divorce, often including bigamy, adultery, impotence, desertion, a husband's refusal to provide support, imprisonment or conviction for an "infamous crime," and extreme cruelty. They implied that a spouse had a responsibility to stay sexually faithful, abide laws, be civil, forgo drug addiction, and live at home. A person should no longer have to stay in a marriage if his or her spouse seriously violated these marital responsibilities beyond limits allowing redemption. (Notably, the explicit grounds allowing divorce emphasized transgressions by husbands. This probably reflected the presumption that wives were dependent and husbands were supposed to be responsible.) Some states, particularly those in the West, generalized this standard by including "omnibus clauses." These gave courts the discretion to grant divorces under any conditions causing the court to conclude that the marriage was a complete failure.

Over time, divorce continued a meandering course away from moral restrictions and toward practical responses. Pioneering social scientists who began studying divorce clearly attributed rising divorce rates to social and economic conditions rather than to moral flaws. By the 1930s, American movies often depicted divorce as a straightforward, if unfortunate, solution to marital discord. Still, the law and social opinion persistently regarded divorces as failures that raised serious questions about the character of the women and men who had made such a mess of a grand institution. Divorce laws kept gradually shedding moral strictures in the second half of the twentieth century. An acceptance slowly emerged that marriages regularly fail because two people proved overwhelmingly incompatible. More and more people petitioned for divorce not because a spouse had violated his or her fundamental obligations, but because the marriage was a miserable experience. Finally, during the 1970s, states began to accept the policy of divorce without fault. In 1969 California led the great break with the past by adopting a law allowing divorce on the grounds of irreconcilable differences. Other states soon followed with a variety of laws that, in their strongest form, ensured that either spouse could divorce the other simply by asserting a wish to do so.

In principle, these laws transformed marriage into a private contract that two spouses could end just as readily as they began. The state's role in divorce became similar to its role when a business partnership ended. It certified the dissolution and, when needed, resolved competing claims over joint assets. The new laws shunned moralistic attribution of blame. When both spouses agree to dissolve a marriage, the courts merely ratified their decision. If one spouse rejected divorce or disputed the division of property, custody of children, or future obligations, proceedings could still be complicated. The thrust of the law, nonetheless, converted divorce into a right. This added to the transformation of marriage from a legal bondage to a conditional partnership. As a partnership, marriage need endure only so long as both spouses wished to preserve it.

Divorce has gone from an extraordinary to an ordinary event. In the middle of the nineteenth century, divorces were unduly hard to get, people considered them scandalous, and they were rare. By the first half of the twentieth century, people found divorces moderately available if they had money or endurance. Most people disapproved of divorce but accepted it as necessary yet repugnant, and it became increasingly common. During the past few decades, popular opinion has accepted divorce as an unfortunate but normal part of life. Divorce has become easy to get. Today, marriage is as likely to end through divorce as through death.

The progress of divorce laws both reflected and reinforced the other changes in women's status. As women's opportunities grew, so did the likelihood that a woman with a bad marriage would prefer to end it or that she would act in ways that would motivate her husband to end it. As ending marriage became a more feasible alternative for women, men's superior bargaining position within marriages also declined.

Though increasingly individualistic, families did not become romantic, egalitarian oases. They remained battlegrounds for influence in which most men had sufficient resources to gain the advantage.[43] With this advantage, men have held sway in family decision making and presumably extracted a better balance of rewards from family life compared with their contributions. Over time, however, men's family power declined in proportion to their declining overall status advantages in society. As a result, men's family power has dropped considerably over the past 150 years, although husbands still typically have more authority and centrality than their wives. Family power has not been a stable foundation of men's dominant social position. Instead, family dynamics have sustained a continuous pressure toward more egalitarian family organization as the external alternatives available to women and men shifted.

The data on family power are not precise. Even with direct and intensive research on people living today, family power is difficult to assess. For past periods we will never have more than crude estimates. Nonetheless, the rough outlines of changing family power seem fairly clear. In the early nineteenth century, people took men's family authority for granted. By the early twentieth century, commentators were beginning to talk about the companionate family, in which sentiment and mutual respect between husband and wife tempered men's authority. Today, principles of family democracy and equality have much more legitimacy than masculine claims for deference from wives, especially among young adults. While men may still commonly have the upper hand in families, the average power of husbands over wives has become much less than it was 150 years ago. The expectation that half of all marriages will end with divorce is powerful testimony to this change.

In the nineteenth century, analytical women and men saw women's legal disabilities and political exclusion as the principal source of spousal inequality, as portrayed in John Stuart Mill's influential essay, *The Subjection of Women.* Yet even after married women gained property rights (and other legal rights) and the vote, men seemingly retained authority within the family. The durability of husbands' authority and privileges suggested that the problem was more complex and difficult to solve than nineteenth-century thinkers had realized.

During the Great Depression of the 1930s, Mirra Komarovsky did a classic analysis of familial inequality, called *The Unemployed Man and His Family.* This considered the possibility that a husband's authority depended on men's near monopoly of paid employment. To test this possibility, Komarovsky studied families in which the husband had been continually unemployed for several years. She found that men's authority broke down in one-fifth of the families. According to Komarovsky, the loss of work weakened men's capacity for economic coercion, lowered their prestige, and created new tests of authority and role performance under the austere circumstances. Men's job loss did not change their wives' sentiments, but made explicit the already existing negative sentiments.

Komarovsky's finding that husbands' authority broke down in one-fifth of the families enduring prolonged unemployment leads to two dramatically opposing inferences. The finding that the wife continued to defer to her husband's authority in four-fifths of the families suggests that something other than men's current employment or economic resources must be decisive. The finding that a wife rejected her husband's authority in one-fifth of the families after he failed to provide income for only a couple of years suggests that the pattern of male family authority can begin to unravel quickly if certain sustaining conditions are lacking. While the second point better fits the analysis developed in this book, the first point aims more directly at the immediate question that Komarovsky could not answer. Why did men without jobs remain dominant in the majority of these families?

The answer seems to be that the crucial alternatives affecting family power concerned the availability of jobs and the obligation to care for children. Husbands' higher earnings gave them influence, while wives' inability to earn a decent income made them dependent. Men's income gave them domestic power over their wives because they had the capacity to give or withhold the money women needed and wanted. Women had less attractive choices outside marriage than did men. Women usually had to raise the children a couple had. They found it harder to support themselves. They usually also had a harder time finding a new spouse. Women, who had few opportunities for independence, therefore deferred to their husbands.

An idea termed *principle of least interest* specifies a key link between differential opportunity and power within families. The sociologist Willard Waller identified this connection a half-century ago.[44] Waller contended that the party who cared less about preserving a relationship would have a strategic advantage. The less important a relationship is to a person, the lower the threshold at which the person will withdraw or use threats of withdrawal as a strategy. During disputes, the less committed person will commonly start to withdraw or threaten to withdraw sooner and more freely than the other. This withdrawal or threat can take varied forms, such as an impassioned argument, a refusal to talk further, a symbolic departure, or an explicit threat. At this point, the more committed person often capitulates because sustaining the relationship is more important to her or him than the issue under dispute. The more indifferent person therefore has won.[45] More generally, withdrawal can be manifested through a spectrum of possibilities, including permanently abandoning the relationship, temporarily abandoning the relationship, a refusal to fulfill obligations, or a rejection of the rules and understandings governing the relationship. Any act that seems destructive to the relationship implies withdrawal. Even a small difference could give the less committed person the upper hand. The power induced by unequal dependence in a relationship often grows over time as people adapt to it, although it also could decline if its use (or other things) diminished the other person's commitment.

Applied to Komarovsky's study, for example, the principle of least interest suggests that most women in the study continued to defer to their husband because women's inferior alternatives seemed an unquestionable, permanent fact of life. However long the husband was unemployed, these women could anticipate that when jobs eventually became available, the openings would go to the husband, not to them. If they forced a split in the family, the women also knew that they would retain the responsibility for raising their children. Even long without a job, therefore, men had a considerable advantage. Realistically, most of these women faced two alternatives: they could defer enough to gain the husband's acceptance or they could reject the husband's authority at the cost of seeing him leave. For most women, deference was less risky. (Presumably, some women simply preferred a husband exercising family authority, but no evidence suggests that this feeling was widespread.) In a minority of families, women abandoned their former deference, as they discovered that they could defy the husband's authority without risking his departure or the balance of interests favoring the wife's deference when the husband provided an income too small to sustain his power without that income.

More generally, according to the principle of least interest, circumstances altering women's and men's relative dependence on marriages explain the historical shift in power between spouses. The growing use of divorce gave concrete evidence of expanding alternatives to staying in unhappy marriages and people's willingness to carry the strategy of withdrawal to its extreme. Neither wives nor husbands could rely on threatened withdrawal as a strategy to gain family power, however, unless family relationships were discretionary. The more discretionary family relationships became, the more important threatened withdrawal became.

Women also made gains as daughters through rising familial individualism. What parents did for their children always reflected the combined influence of parents' interests, sentiment, and impinging circumstances. Before the modern era, parents' interests and social conditions left daughters in a secondary status regardless of parents' sentiments. Over the past two centuries, daughters have gradually gained ground on their brothers in the United States. The restructuring of family interests has made the particular characteristics of children more important to parents and their sex less important. This change has resembled organizational interests' increasing indifference to sex.

Daughters' rising family status owed much to the decay and ruin of the family economy. When families had owned the means of making income, they had felt obliged to keep the family property intact.[46] They did this by passing the family business from father to son. Before capitalism emerged, a need to keep family capital intact decisively shaped inheritance patterns. How to pass control over their family property to the next generation was the most important inheritance issue facing families who controlled productive property such as a farm, a manor, or a shop. How to divide their family wealth among their heirs was a lesser concern. Before the transition to the modern economy, society was organized around a fixed set of productive properties. Over time, the people controlling these properties changed, but farms, the fields, the craft shops, the markets, and the hostelries remained unaltered.[47] As those controlling one of these properties grew old, they had to decide to whom they would pass control. The property was not liquid wealth they could divide at whim. Even more than a family business, it was the foundation on which a family was built.

In a world in which only men held political power and legal rights, passing control of the family property to a son served family interests most dependably. As well as they could, families tried to help daughters on their way with dowries and additional sons with gifts or bequests to start their own family properties. Preserving the family capital was usually a decisive goal, however, and people would disperse funds or wealth to their departing children only within limits avoiding threats to that goal.

These circumstances were reversed in the modern family. Enterprises ceased to be family concerns. More men earned their income through employment. Those who still owned businesses found their wealth much more fluid and unstable than in the past.[48] Favoritism for sons became a less attractive investment as the family capital fell. Without a family business, parents' interests were better served by the promise that all their children or the children who were most responsible to their parents would inherit property, whatever their sex. Even families who had a business often found children would seek opportunities elsewhere, forcing the parents to treat the business as an asset. Fathers probably still regularly gave sons more economic support than they gave daughters. Nonetheless, they commonly tried to take care of their daughters and to guard their well-being.

Declining family size forced more parents to focus their dreams and aspirations on daughters. The new economic conditions led to smaller families. As a result, more families had no sons (and more had no son they regarded worthy or reliable). Among families who had five children, only about 3 percent had no boys. When families had two children, about 25 percent had only daughters.[49] During the nineteenth century, the proportion of families who had daughters but no sons probably rose from about 5 percent to above 15 percent as the average number of children declined from more than six to about three. These proportions were higher in urban areas.[50] Many others with daughters had only one son, who might prove to be untrustworthy, unlikable, or who migrated away. Over time, therefore, a growing minority of parents had every reason to give all their love and pride and wealth to their daughters.

In short, parents became more likely to give equally to their daughters and sons. If advancing the quality of parents' later years dominated the interests influencing support for children and inheritance patterns, children's sex gradually lost a role in assessing those interests. A good daughter was at least as likely to reciprocate a parental investment through caretaking, respect, and monetary assistance as was a son. Without a need to preserve the family enterprise, families, and fathers in particular, had more room to treat both sexes sentimentally.

The individualistic family arose through a series of related changes, both external and internal. As it gradually became independent of economic and political organization, the family gave men progressively less authority to secure women's intimate subjection. Increasingly, government and business treated people as autonomous individuals rather than as members of a family. Men lost their position as intermediaries linking women to productive property and the state. Sentimentality's growing role as a binding force of family life improved daughters' standings and wives' resources. The transition to employment in jobs and professions, the dismantling of family enterprises, the increasing importance of education, and the declining size of families combined to alter family interests. Parents' interests became better served by supporting all children without regard to their sex. Men's interest in sustaining their family power declined as the value of that power diminished. Simultaneously, through the principle of least interest, family dynamics rapidly adjusted the power of women and men to the changing alternatives available to them. The rising availability and use of divorce reflected and magnified the voluntaristic interpretation of marriage. This complex transformation toward an individualistic family occurred slowly and unevenly. It is not complete even now. Nonetheless, the authoritarian family as an instrument of male dominance has become a declining remnant.

THE RISE OF THE INDIVIDUAL

Modern individualism arose from the reconstruction of economic and political life. The economy and the state gradually absorbed the mechanisms of power. Pursuing their organizational interests, the economy and state increasingly treated everyone as individuals, eliminating the family's role as a mediator. Economic and political individualism led to individualism's expansion into other institutions and into ideology.

When guided by their interests, those with influence in these institutional contexts responded to gender inequality almost amorally and impartially. They pursued their organizational interests without significant concern if their actions aided, complemented, or subverted gender inequality. They rarely treated women and men equally. Because men ran them, they paid greater attention to men's interests. Yet modern organizational interests did not include gender inequality, and the men in charge did not spend much effort considering it. When it suited their organizational or positional interests, they adopted policies and ideas that benefited women over the long term. Often no one realized that new policies or ideas would eventually affect sex inequality. Even when the effects were predictable, they became subsumed in the calculation of institutional interests.

The history of the public school system typifies these discrepant effects. Schools were largely bureaucratic workplaces for the young, who labored competitively for grades, promotions, and credentials. Schools openly treated the sexes differently. They promoted sex stereotypes and channeled girls and boys toward divergent goals. Schools offered somewhat different curricula for girls and boys. A few courses teaching vocational skills such as cooking or mechanics were strictly segregated. Most academic courses were open to both sexes, but informal mechanisms channeled children to conform to sex stereotypes, especially in the higher levels. In particular, the programs that prepared students to enter high-status occupations were largely male domains until women's access to these positions was opened after the 1960s. Through these mechanisms, the school system has helped to perpetuate women's lower status.

Yet even as they sought to preserve sex-role distinctions, schools and colleges gave women and men considerably more similar experiences than they would have later in life. Women studied most of the same subjects. They read the same books. They learned the same basic skills and knowledge. Usually they attended the same classes. Repeatedly they vied directly with males and discovered they could do as well or better. This similar educational experience belied gender inequality. Even as the schools tried to treat the sexes differently, they did more to subvert inequality than to sustain it. They prepared women for careers and a style of competition with men that they would find denied them after they left school.

Meritocratic ideas also reflect the unintended consequences of institutional individualism. Meritocratic ideas and practices originated in diverse institutional contexts—among businessmen defending their status against the established elite and seeking ways to tame their growing firms, among politicians seeking legitimacy for the state and contending with the government's bureaucratic expansion, and in schools applying bureaucratic standards to the educational process. They arose because they met institutional needs. Regardless of origins, meritocratic customs propagated the belief that qualifications should decide who gets promotions and rewards. These ideas and practices implied that suppressing qualified women was both unfair and counter to organizational interests (in getting the best personnel at the lowest salary). Sex inequality had nothing to do with their origin or development. Yet even if the men controlling these institutions had thoroughly understood how meritocratic ideology would affect women's claims for equal treatment, they would have been unlikely to reduce their support for these new ideas. The abstract issue of gender inequality's fate over the long term was too vague and remote compared with the immediate and self-interested reasons for adopting meritocratic ideals.

Institutional individualism also penetrated the family as it slowly shifted toward less hierarchical, more voluntary organization. Increasingly, family life stressed companionship and mutual emotional support. Divorce rates rose steadily, with marriages lasting only as long as both wife and husband chose to preserve them. When emotional goals displaced material goals in families and staying married became voluntary, the family ceased to provide dependable support for women's subjugation.

Expanding individualism did not rob people of all alternative forms of attachment and organization. People have preserved kinship and community ties. To sustain these ties, however, people had to change them. Kinship and community bonds gradually lost much of the authority and dependency they once had. The attachments and private institutions that people care about today usually concern ties of affection and mutual support among autonomous individuals.

Whatever its specific form, the institutional individualism that emerged in these diverse social contexts was generally inconsistent with exclusionary status inequality. Sustained status inequality must be embedded in positional inequalities, particularly economic and political inequality. This embedding enables advantaged status groups to control high-ranking positions and to restrict access to people like themselves through discrimination and oppression. By generalizing the effects of the concentration of social power in economic and political organizations, institutional individualism directly contravened such exclusionary practices.

Institutional individualism comprises social beliefs, practices, and relationships that recurringly make status inequality seem arbitrary, impractical, and unjust. Institutional individualism can coexist with status inequality, producing neither direct contradictions nor challenges. Such conditions are unlikely to be stable, however. The more that individualism pervades a society, the shakier the supports for status inequality become. Individualism both practically and ideologically erodes people's commitments to the discriminatory practices needed to sustain status inequality.

Institutional individualism reflects two fundamental principles of modern social organizations: they have no integral interest in gender inequality, and they do have inherent tendencies to produce interests that ignore sex-role distinctions. Organizations might exploit opportunities stemming from existing gender inequality, as when employers hired cheap female labor. Organizations might adapt to gender inequality, as when schools created specialized courses to fit women's and men's distinctive roles in society. The men running organizations might generally prefer to honor and support gender inequality because they share the prejudiced ideals and perceptions of their sex. Nonetheless, modern organizations have no inherent interest in preserving gender distinctions. Instead, they generate interests in treating all people by criteria related to the functional activities of the organization. People are increasingly recognized and responded to in terms of their role in relation to the institution, as workers, managers, consumers, voters, criminals, students. Institutional individualism may not have been a primary cause of gender inequality's decline, but it reinforced the movement toward greater equality and made it easier to attain.

CHAPTER FIVE

WOMEN'S REJECTION OF SUBORDINATION

Once the conditions supporting gender inequality started to change, women (and men) began to face new choices. Circumstances beyond any individual's conscious control dictated the choices available to women and their probable outcomes. How women could or should live their lives became less well defined. If men have increasingly ceded more of women's aspirations and demands, women have increasingly aspired higher and demanded more. If structural changes generated new opportunities and reduced the obstructing interests, women still had to seize those opportunities and champion their interests. Real women and men had to take all the actions that created, preserved, challenged, and eroded gender inequality.

Women helped erode gender inequality through several levels of action, including passive responses to altered circumstances, active efforts as individuals, and collective action in social movements. As the economy and political orders developed, in an unobservable systemic process, gender inequality underwent a gradual structural disembedding from positional inequality. Women (like men) responded to a complex realignment of interests and relationships that were not reducible to a simple series of historical events. Reducing childrearing, taking unwanted jobs, and going to school were but a few of women's important adaptations to changing circumstances. Individual efforts at advancement by ambitious women rose above simple adaptation, quietly but continuously. Women sought to better themselves, to achieve new identities, to acquire new freedoms. Taken together, these actions left a marked historical trace. Individually, they were part of people's biographies rather than public history, and their traces died with the people who experienced them. Feminist activity transcended the limits of individual actions, occurring in sporadic but conspicuous bursts. These movements were public historical events. They were able to influence changes in social structures and norms directly.

Only in the past 150 years have women organized against subordination. Both the woman suffrage movement of the late nineteenth and early twentieth centuries and the modern feminist movement attracted wide followings and captured public attention for a long time. These movements played a crucial role in the transformation of women's status and in the long-term process that disembedded gender status inequality from positional economic and political inequality.

Women's private and public rebellions fueled an uneasy public awareness that women's status was an issue. Since the 1830s, women's changing role and identity have been continuously debated in the news media and popular culture. Books and articles about women's place have been published with great regularity, including many early practical guides such as *Employments of Women: A Cyclopaedia of Woman's Work* (1863) and *Women Wealth-winners: Or, How Women Can Earn Money* (1893).[1] Many works that we no longer remember appeared beside those that are still renowned, such as Elizabeth Cady Stanton's *Suffrage a Natural Right*. The concrete issues changed over time, but they usually centered on women's rights to jobs, equal treatment, self-expression, and political influence and on women's obligations to children, husbands, and society.

Similarly, although magazine articles about women's identity tended to advise women not to transgress the boundaries between women's and men's roles, even the most conservative tracts demonstrated a widespread concern about women's status. Works extolling women's role as guardian of domestic virtue were common in the nineteenth century. Conservative twentieth-century advice was more likely to stress women's contribution as childrearers, but the concern with role boundaries was unchanged.

Throughout these public debates, the key point was constant. Women had some freedom to choose how they lived their lives. In particular, they could acquiesce in the social constraints that had limited women's lives in the past, or they could rebel against them. People recognized, although few could clearly articulate the idea, that women's responses to these choices in one generation had the potential to change the choices facing the next generation. Those who saw this possibility vied to promote, to impede, or to pilot these changes.

THE INHERENT REBELLION

Before the modern period, women's resistance to the constraints upon their lives could not budge the social structures sustaining gender inequality. Only under modern conditions, starting in the early nineteenth century, did women's individual efforts to gain greater status become more effective. Then social power migrated from households into organizations, powerful men's interests and ordinary men's interests shifted, and women found new possibilities for improvement in their status.

The changing patterns of women's individual efforts to achieve greater freedom and status have less dramatic appeal than the suffrage movement or modern feminism. Yet they probably helped to reduce gender inequality at least as much as did organized rebellion. Women sought education, they took jobs, they had fewer children, they joined voluntary associations, they entered the political party system, they joined unions, they demanded a greater voice in family decisions, and they divorced husbands to escape bad marriages. All these actions, and others, challenged constraints on women's identity. Although these were individual actions, they had historical impact because they represented the shared interests and ideas produced by women's changing social circumstances.

To be sure, men and women still often found themselves responding to similar conditions. As spouses, siblings, and parents and children, women and men were bound together by sentiment. They lived in the same households, usually had the same class and ethnic identity, and shared the same fate. Divergent, crosscutting systems of social inequality and social identity—such as class, ethnicity, and religious affiliation—stratified these households. Women and men in the same family or social group often shared more assumptions with each other than with people of the same sex in other strata. Working together, being born into the same families, growing up and dying together, loving (and hating) each other in permanent intimate relationships, raising children together, always dependent on each other, women and men thought and acted similarly. Studies have long shown women and men to have similar attitudes. Even today, some research suggests, working women identify their class position more with their husband's position in the work force than with their own.[2] While inequality and the cultural treatment of gender have stressed the differences between women and men, their attitudes, their ideas, and their agendas were strikingly similar. Women and men were more similar than different. These similarities ruled people's actions much of the time.

Yet gender inequality permeated peoples' lives, placing women and men in disparate social positions that affected their outlooks and their actions. What distinguished the actions of women from those of men were their circumstances, not their motives. Both women and men tried to fulfill their socially defined obligations and to advance their interests in a practical way. However, inequality gave women different opportunities and different resources from men, making women's actions in pursuit of their interests less effective than men's.

Although there have always been both women and men who resented the constraints of their gender roles, women's expressions of this resentment produced pressures against inequality and men's did not. Two reasons stand out. Women were more likely than men to act against the system of inequality because they suffered net disadvantages while men enjoyed net advantages. Moreover, their rebellious acts were much more likely to challenge the system of inequality.

The differing circumstances of women and men directly affected their interests and their roles in changing inequality. Women's personal resources were fewer than men's in their social stratum. Women had an inferior legal status, fewer political rights, and fewer economic resources. They also confronted cultural constraints on their behavior. This strategic disadvantage meant that most women had little opportunity to improve their circumstances individually through direct conflicts with men. To avoid the typical dependency on a husband, father, or other man, women had to endure the costs of marginal life choices, such as setting up independent households with meager income or joining a religious order. To achieve more, they had to await new opportunities or engage in collective action.

Selective mating commonly assured men's resource and status advantages in marriages. If mating had ignored other sources of status such as social background, wealth, race, and, to a lesser degree, income, then marriages would have created more variation in spouses' relative resources. Wealth, education, or family resources would have given a minority of women leverage over less well-endowed husbands. This rarely occurred. Because most marriages took place between women and men within the same social stratum, all men had a resource advantage over their wives. Middle-class women may have fared better than both poor and more affluent women. A wealthy, prominent, or influential man usually commanded resources greatly exceeding those of his wife (even if she came from a high-status family, although such a background might sometimes mitigate the resource disparity). In poor, low-status families, where scarcity gave rule to need, any gender advantage could give men considerable power over their spouses. Such men gained advantage even though their resources seemed few compared to those of people in higher strata (although low-status men's gender advantage might have effectively disappeared, if their resources fell extremely low). Gender inequality varied in some ways by class, but women were uniformly disadvantaged.

Reflecting their contrasting circumstances, women and men had opposing relations to inequality's traditional distribution of restraints and opportunities. No matter what motives or understandings they had, men reinforced inequality by fulfilling their traditional role obligations and using the associated opportunities. No matter what motives or understandings they had, women challenged inequality by resisting unequal arrangements. Thus, when thoughtlessly pursuing normal role expectations, men's actions reinforced inequality while women's actions strained the system of inequality. These opposing stresses actively influenced inequality if, and only if, altered circumstances shifted the imbalance between them.

Throughout most days, a woman repeatedly has either to contest or to concede gender inequality. (So does a man, but the tensions are different.) The issues and alternatives have changed over time, but the pervasive implications of inequality have not. Does a young woman challenge a stereotyped comment on women she overhears her brother make to her mother (or her husband make to his buddy), or does she silently assent? If a man on the street or in some gathering makes a lewd comment on her appearance, does she smile, ignore him, frown, call him names, or kick him between his legs? If a friend bubbles over excitedly because she has found a man to make her life meaningful, does a woman make a toast to her friend's good luck or advise her to quit throwing her life away on men? Does she adopt her husband's name when she gets married? Does she accept or reject responsibility for the kids' lunch? Much of life's ordinary activity assumes or occurs along the boundaries between male and female identities, always making these boundaries a potential object of contention.

Women's part in the give-and-take of normal female-male interactions commonly strained against inequality while men's part defended that inequality. As women and men negotiated responsibilities, joint decisions, and the shared definition of reality, they pushed and pulled against the normative definitions of their gender roles and their respective resources. Usually they did not think of these exchanges as conflicts over gender inequality. Rather, they saw them in personal terms. Yet except in extraordinary cases men held an advantaged position in these negotiations. As both women's and men's claims reflected their distinctive gender interests, they necessarily pushed in different directions.

On balance, women's preferences pushed toward greater gender equality while men's pushed away from it. This might not happen when people were mistaken about the effects a choice would cause, when they were indifferent to the particular effects, or when they were exposed to peculiar circumstances that made the expected effects of actions different for them than for most others (for example, because they were employers). However important such exceptions, inequality channeled women's interests and their resentments. Therefore, women usually contended for greater equality with men, even if they did not think of their conflicts in these terms.

Similarly, women were more likely than men to adopt a sustained strategy that challenged inequality. Men did experience resentment derived from inequality. Their resentment concerned either male responsibilities, such as those for holding jobs and providing income, or the norms that restricted men from "feminine" actions, such as the expectations that men would not care for children or express "weak" emotions. Resentment caused some men to reject the responsibilities or constraints of the male role; for example, they became criminals, dropouts, or sexual deviants. These men's violation of male role expectations did not, however, directly threaten other men's advantages. The men who rejected the typical male role also did not win any increment in status or resources to offset the social disapproval they provoked. Nothing occurred to motivate other men to follow their lead. Sometimes women rejected their gender-role responsibilities, such as rearing children or caring for a household, also without trying to gain any position with greater status. Like men who cast off some aspects of the male role, these women's rebellion did not place pressure on gender inequality. In contrast, some women tried to enter positions usually reserved for men. These women did directly threaten male advantages. If successful, they did win some increased status and resources that served as a model for other women.

These observations stress ordinary women, but most women were ordinary in this sense. Women wielded little influence through positions of power, which men largely monopolized. The actions of powerful men had special importance, because such men exercised influence and had distinctive interests. Because very few women held positions with power, they had no comparable group. Women therefore did not influence change through decisions over institutional policies, because they did not control institutions.

Women's collective power was also less than men's. Men's gender interests received a collective defense without explicit organization toward that goal through men's economic and political links. Male-dominated government and business sustained policies favoring men. Women could achieve a countervailing collective power only if they either penetrated the institutions of power in significant numbers or created effective organizations to promote their interests. Because of women's fewer individual resources, they could successfully pursue these strategies only when changing circumstances gave them new opportunities.

Women and men had opposing experiences of the changing circumstances that led to reduced inequality. Not surprisingly, women more often welcomed and gratefully used new opportunities to engage in traditionally male activities while men more often resented and resisted an apparent erosion of their rights. Many women experienced increases in women's opportunities, available resources, and potential statuses as both practically and symbolically valuable. This positive experience prompted them to welcome and champion the changes. Some women, particularly those who could foresee no personal benefits from the changes, did sometimes feel threatened by these changes. Still, on balance, women reinforced changes that reduced inequality by using new opportunities, regardless of their motives or understandings. In contrast, men repeatedly experienced women's efforts to improve themselves as threats to legitimate rights that men had earned, and responded with resentment and opposition. As their interests and resources shifted, men's resistance became both less energetic and less effective. Simultaneously, women's pursuit of new opportunities and struggle against their inferior status became more vigorous and more successful.

One response to changing conditions was women and men trying out aspects of the roles traditionally assigned to the other sex. People's experiments with crossing sex-role boundaries depended on structurally determined opportunities and on their perception of the risks and rewards. Inequality meant that women often experienced their chances to enter male roles as opportunities, but men were less likely to value their chances to enter female roles. Not surprisingly, more women were likely to try employment when jobs became available than men were likely to try childrearing. In contrast to women's long, slow movement into the economy, research has shown that men's participation in childrearing has begun to rise only in the past two decades and is still limited. While they can experience some facets of childrearing as an opportunity, people typically see much of it as a burden.

Neither women nor men willingly adopted the obligations of the other sex, no matter how much they tried to avail themselves of the other sex's opportunities. Despite men's collective dominance, men's individual responsibilities may have been even more inescapable than those of women, and this unavoidable responsibility may have significantly reinforced male resistance to change. Both women and men retained their traditional role obligations if they adopted some activities from the prescribed role of the other sex, but the perceived value of the changes differed. Women crossing the sex-role boundary to take a job were aiming at a status-enhancing activity and would commonly anticipate reducing their household labor somewhat, though not a commensurate amount. Working women still did more household work than their husbands.[3] For example, a middle-class woman taking a job might hire someone to take care of her children, to clean her house, and to cook her food. A working-class woman might pass some of these duties to a relative instead of hiring someone, but the effects were similar. Analysts have noted that this household burden both reflected and sustained women's lower status.

Men crossing the sex-role boundary to assume household tasks were taking on a low-status activity and would usually expect no reduction in their job responsibilities. Theorists have largely ignored the inflexibility of men's traditional role responsibilities. A man taking household responsibilities could not get someone else, other than his wife, to provide income for his family. Women's lower income, the rigidity of employment alternatives, and cultural expectation left most men with no reasonable strategy for lowering their economic activity if they increased their household involvement. Because women's role activities held less prestige than men's, men were not falling over each other trying to adopt women's household activities anyway. As men were also unable to shed their traditional responsibilities, those who did experimentally adopt female role activities besides their male role activities were unlikely to provide an attractive example for other men to emulate. The uninspiring images of men who rejected traditional roles contrasted strongly with the positive models provided by many women who experimentally tried male role activities.

Sometimes women and men rejected traditional gender roles by defying or withdrawing from conventional society rather than challenging it. Most of men's rejections of the masculine role and many of women's rejections took this form. Sometimes this produced a deviant subculture, such as outlaw men, who rejected the responsibility of steady employment. Sometimes it reinforced a deviant stereotype. Still, individual rejections of gender-role definitions that did not involve a status improvement were unlikely to have a lasting effect because they did not inspire imitation.

Women have always resisted and challenged sex inequality through individual actions. While sex inequality was securely embedded in the structures of economic and political positional inequality, these efforts had no cumulative effect. Women's resistance to inequality may have prevented it from getting worse but could not make it better. Women could not pursue new individual strategies that altered the conditions under which future women made choices or that set examples attracting others to follow.

As modern economic and political organization became increasingly individualistic, women's rebellious individual actions became important. Through them, women took advantage of new opportunities and forced men to adapt to their altered circumstances. As the resources and rules governing the endless contests between women and men changed, so did the outcomes. Unlike in the past, the rebellious pioneers found their successes did alter the situation for those that followed. The pioneers served as examples. Their presence in new roles (for example, the women working in a firm) also altered the situation and enhanced the opportunities for those who followed. Resistance could finally have a cumulative effect.

As the constraints on women's roles eroded, new, sometimes substantial choices became active. A woman had to decide how much education she should try to get. How hard should she compete with males in school? Should she seek a job? If so, what kind of job? What kinds of organizations should she join? What goals should she pursue in her life? These choices involved costs and demanded sacrifices, which could be severe. The opportunities that did exist were often available only to some women. Nonetheless, even small and costly opportunities gave women new chances to rebel against their constraints.

The aggregate actions of women rebelling against their circumstances had significant effects on gender inequality, even when their individual actions seemed insignificant when considered alone. Once the number of women who did choose to try new opportunities crossed some threshold, the circumstances constraining all women were altered. For example, the first women hired stood out as oddities or tokens. As their numbers in some jobs grew, they came to be regarded as ordinary. They also gained the potential for collective action.

The major prospect for a lasting effect of individual actions was changing the actions of other individuals. When women's individual rebellious actions succeeded and secured them higher status, greater resources, or more freedom, they set a new standard and they often inspired other women to imitate. When the number of women whose activities had changed grew large enough, the aggregate impact changed even the conditions that affected action.

While personal ambitions motivated most women pursuing goals such as improved education, employment, and political activity, their actions' cumulative impact surpassed any individual intentions. As more women engaged in an activity, adopted a role, or entered an organization, their presence created a different environment for all concerned. Perceptions, expectations, arrangements, and interests were adjusted and readjusted. Male politicians, employers, administrators, educators, students, co-workers, fathers, and husbands all had to adapt. The next wave of women faced new choices, influenced by what they now saw as women's alternatives and the reactions of men and institutions. On occasions when women's rights became an explicit public issue, the divisions between women's interests and men's interests became more evident to all.

ORGANIZED REBELLION

Women's organized rebellion against their inferior status complemented their continuous individual resistance to inequality. Through individual resistance, women created a constant pressure toward equality. This pressure assured the erosion of inequality as conditions changed. In comparison to this individual resistance, organized resistance created a more concentrated pressure for increasing equality, but only under special conditions.

Mainly, organized rebellion occurred when women's capacity and will to resist outpaced the improvements in women's status. While women's movements have spent much effort opposing economic and political institutions, these movements largely grew out of and reinforced integral, long-term structural developments driven by these institutions. The impetus of structural change in the economy and the political order coincided with the impetus of women's movements seeking women's equality through assimilation.

Women first organized effectively to improve their social status in the nineteenth-century United States and other Western nations. Efforts to organize rebellion against gender inequality went through several distinct phases. At first, pioneer American critics of women's low status (like those in other countries) objected most loudly to laws restricting middle-class women's economic activity. As the government gave women greater property rights, female activists shifted focus and agitated for the vote. When the government granted women suffrage, the movement lost its spark and stalled during the 1920s. Modern feminists protesting anew about women's experience and status began a new movement in the 1960s.

For simplicity, the term *feminist* refers loosely to all the ideas and actions devoted to improving women's status. Extending the term to cover all collective rebellions against women's lower status is imprecise. Still, this loose terminology usually produces less theoretical confusion than imposing arbitrary distinctions to refine the term's definition. Admittedly, feminism as a self-conscious ideology did not emerge until sometime in the twentieth century.[4] Earlier women's rights and

suffrage ideology did not clearly attribute all gender inequality to social processes (rather than to biological or divine origins), nor did it
reject all gender inequality as unjust. Still, the break with the past by
nineteenth-century women's movements was much greater than the
differences between their ideas and those of modern feminism. The
nineteenth-century efforts to improve women's rights were self-
conscious, collective rebellions against women's inferior status, accompanied by attempts to understand and interpret that status. For
these reasons, we can use the term *feminist* inclusively rather than
restrictively.

The women who fought for suffrage and the modern feminists who
have struggled to give women full equality have thought differently,
lived differently, and had different circumstances from the women
who lived before them. Most important, the changes in their economic and political surroundings gave them better opportunities and
resources while diminishing men's interests in opposing their advancement. As women used these opportunities, their changing social position allowed them to see their circumstances differently. As the resulting feminist insights combined with women's altered circumstances,
women organized themselves to change those circumstances even further. Organization and collective action then allowed feminists to develop their insights even more.

Through feminist organization and ideology, women shaped their
own collective future. Yet, like architects constrained by a developer's
goals, building codes, and physical laws, women's movements oper-
ated within a highly constrained environment. Changing circumstances produced feminism and defined its potential. After long struggles, the state and other institutions—such as businesses, schools, and
churches—repeatedly conceded feminist demands. However, these
same institutions also rejected many feminist demands. Moreover,
they repeatedly adopted policies that benefited women without any
feminist agitation. Feminist movements had considerable room to act
effectively when they sought goals consistent with the direction of
general economic and political development. They had very little
chance to achieve goals inconsistent with structural trends.

Several conditions foster social movements dedicated to change, according to the extensive literature on this subject. First, the more that
people experience both shared dissatisfactions and hopes, the more
motivation they have to act collectively. Second, the more individual

freedom and resources that people in a group possess, the more able they are to join a movement. Third, the more that a group's circumstances ease organization, the more likely it is that pioneering experiments with collective rebellion will accumulate, grow, and stabilize. Fourth, the more that a movement's aims can be accommodated without threatening the interests of those in power, the more likely it is to succeed.[5]

These conditions suggest several questions that can help us to explain the woman suffrage movement or modern feminism's rise in the 1960s. In each case, did more women than in previous times acutely feel dissatisfactions and, perhaps, more sharply perceive alternatives?[6] Did more women possess the freedom and resources that allowed them to voice their feelings and act to further their interests in these two periods? Were more women in circumstances that gave them both the knowledge and the means to create organizations?[7] Most important, why had such changes occurred?

The woman suffrage movement was a revolutionary break in the history of women. It lasted throughout the second half of the nineteenth century and the first two decades of the twentieth. For the first time, women created and sustained an organized movement dedicated to improving the status of women. While women eventually got the vote, this movement's own history embodied its greatest achievements: its emergence, its growth, its public recognition, and its perseverance.

Through the nineteenth century, middle-class women gradually achieved a circumscribed liberty. An ever-growing proportion of these women had some experience of early independence from families through education or employment or both.[8] Although even a high school degree was still uncommon by 1900, those who attended schools often experienced autonomy from families coupled with competitive strivings for excellence. These experiences contrasted sharply with their traditional prospects of domestic dependence and social inferiority. A small but notable and growing number attended college.[9] Many young women, even in the middle classes, held jobs for a while before marriage (and much longer if they did not marry).

Marriage curtailed this youthful independence, but married women were also gaining greater independence. Middle-class families gradually reduced married women's domestic labor obligations by buying more of the goods they used in their homes while still hiring servants. (According to the rough figures of the census, the proportion of adult women employed as servants began to decline significantly only between 1910 and 1920; the absolute number of women employed as servants began to decline significantly only after 1940.)[10] Because their husbands now worked in businesses located away from their homes, wives spent a significant proportion of their time outside their husbands' observation. The separation between economic production and the household has often been invoked as a process that isolated women in the home. It did, but another side of this separation was women's increased freedom from men's supervision. In combination with declining domestic labor responsibilities, this increasingly separated life gave some middle-class women time and space in which they could nurture an incipient independence.

As women became freer from both domestic labor responsibilities and husbands' oversight, they participated more in pursuits outside their homes. Varied arenas and activities drew women, especially middle-class women, outside their homes. Many poor and immigrant women continued to hold poorly paying jobs as before.[11] Many women met in the quieter pursuit of culture and entertainment associated with the explosion of women's clubs.[12] Membership in women's clubs had become commonplace by the beginning of the twentieth century. Significant numbers of restless, educated middle-class women also joined various reform organizations, the largest of which was the Women's Christian Temperance Union.[13] The *History of Woman Suffrage* volume published in 1902 listed more than 100 national associations of women, such as The National Council of Women, The General Federation of Women's Clubs, The National Association of Colored Women, The Women's Relief Corps, The International Board of Women's and Young Women's Christian Associations, and the Supreme Hive Ladies of the Maccabees of the World.[14] These groups claimed up to a million members and pursued a wide range of goals, including politics, charity, recreation, moral uplift, and religion.

In this general expansion of women's realms of activity, the suffrage movement stood out as the pinnacle. Even as many disparaged them, the suffrage activists became heroines and objects of awe to both women and men. Ridicule and respect came side by side. The suffrage activists' knowledge, determination, and hard work won them grudging admiration from all sorts. Politicians, in particular, discovered that the suffrage activists were among the most politically knowledgeable people with whom they had to contend and that suffrage organization often rivaled that of political parties.

Circumstances, not ideology, focused women's collective rebellion on the goal of suffrage.[15] When a few advanced women made the first organized demand for women's rights at the Seneca Falls convention in 1848, the right to vote was one of a handful of demands. The others emphasized education and various legal rights centered on ending women's legal subservience to their husbands. Two circumstances gradually centered the attention of women's organized rebellion on the vote. First, the state extended suffrage to white working-class men in the 1830s and to black men after the Civil War. Second, women experienced many, though gradual, concessions of the other rights, but suffrage was particularly unyielding. In part, the difficulty in getting the vote reflected a limitation in the structure of the law: women could obtain suffrage only through a constitutional change—at the state or federal level. This was difficult to achieve. In part, the resistance to giving women the vote probably represented the symbolic and practical association of the vote with power. The early extension of the vote to women in some western territories and eastern localities showed that the goal was feasible. These conditions combined to focus women's organized rebellion on the suffrage issue.

While middle-class women had enough independence to organize in favor of suffrage, they were not ready to agitate for economic advantages. Few of these women had the prospect of independence through careers. Jobs both available and acceptable to middle-class women were scarce. The number of women holding middle-class jobs was still far too small to form the basis of active organization against employment discrimination. Probably most married women actively campaigning for suffrage had gained their husbands' support (even if unenthusiastic) for the vote, but husbands would have been much more resistant to a campaign for women's careers. It was one thing for a man's wife to go to an occasional meeting in support of suffrage; it was quite another for her to take a job. Moreover, most middle-class women probably also did not find the possibility of permanent employment inviting enough to adopt a strategy of protest aimed at securing careers. Most of these women were already committed to a domestic life and had no visible prospects of a career. For them, holding a job was more likely to seem a burden than an opportunity.

How, then, did the circumstances of middle-class women fit the conditions needed for a social movement to obtain suffrage? The dissatisfactions and hope that motivated women's participation came from the increased liberty they experienced, their greater temporal independence from men (constrained by an unchanged economic dependence), the awareness of public life produced by education and associational activity, and a sense of injustice increased by the extension of suffrage first to working-class white men and then to black men. The freedom needed to organize came from the reduction in domestic responsibilities joined with men's absence during their hours of employment. Women's widespread voluntary associations and the absence of any violent suppression also eased the organization of suffrage groups.

Thus, gradual changes due to structural developments and to the cumulative impact of dispersed women's private actions produced precisely the conditions known to stimulate social-movement activity. Changes in economic and political organization gave women more liberty and reduced ordinary men's relative resource advantage. Women who used, and helped create, their new opportunities produced the educated elite with organizational ties and skills who inspired and led the suffrage movement.

The suffrage movement revealed the growing rift separating women's stagnated political rights from their otherwise improved social status. The suffrage movement was thus a product of women's uneven progress toward greater equality, an outgrowth of the transformation toward a modern economic and political order.

The suffrage movement itself, not the vote for women that it sought, was the key historical process through which women successfully entered the political realm in the United States. The vote for women initially reduced women's collective political voice, because the suffrage movement was a more potent political force than the disorganized impact of women's votes. The suffrage movement brought women into politicians' offices and into legislative chambers. It forced politicians into long negotiations with women representing the suffrage organizations. It made women's status a central political issue for many years. For decades, it repeatedly placed women's status on the front pages of newspapers. Through the suffrage movement, women achieved an active political presence.

Although suffrage failed to induce any dramatic improvement in women's political position, woman suffrage was an extremely important change in the organization of gender inequality. After the national suffrage amendment was ratified, women did not turn out to vote in large numbers, women who did use the ballot did not vote significantly differently from the men in their social milieu, and women did not move into political office in significant numbers. Yet the social changes that resulted in a few years or even a few decades should not measure the effectiveness of woman suffrage. A century is a more appropriate time span. Fundamental changes in social organization, such as removing gender inequality, can happen only over long periods, despite our hopes, desires, and expectations for faster remedies. We already know that women's vote has had significant influence. In contemporary politics, every elected official has to consider how women and men vote differently. After women gained the vote, political actors (including the state apparatus) did become increasingly responsive to women's political impact. It has taken time for the promise of woman suffrage to be fulfilled, because political processes are not simple reflections of the most obvious political rules and laws. Winning the vote was not so much a culminating event as the beginning of a new process. Suffrage was the breakthrough that opened the gates to women's political assimilation.

The history of women's suffrage suggests that women's agitation for the vote was neither an independent, exclusive cause of suffrage nor an unimportant sideshow. Over time, some industrial nations developed strong woman suffrage movements, some produced weak movements, some produced almost no organization for woman suffrage. Ultimately, all granted suffrage to women.[16] If woman suffrage emerged in countries without agitation by a women's movement, some other social conditions or processes must have been crucial. The experience of achieving woman suffrage at the state level in the United States showed that timing of adoption was poorly related to the degree of organization. This experience was replicated internationally, as countries that granted woman suffrage early often had low levels of organization among women. Examples include Finland, Norway, Austria, Czechoslovakia, Poland, and Ireland.[17] These comparisons show that a woman suffrage movement was not a universally necessary condition to the extension of the vote to women. They also show that suffrage organization was not a simple determinant of the timing of woman suffrage. It did not consistently give women the vote earlier in countries or states with higher levels of organization. Rather, the woman suffrage movement in the United States (and other countries) was an integral part of a larger process that changed the status of women.

While the structural changes in economic and political organization progressively undermined the supports for gender inequality, they did not directly determine *how* the decline in gender inequality would come about. Differences among the states showed this clearly. Some American states granted women suffrage before women organized or agitated. Others gave in to the demand after a long struggle. Still others gave women the vote only because the national constitutional amendment forced them to do so. In this social and historical context, the American woman suffrage movement was a necessary and essential part of the process that brought women the vote. The movement was not the exclusive, fundamental cause of woman suffrage. The structural and organizational transformation created the potential for equalizing women's political status. Nonetheless, the movement was the crucial historical "agent" that did the most to realize this potential for raising women's status through the vote.

The disembedding of gender inequality from economic and political inequality did not involve or produce a moral commitment to raising women's status. Ordinary men's resistance to women's efforts declined over time because their resources and interests altered. Men with power also responded to changing personal and organizational interests that sometimes caused them to introduce policies that benefited women and further eroded gender inequality. Neither ordinary nor powerful men's interests became associated with a general goal of raising women's status, and neither group was infected with a moral commitment to end inequality.

Some aspects of gender inequality evaded the effects of gradually changing conditions. Women's exclusion from power and their responsibility for children were the most important. Economic and political development did not produce male or organizational interests that were inconsistent with the persistence of these limitations on women. Men's pursuit of new opportunities for profit and power did not produce policies that contested these facets of gender inequality. Instead, men's ordinary individual efforts to fulfill their responsibilities and succeed continued to sustain women's exclusion from high-status posts (and their responsibility for children). This happened even when men were not directly concerned with women's relative status.

Yet men had no compelling interest in keeping the vote from women. By this, I do not mean that men felt simply indifferent. Many politicians feared the unpredictable risks inherent in a dramatic expansion of the electorate. Many ordinary men were suspicious of the symbolic rise in women's status. These anxieties did not represent any substantial interests, however, so they induced only a passive resistance. Men's passive resistance was long effective, because women could gain the vote only through male actions. Some men, usually politicians, first had to support a proposition to give women the vote. Other men had to ratify this proposition. For state constitutional changes, this usually meant the male electorate. For the national constitutional amendment, this meant the men in state legislatures.

Initially, men could block woman suffrage by doing nothing. Wherever sufficient support had made woman suffrage an issue, men could block it by simply voting no. Woman suffrage lagged behind other legal and social changes that benefited women because such mild, passive male resistance to change was so effective.

In these circumstances, women's collective efforts to gain the vote seem much less difficult to explain than would have been an absence of such efforts. Middle-class women were receiving greater status, liberty, and resources while being denied a major component of citizenship that the state awarded to men of a lower class. They could not hope to gain the vote through individual action. They had the resources they needed to act collectively. The opposition they faced was largely passive, even if sometimes hateful and oppressive. These circumstances included all the materials that typically produce a social movement. The opportunities for a movement to begin were greater than in many other countries. The decentralization of American government meant that each state (and many municipalities) offered separate platforms on which to launch a suffrage campaign. A women's movement for suffrage would have become unlikely only if suppressed by some highly influential historical conditions, such as a prolonged depression or some other enduring social tension.

The modern feminist movement that arose during the 1960s was the second major episode of women's collective rebellion against inequality. While its history is very different from that of the suffrage movement, its causes and consequences reveal many parallels.[18]

The stage for modern feminism was set by a combination of long-term and short-term changes in social life that widened the gap between women's expectations and experience. This gap magnified the dissatisfactions of women in varied walks of life. The same changes in society that caused more women to be acutely dissatisfied also gave more women the freedom to rebel and the capacity to organize. A rapidly growing group of women earned college degrees in the twentieth century. They then found the promises of their learning achievements denied by the closed doors of professions and business. A growing group of women nonetheless sought, owing to extraordinary commitment or circumstances, to fulfill those promises by pushing their way into business and professional occupations. They found their limited successes hard fought and their progress blocked, leaving them frustrated and angry. Many middle-class women increasingly found themselves victims of the failed social experiment of the suburbs that, after World War II, promised an idyllic domestic life. For many educated, often ambitious, women, this suburban domesticity all too soon proved to be more a breeding ground for malaise. Simultaneously, ideological norms of meritocracy and equal opportunity had progressively eclipsed the formerly blinding effects of ideological justifications that described sexual inequality as necessary and beneficial. And the dramatic, widespread civil rights and antiwar movements of the 1960s gave numerous young women (many the children of suburban mothers) a profound confrontation with sustained male domination all too clearly contradicting the essential premises motivating the movements.

Thus, by the 1960s the development of major social institutions had placed ever larger numbers of women in circumstances in which seemingly legitimate expectations were thwarted. Greater education, higher female employment, a stronger meritocratic ideology, and liberal social movements gave high aspirations to more women than ever before. These aspirations were then dashed against the rocks of employment discrimination and social prejudice. Discontent is endemic to the human condition, and the universal subordination of women has everywhere exacerbated that discontent. During the century ending in the 1960s, however, social circumstances forced progressively more women to suffer a severe disparity between expectations and experience, a disparity that was increasingly difficult to disguise or justify, a disparity, moreover, that appeared straightforwardly susceptible to remedy.

Most accounts agree that the women's movement in the United States grew along two lines. Both were composed largely of college-educated women from affluent circumstances.[19] The branch exemplified by the National Organization for Women drew employed professional and business women seeking to use political organization to eliminate sexual discrimination and further their collective interests. Women frustrated with the experience of women in the civil rights, antiwar, and student power movements started the branch better known as the Women's Liberation Movement. It blossomed about universities, drawing its membership from current and past students. The new feminism grew mostly among educated women who had grown up in affluent families. The affluent beginnings gave these women the aspirations and resources to pursue higher education and careers.

Following these goals, many women had become enmeshed either in the culture of urban professionals and business people or in a college culture (most commonly a prestigious university). By the mid-1960s more than 2 million women were attending college. Of the more than 25 million women in the labor force, more than 4 million held positions classified as white-collar professionals, technicians, managers, proprietors, and the like.[20] The growing number of women in these special cultural settings had freedom to voice their dissatisfactions with women's lot. Some were independent of men. Others found that the men on whom they depended were unwilling or unable to restrain their rebellions against restrictions based on their sex.

Affluent college students living away from their parents' homes had largely escaped both parental supervision and economic responsibility. Fathers had lost their control, and husbands were still in the future. Moreover, the intellectual life of the university, however flawed in reality, gave students the freedom to think beyond the confines of their upbringing, a freedom temporarily magnified by the social movements that captured the imagination of activist students in the 1960s.

Women employed in professional or managerial positions possessed significant status and income even if discrimination denied them the responsibilities and rewards that men achieved for equivalent education and performance. These employed women's resources restricted the ability of men to exercise control over their private lives. Also, as a result of the mutual selection process governing the choice of marital partners, such women probably married men who were more likely to sympathize with their wives' status frustrations.

An ever-increasing number of women had the freedom to express their dissatisfactions, because the prestigious universities accepted more female students and the professional and managerial strata employed more women. These women had less fear of restriction by men (or women) on whom they were seriously dependent. This freedom was relative, not absolute, of course. Not all women in college or white-collar jobs had this freedom. Many who did have it may have lacked the ability to recognize or use their freedom. Granting these limitations, the trends were unmistakable. Ever more women exposed to strong, legitimate dissatisfactions due to sexual discrimination were in circumstances that allowed them to express their frustrations and share their plight with their peers.

From similar circumstances, more women than before possessed the knowledge and capacity to organize themselves. Again the key was participation in settings separated from their households. Colleges tied together students. Facilities were readily available for organizations. The civil rights, antiwar, and student power movements also brought students together under movement banners. These students also received special training in organization. Professional and business women met each other through their occupations. They also participated in occupationally related associations. Their shared experience of discrimination made it easy for them to discover their common interests.

Women in these social worlds possessed greater knowledge about organizing, and their institutional relationships lessened the difficulty of organizing. Thus, as gender inequality disembedded from economic and political inequality, women participated more in universities, professional and business occupations, and social movements. These experiences allowed women to escape the confines of domesticity. Within these contexts, women gained the opportunities and skills to organize a sustained, collective response to their shared dissatisfactions.

Modern feminism, like many social movements that aim to improve the circumstances of a disadvantaged group, arose in response to institutional changes that had bettered women's position in society. Increasing numbers of women from affluent families were going to college and seeking careers, meritocratic norms had become dominant in ideology, and contemporary social movements placed women in ever more conflictive circumstances. These changes yielded progressively more women with acutely frustrated ambitions, personal independence, and the capacity to organize. Accumulated long-term changes in society had been progressively raising the potential for a feminist movement for decades. The higher that potential, the more likely that historical events could trigger collective action and organization. By the mid-1960s the potential for a feminist movement had become so high that avoiding its emergence probably would have been more difficult than inducing it.

In the face of this potential, the 1960s produced conditions and events that seem, in hindsight, ideal for igniting the feminist movement. As an offshoot of civil rights legislation, the federal government passed measures that opposed discrimination against women. Social movements for blacks' civil rights and against the Vietnam War provided a political, ideological, and organizational training ground for feminists. These historical conditions were effective catalysts, igniting the latent potential for a social movement produced by women's changing circumstances.

To understand the impact of modern feminism, we must return to the issue of uneven change. Long-term structural changes and individual women's efforts to better themselves largely account for the circumstances in which the modern feminist movement arose. The path of these gradual processes led to women's assimilation in lower-status positions. Women's movement into higher-status positions was far more problematic. Neither organizational interests nor the personal interests of powerful men prompted anyone to bring women into high-status positions. No obvious advantages accrued to men who promoted women or sponsored their careers. Instead, women were riskier choices for organizations and powerful men, because they were less likely to succeed than were men who had similar credentials. Men controlling policies and promotions were concerned with their personal interests, the interests of their network, and the interests of their organization. Moral uplift and altruism had no role.

In these circumstances, organizations did little to initiate policies bringing women into high-status positions, and, as individuals, aspiring women could rarely overcome these obstacles. Without any interests at stake, organizations had no incentive to promote women upward. Without affirmative organizational policies favoring their advancement, women had no path that led into high-status realms.

Yet organizations and powerful men lacked a strong interest in excluding women. While prejudice against women was commonplace among powerful men, few organizations exhibited a high commitment to preventing women's entry. The key to women's effective exclusion from high-status positions was not the effort expended to keep women out. On the contrary, most organizations sustained women's exclusion with little effort and low costs. When affirmative action policies and judicial decisions raised the stakes, few organizations risked anything to resist women's entry into high-status positions.

Nonetheless, the barriers against women were almost insurmountable through individual effort. To advance into high-status positions, people usually pass through a chain of entry points and promotions. They must go through a series of educational institutions, join some organization such as a firm or a political party or profession at an entry-level position, and then rise through some hierarchy of statuses and positions. However able and ambitious an individual is, she or he depends on the goodwill, cooperation, and support of others for success. This dependence occurs at every level in this process and affects advancement to every new level. To prevent women from rising individually, organizations and powerful men normally had only to withhold that support. No one needed to exert a dynamic effort.

Wherever these low-effort exclusionary practices were absent, women did advance. For example, this sometimes occurred in businesses and organizations where all-female sections gave women the chance to rise into supervisory positions; it also happened sometimes in professions in which promotion limitations or a female clientele avoided the development of male strongholds. Women were also elected or appointed to a few political posts. Usually such achievements meant both that men were not overly interested in the position and that it was "assigned" to a woman as a reward for women's political party work.

Curiously, the selection processes and ideology used to choose which men would advance to high-status positions were flagrantly contradictory to women's exclusion. Organizations increasingly stressed that merit should decide promotions, even if those making decisions preferred to follow their whims and fancies. Merit implied that criteria such as education, knowledge, skills, dependability, and performance history should decide who gets ahead. Although organizations could and did apply these criteria discriminatorily, deference to these criteria ideologically controverted that discrimination.

In contrast to the impression often conveyed in the popular press, the main goals of the modern feminist movement coincided with the trends of institutional development. Those defending the barriers to women's advancement into high-status positions, not the feminists, were the ones opposing the momentum of history and the logic of organizational development. Feminists sought assimilation into high-status economic and political positions and a general end to discrimination and unequal treatment based on sex. These goals were entirely consistent with organizational rationality, economic optimization, egalitarian representative government, and meritocratic ideology. The compatibility between modern feminist goals and the logic of institutional development has largely created the opportunity for feminist successes. It has also defined the limits to those successes.

Those defending women's exclusion were butting heads against destiny. Realistically, they were not even defending the status quo. The present was not a static entity that could be preserved. It was a system in movement. Instead, their implicit goal was to reverse some essential consequences of organizational, economic, and political development while retaining the rest. This was a romantically implausible quest.

Women's position in society has improved in many ways since the rise of modern feminism. More women are employed, including those with young children. Most important, more employed women hold high-status professional and managerial jobs. More women are seeking and achieving advanced educational degrees. More women hold political office. Fewer women willingly accept subordination to men. Women have more legal rights, particularly for abortion, divorce, financial credit, and protection against sex discrimination.

Inevitably, men instituted most of the changes in social policy that have improved the collective status and opportunities of women. This was unavoidable because men have held most positions of social power. Male legislators, judges, employers, and educators have enacted most policy changes in government and business that benefited women. The issue, however, is not who enacted the changes, but why they did so. Men, as a group, did not have an interest in reducing sex inequality, few men conceived greater sex equality as a valuable goal, and the goal of enhancing women's status rarely motivated the male actions that did benefit women. The gap between men's motives and the effects of their actions pinpoints an analytical issue. It suggests that we need to show how circumstances induced men to adopt policies conducive to increased gender inequality.

Men were the gatekeepers. Why did the men controlling the gates to high-status positions open them to women? Two hypothetical scenarios that might account for the policy trends seem so inconsistent with the historical evidence that we can discount them. Powerful men could have conceded these policy changes because a dominant women's movement compelled them to act against their own strong interests. Or, powerful men could have enacted these changes because an ideological epiphany converted them into true believers in the justice of feminist claims. Neither of these alternatives seems plausible.

While trying to influence changes in the position of women, the modern American women's movement acquired neither integrated, disciplined organization nor irresistible political power. Since its origins, the women's movement has been fragmented, and the factions could not agree enough on goals and methods to join in one association. Groups who voiced the least controversial goals and committed themselves to the least controversial methods have obtained the greatest organizational success, like the National Organization for Women. While appearing well regulated and enduring, however, even these groups lacked a disciplined membership and were unable to rule their members' actions predictably by collective policy decisions. Therefore, strategy could not extend beyond policies sure to gain voluntary compliance of the membership.[21]

The women's movement also failed to achieve much legitimate political power by winning political offices for its members. Nor did it effectively threaten the power of male-dominated government. It did not accumulate the capacity to control elections, to deter the normal progress of political and economic institutions, or to mount a civil insurrection.

Women's vote was the feminist movement's greatest hope for political influence, but this strategy has also fallen short. Women's voting behavior remained too erratic. For women to gain a gender-based influence over the political process through the vote, women's and men's voting preferences have to reflect the difference in their gender interests. Also, the issues revealing these differences have to become prominent. The distribution of attitudes about public issues does differ by sex, but the differences are commonly less dramatic than the similarities. Also, gender-relevant issues commonly get diminished by other issues during elections.

Politicians *have* become highly aware of women's potential political clout and the possibility of gender differences in attitudes about some issues. A concern with the consequences of alienating women voters (or the hope of wooing them) has become more explicit and important to the political process. The gender gap in voting has increased in recent years and may become a significant force in the future. It was not that large during the decades associated with modern feminism's influence, however.

Without effective political power, the women's movement was repeatedly a supplicant before men's institutional dominance. Instead of coercion, it relied on moral courage, moral suasion, and the clever manipulation of legal and political conditions. It tried to gain by finesse what it could not win by power. Yet, sympathy with the arguments of feminism also seems rarely to have motivated the men who enacted policy changes benefiting women. Although many politicians and many businessmen ultimately adopted public positions supporting women's assimilation, true advocates of feminist causes seem to have been rare in these circles. During the period when any particular policy was being contested—whether it was a very local issue such as women's bathrooms in a manufacturing plant or national issues such as laws governing loan practices—men responsible for policy decisions were generally resistant to feminist demands. The moral arguments justifying women's demands for equality had been widely known for many years before the modern feminist movement emerged. If the justice of women's resentments had swayed men in power, the feminist movement would never have arisen, grown, and lasted as it did. Of course, those running businesses, government, and other organizations are primarily practical, not moral, actors.

Why and how, then, did many policies change in the direction sought by feminists? The key was that no significant interests of organizations and powerful men conflicted with these goals. By the 1960s, gender inequality was sufficiently disembedded from political and economic inequality that organizations had little interest in defending it. Organizations had not gained interests that propelled them to oppose gender discrimination as a general policy or to recruit more than a few women into high-status positions. However, the changes had effectively diminished these actors' interests in preventing women's entry or sustaining discrimination. Many, probably most, men with organizational power harbored personal prejudices against women. When organizational interests were neutral, powerful men could satisfy those prejudices through continued discrimination. Such actions became problematic when they conflicted with organizational interests.

The feminist movement could achieve some of its major goals because limited changes in costs and risks were enough to alter an organization's balance of interests. When organizational interests shifted, so did the interests of the men who got their power from those organizations. The barriers against women's progress into high-status positions by individual endeavors had been effective because they did not cost much, required little effort, and held no risks. Most of the time, men really did not have to keep women out. They simply had to withhold the support women would need to gain access.

Collective action by women suddenly introduced new costs and risks. Feminist organization was erratic and fragmented, but it was also spirited and widespread. Suddenly such risks as electoral reprisals, social unrest, work stoppages, or lawsuits entered the calculations of policymakers. For many issues, women's collective actions nearly reversed the risks and options facing men running organizations. Before, these men could foresee almost no likelihood of gain by introducing policies to give women equal access to high-status positions and equal treatment generally. Yet they could easily imagine many risks and costs if things went wrong. After women began a wide range of collective actions, the policymakers saw their expectations undergo a sharp shift. Refusing to give women equal treatment risked varied costs. Because no significant, equivalent organized opposition to gender equality existed, granting *reasonable* feminist goals held lower risks.

How balanced were the organizational interests favoring and opposing egalitarian practices before modern feminist agitation began? We can assess this only indirectly. Let us recall here that institutions began to assert some more egalitarian policies benefiting women in the decades before modern feminism emerged. The equal pay acts and the inclusion of women in the Civil Rights Act were examples in the political realm. Employment statistics show that women had gained somewhat better access to high-status positions by the mid-1960s, although progress was slow. Similarly, young women were catching up with men in higher education. These observations show that men in power were already adopting more egalitarian measures when circumstances particularly supported this strategy, even when they faced no risks as a result of women's collective action.

After the modern feminist movement began to agitate for changes, the fate of each egalitarian goal seemed to depend most on how much active opposition it provoked. Men in positions of power found it increasingly practical to adopt policies that favored the status and opportunities of women. The emerging institutional structure of society made the continued domestication of women more costly and difficult to defend ideologically. Yet some issues—such as women's status in the military, abortion rights, and preferential hiring treatment—aroused strong opposition. Significant opposition on any issue, whether based on interests or on ideology, generally stymied feminist efforts. Because feminist organization was weak, even moderate opposition could be enough to stymie a feminist goal.

Government responses to modern feminist agitation suggest that feminist efforts to affect national legislation succeeded only when they defined the issues narrowly, minimizing potential effects on gender roles.[22] Feminists did influence legislation, such as laws that provided women equal access to credit, required schools receiving federal funds to give equivalent support to girls' athletics, and required disability plans to cover pregnancy leaves. These successes seem to have occurred because none of these laws threatened to initiate significant changes in the status of women or the relations between the sexes.

Feminist successes seem mainly to have involved rational adaptations to past changes in the activities of women. Therefore, they did not threaten any substantial interests. Much the same has been observed about the earlier suffrage movement. Speaking of the movement at the beginning of this century, Viola Klein argued that "in spite of all their failings feminists saw almost all their demands gradually realized . . . simply by force of practical necessity, and because their claims were in accordance with the general trend of social development."[23]

These interpretations suggest that modern feminism could be interpreted, in part, as an adaptive response to unavoidable changes in the relations between the sexes.[24] Women were being pushed out of domestic life and into the economy. Men (as Barbara Ehrenreich argues) were increasingly rebelling against family responsibilities. Nonetheless, cultural norms and institutional practices largely continued to assume women's subordination and domesticity. Women, as Mirra Komarovsky argued in 1946, faced inconsistent and contradictory role expectations.[25] Feminism responded actively to the painful inconsistencies arising in the midst of the long-term transformation in women's social position. Although modern feminism has exhibited

many distinctive ideologies, the principal shared goals of feminists—
equal opportunity, freedom from discrimination or harassment, and a
right for self-determination—have been a practical and effective response to the contradictory circumstances facing women.

While the modern feminist movement apparently achieved its goals
only when they were consistent with long-term developments in society, the movement's efforts had a marked effect on history. True, the
historical evidence suggests that feminist agitation rarely overcame
significant contradictory organizational interests or defeated determined opposition rooted in such interests. However, the most fundamental feminist goals fitted within these limits.

The evidence also suggests that feminist activity was the principal
reason that egalitarian policies (though limited to ones consistent with
structural developments) rose dramatically and realized their historical form. Before then, the passive resistance of men and organizations
effectively preserved discriminatory practices against women's individual efforts to improve their status. The collective action of women was
the decisive force that overcame this roadblock.

WHY WOMEN AVOIDED OR OPPOSED FEMINISM

Gender inequality has always given women an inherent interest in
changes increasing equality, an interest that most women confront
repeatedly in their daily lives. When changing circumstances gave
women new opportunities, some vigorously pursued the new chances
to get ahead. Through acts aimed at personal improvements, women
gradually altered the social environment. Some aspects of women's
status, such as voting rights and access to high-status jobs, were less
amenable to the processes gradually improving women's status. Eventually, a sharp discontinuity arose between these retrogressive facets of
women's lives and those aspects that had improved. This discontinuity
induced collective actions. Through such actions, women were able to
shift the balance of interests influencing men's actions in their favor.

Yet how do we explain the actions of women who opposed the
social changes that reduced gender inequality? Not all women have
embraced feminism. In recent decades ever more women (and men)
have acknowledged sympathy with the egalitarian goals of feminism.
Not surprisingly, research has consistently shown that most women
enjoyed the recent improvements in women's status associated with
the goals of feminism. Nonetheless, most women have resisted identi-

fying themselves as feminists. A significant minority of women went further and opposed change. At its extreme, women's opposition has produced organized efforts to stop the passage of woman suffrage and to deny passage of an equal rights amendment to the U.S. Constitution.

We need to distinguish women who simply did not support feminist goals from those who actively opposed them. Many withheld support, but only a few women actively opposed the principal feminist goals aimed at reducing inequality. (By the principal goals of feminism, I mean the major goals accepted by most segments of the movement, including ending general sex discrimination, gaining equal access to high-status positions, establishing equal treatment by bureaucratic processes, and ending sexual harassment of women by men. This list omits popular goals that did aim directly at inequality, such as abortion rights, and goals associated more with factions, such as lesbian rights.)

No difficulty arises for explaining why many women never directly conceived feminist goals as a possible part of their lives. Usually, such women simply had never been part of a social network that made feminist ideals or a feminist identity into feasible alternatives. Most people's ideals, relationships, and actions conform to the patterns and expectations made familiar by their biography and reinforced by their surroundings. Most people understand the world and their place in it through the ideas that they receive from the surrounding culture. Under stable conditions of gender inequality, the dominant ideology presses both women and men to accept the current standards of feminine and masculine behavior. The culture depicts sex roles as just, valuable, and necessary. Most people step outside this familiar terrain only when circumstances render ineffective the strategy of unthinking conformity or when events force them to accept or reject some alternative action.

People's tendency to conform to the expectations of their social circle is one reason that social movements commonly draw their new members from the social networks of old members. People who have no relationship with a member of a social movement are unlikely to consider its point of view. In short, most women who did not support feminist goals commonly did not support antifeminist goals either. If asked about a specific issue, they might give an opinion in either direction. The overall conflict between feminist and antifeminist ideology did not loom large in their lives.

Now we must account for the women who directly opposed

changes meant to reduce sex inequality. Why did they seemingly act against their own interests?

Our culture has a deep concern about inequality. We care about its effects on people's lives. We believe that being a member of an advantaged group is always more desirable. We think power is better than subservience, that autonomy is preferable to dependence, that wealth surpasses poverty, that status is more desirable than obscurity. These beliefs seem so encompassing and self-evidently shared that we rarely bother to make them explicit. Therefore, it is perplexing that members of a subordinate group would withhold support from changes that should improve their circumstances.

No evidence shows that women who opposed feminist goals were more ignorant about the consequences of those goals than women who supported them. Realistically, both women for and women against feminist goals have had a limited understanding of inequality and social change. Women who resisted change were commonly ignorant about social policies and the determinants of social conditions. The average woman opposing change did not know why women have a lower status than men. She could not give a clear, accurate description of feminist goals. However, not all women who supported feminist goals were experts either. The average woman who supported feminist goals had not read a pile of theoretical books. She had not tried to learn the social statistics that documented discrimination. Feminists and antifeminists were much more distinguishable by their interpretations of women's circumstances than by the amount or quality of their knowledge.[26] Activists on both sides were much more knowledgeable than other women. Women on both sides of the issue have had easy access to the ideas of women on the other side. Women sought the information that supported their expectations and turned a blind eye to evidence that cast doubt on it. Those on both sides believed they had a truer and more comprehensive knowledge than their opponents.

Alternatively, women opposing changes might have been more devoted to traditional values. Women who opposed feminist goals did claim more traditional values and higher church attendance than those who supported change. Yet feminists also claimed that they were pursuing traditional values. The bundle of traditional values is so general and internally inconsistent that feminists and antifeminists could draw on them equally.

Neither ignorance nor traditional values seem sufficient to explain antifeminism. Some women may have resisted change because they did not understand the issues, and some may have wanted to preserve traditions. Nevertheless, these possibilities do not appear adequate to explain the patterns of committed resistance evoked by feminist movements. Not many women were so isolated from alternative perspectives that inescapable ignorance blocked them from discovering the meaning of what they did. Similarly, few women seemed so committed to traditions that they were ready to choose a worse life to preserve them. Instead, these women seemed to believe their lives would be better if they resisted change than if they promoted it. Rather than assuming that ignorance or inflexible values blinded these women about their interests, let us ask why they might have had good reasons to oppose change.

The status quo served some women's interests better than the promises of change. Those women had more to lose than to gain. Women could reach this conclusion by two routes. Some women had such a large investment in the current system that their future well-being was tied to its persistence. Other women's values, talents, and aspirations better fitted the limited opportunities and female role available under the system of sex inequality than did the expanded, but different, opportunities promised by equality. Some women apparently felt that feminists sought to draft them as footsoldiers in a war that could only bring them harm. Lofty rhetoric did not meet their practical needs.

Most women had made a workable accommodation with inequality. A woman who had spent youth's choices and made lifelong commitments no longer saw a future in which anything different was possible. A married, middle-aged woman with children, for example, rarely aspired to going to law school and starting a trail-blazing career. Such a woman wanted to protect the life she had. She wanted her husband to stay faithful and obligated to support her. How could she use women's new career channels or new sexual freedom? Feminist agitation asked her to bear the costs of a social transformation. If she saw little hope of reaping its rewards, her interests lay elsewhere.

Some women could reasonably believe that they could do better in life using their opportunities under the existing system than by the prospects promised by gender equality. They might value the life offered women under the status quo more than that promised by the system of equality. Some women valued the secondary benefits of inequality more than the primary benefits promised by equality. For example, sex inequality could give women freedom to avoid men's responsibility for holding jobs and providing an income for a family. If a woman really preferred taking care of a household to holding a job, she had reason to oppose the removal of sex-segregated work roles. Similarly, some women found marriage a better route to a good life than competing as an individual in the labor force. Economic inequality cut across sex inequality. Some women gained economic and status advantages through the personal ties of subordination to successful men. Such a woman achieved an affluent lifestyle and high community status through marriage. This could give her a better life than many other people, both women and men. She could reasonably decide this was more than she could achieve through an education and career.

In her well-known study of women in the professions, Cynthia Fuchs Epstein argued that "the American middle-class woman has a substantial interest in the status quo. The commitment is clearly linked to the secondary gains that have accrued to her, seemingly as rewards for service to her class, her husband, and her society."[27] Middle-class wives, Epstein suggested, could get a good income and high social status but escape their husbands' need to work hard and continually, compete successfully, constantly prove themselves, and bend to the requirements of their jobs. Essentially, her portrait suggested that to achieve more success, husbands had to have more talent, work harder, and endure more stress, but the more successful the husband, the less his wife had to do to enjoy the privileges she derived from his success. By this means, some women experienced relative advantages through the system of gender inequality. To many of us today, the relative advantages may not sound appealing, but we should recognize that others found them highly desirable.

Some women, then, resisted changes meant to reduce gender inequality because they judged those changes harmful to the conditions that gave them individual advantages. Changes that improved the general status of women might make their lives worse. The ideology and social characteristics of women who opposed feminist policies confirm this conclusion.

Women's organized resistance to feminism focused on defending the family and women's place in it. Antifeminists were generally much more concerned with maintaining men's obligations than with limiting women's opportunities. Organizations that opposed women's suffrage early in the century stressed fundamental and immutable differences between men and women. In recent decades, women's groups who opposed the Equal Rights Amendment used similar rhetoric.[28] The differences that concerned them were those defined by sex roles.

Groups resisting feminism aimed to defend what they saw as women's special rights and to reinforce men's traditional obligations. The women opposing gender equality argued that progressive policies placed the family in jeopardy. They proclaimed their mission to be the preservation of the traditional family. To them, the traditional family meant a middle-class ideal of a permanent alliance between an employed husband and a wife fully dedicated to home and children. They believed this gave women advantages they could lose. In 1910 an antisuffrage writer warned that "if women claim equality, they must lose their privileges."[29] Similarly, modern antifeminists argued that feminism would rob women of their rights to avoid the military, to stay home with their children, and to have their husbands supply an adequate income.

Antifeminists in both periods claimed that women's moral virtue and nurturing capacity made them ideal domestics and childrearers. Men's aptitudes and competitiveness suited them for economic and public life. According to the antifeminists, they were defending God, religion, prosperity, and democracy. To sustain these values, they claimed, it was necessary to maintain the traditional family and women's place in society.

In her study of the politics of abortion, Kristin Luker found that women leading the opposition to abortion rights had similar conceptions of their mission. They also emphasized intrinsic differences they believed distinguished the sexes. They proclaimed that those differences made women and men ideally suited to the distinctive roles of the traditional family. They argued that women should be wives and mothers. They felt that this job was so demanding that women must devote themselves exclusively to it and that it was so fulfilling that every normal woman should desire it. The anti-abortionists emphasized the value of children, disapproved sex outside marriage, and appealed to religion as a moral defense of their goals. They believed abortion is associated with free sexuality, declining interest in children, and the erosion of differences between the sexes.

In their arguments, anti-abortionists expressed a fundamental fear of social changes that would undermine the traditional family. Abortion symbolized all these changes. These changes jeopardized the moral and structural assurances that women could choose the role of homemaker and mother. They threatened homemakers' confidence that their husbands would provide for them and that society would honor them.[30]

This rhetoric appealed to women who believed that feminist goals threatened their past lives and future expectations. They had invested their lives in the family and the division of labor between the sexes.

Comparing anti-abortion activists with activists defending the availability of abortion, Luker found that those actively opposed to abortion were less educated, much less likely to have careers (indeed, rarely did they have jobs), married earlier, and had more children. Other studies found similar characteristics for activists opposing the Equal Rights Amendment and the ordinary women who supported them. Having made a large investment in family life and having low expectations for personal economic success motivated women to oppose feminist goals. These women had made a commitment to family life. Having made it, they feared social changes that threatened that commitment. These threats included changes that would challenge the beliefs that gave meaning and value to their memories. They also included changes that would diminish the security of their future.

Social policies that attempted to increase gender equality by eliminating the differences between women's and men's opportunities—and therefore eliminating differences between their obligations—offered little to these women. Such policies implicitly criticized their lives and might jeopardize what they possessed. In short, these women adopted an ideology opposed to feminist change because they realistically doubted that such change was in their interest.[31]

Therefore, some women have resisted feminist goals because their interests were inconsistent with the long-term, abstract interests of women as a group. Policies intended to increase equality threatened to erode their social position and expectations. For some women, being the wives of successful and dependable providers promised a better life than having to work at a poorly paid and demanding job. For women who had already made the commitment to a domestic and mothering role, the proposed changes threatened to diminish their moral worth and to reduce their husbands' obligations. These women's private self-interests contradicted the long-term class interests of women.

The unpredictable risks attached to social change increased

women's susceptibility to conditions that prompted resistance to feminism. For many people, the risks of social change seemed more fathomable than the prospects for gain. They could conceive what it would mean to lose valued aspects of their lives better than they could grasp how their lives might get better.

With every increase in women's status, feminist goals jeopardized fewer women's personal interests. By the 1990s three-fourths of working-age, married women were in the labor force. This was true for both working-class and middle-class women. Fewer and fewer women were subject to antifeminist interests arising from a sustained, exclusive investment in a childrearing, domestic role. Simultaneously, increased equality eroded the opportunities for women to find status and security as homemakers. Fewer men wanted to support stay-at-home wives, and cultural ideals abandoned them. In the long run, changing opportunities seem sure to shrink the number of women with antifeminist interests until they become notable more as social curiosities than as a political force.

WOMEN'S ROLE IN CHANGE

Feminist movements have both reflected and directed social change. Changes in society's fundamental institutional structures—the economy, the state, and the family—diminished the supports for inequality. These institutions removed some aspects of sex inequality because they conflicted with the institutions' own needs. Institutional interests explain, for example, the laws giving property rights to married women and the hiring of women for selected occupations. These institutions did not follow any plan explicitly pushing people toward greater equality. Thus, they left many aspects of inequality in place while they altered the balance of resources between the sexes. The resulting disparities created social rifts when aspects of sex inequality in some realms of social life persisted that did not reflect changes in women's lives. Feminist movements arose out of these crosscurrents.

In a context of gradually improving opportunities, ambitious women could seek to advance themselves through individual efforts or by combining with other women. Collective action was unlikely while the expansion of opportunities allowed women sufficient outlets through individual strategies. Whenever and wherever opportunities appeared, some women found them and sought to improve their lives.

Coordinated rebellion became most likely when accumulated changes and existing constraints placed women in a squeeze. For this to occur, some of women's aspirations had to become *expectations,* and those expectations had to be unachievable because of unequal constraints on women.

Partial assimilation was the key. In the nineteenth century, women who gained legal rights, education, and some relief from domestic obligations came also to expect voting rights like men. In the second half of the twentieth century, educated women who were long-term employees and young women in college became particularly discontented. They came to expect the same job opportunities and the same treatment by organizations as men in similar circumstances. Seeing their expectations as individually unrealizable gave women the motivation to organize. Believing that their expectations were practicable goals that were being unjustly and irrationally blocked made collective actions seem a reasonable strategy. At this juncture, the uneven pattern of advances through economic and political development made collective rebellion more responsive to ambitious women's personal interests than to a strict strategy of individual efforts.

Both the suffrage movement and modern feminism were predominantly middle-class movements brought to life by institutional changes that improved women's social position. These social changes produced more women with acutely frustrated ambitions, personal independence, and the capacity to organize. Working-class women experienced as much frustration but had less capacity to organize, and the lower horizons of their best job prospects produced more ambiguous goals.

Self-interest motivated some women to question and sometimes oppose the demands of the feminist movement. Some women have received secondary gains by accepting their dependence on men. They avoided, for example, economic responsibility and the competitiveness and subordination to bosses characteristic of employment. This attitude applied particularly to older women. They feared that they still could lose the advantages of their middle-class marriages but did not see themselves able to use the opportunities promised by gender equality. Secondary gains also appealed to some young women who believed that they could achieve greater success in the marriage market than in the labor market. Because affluent homemakers generally preferred their circumstances to dull, low-status jobs, and because greater gender equality would reduce the security of homemakers, these women's disapproval of feminism did reflect their interests.

Feminist goals that aroused significant resistance from women can be roughly grouped into three categories. First, any objectives that seemed to threaten the integrity of the family aroused opposition from women (and men) who felt dependent on prevailing family norms and strongly identified with them. Second, any goals that contradicted existing beliefs in immutable sex differences incited resistance from those (including many feminists) who had a practical and emotional investment in those beliefs. Third, goals that seemed to increase women's *obligations* (for example, to serve in the military or to earn an income for their families) incited diverse opposition, often disguised in rhetoric. These direct conflicts between some women's interests and feminist goals caused most of the enduring opposition from women.

Although many women rejected any identification with feminism and opposed some parts of the feminist agenda, an ever-growing majority emphatically supported some of the fundamental goals and accomplishments associated with feminism. Equal opportunities and equal rights for women have received overwhelming support, particularly as established political voices have adopted these ideas.

Feminist movements helped to drive forward increasing gender equality induced by structural changes and helped to direct the changes in women's social identity. As an autonomous entity, neither the suffrage movement nor the modern feminist movement achieved decisive social power. They posed no telling threat to the existing organization of power dominated by men. The feminist movements, nonetheless, had several significant effects. They established a new identity for active participants. They also helped to direct, accelerate, and ease the changes in women's social identity.

Most important, feminist movements supplied the effort, organization, and ideas needed to produce egalitarian changes that were beyond the scope of gradual institutional processes. Even as the gradual changes removed the institutional interests in preserving some key aspects of inequality, they did not supply any mechanism to ensure a transition toward greater equality.

The disembedding of gender inequality from economic and political inequality slowly undermined gender inequality. It did not, however, equally erode all aspects of gender inequality. The shift of power into organizations, the expansion of impersonal profit motives, the development of representative government, organizational rationalization, and related trends transformed interests and redistributed resources. As a result, organizations gradually discovered some interests in treating women like men. And women gradually discovered ways to better their lives, relying on their declining resource disadvantage compared with men and using the new opportunities offered by organizations.

Certain resources were much more resistant to these gradual processes. In particular, the transformation of interests and resources did not produce any institutional process that would directly give women access to social power. Nor did these processes create conditions under which women could hope to gain positions of power or status through individual action.

Women's organized rebellions induced powerful men to concede rights implied by the logic of institutional development but denied by the reality of male dominance. The nineteenth-century women's movement sought to establish equal treatment of women and men by the state. The modern feminist movement sought equal treatment of women and men by all organizations. The major feminist goals were consistent with the inherent tendencies of institutional development. Modern organizations, the modern economy, and the modern state had no inherent interest in the distinction between women and men, but considerable interest in attaining optimal use and control of both. Although feminist movements did not achieve great organization or power, they acquired enough to tip the balance of interests among powerful men.

To understand the role feminist movements played in the long-term decline of gender inequality fully, several points are important. First, the feminists' attack on inequality was much more consistent with the developmental logic of the institutions they engaged than was the resistance by the men who held institutional power. The women's movements had the momentum of history and structural evolution on their side. Second, the episodic pressures of women's movements combined with and depended on two persistent forces: the steady disembedding of gender inequality from economic and political inequality and the constant individual efforts of women to better themselves and resist their subordination. Feminist movements arose because these persistent processes had uneven and incomplete effects. Third, overall, the anonymous women struggling to better themselves probably made a greater contribution to gender inequality's decline than did the much better-documented movements. Over the past 150 years countless women took risks, endured harsh conditions, and defied convention to better their lives. Often acting in isolation, able to depend only on their own resolve, these women provided continuous pressure that propelled gender inequality's decline.

....

CHAPTER SIX

SURRENDERING THE HERITAGE OF MALE DOMINANCE

Over the past century, men have gradually lost the means and the will to defend male dominance. Although they continued to value their remaining advantages, American men's opposition to women's advancement has slowly weakened and become more sporadic.

Men's declining resistance to sex inequality had substantial effects in varied social realms. Male-dominated legislatures and judiciaries enacted and defended policies that gave women ever greater civil, legal, and economic rights. Ordinary men voted in favor of policies, such as woman suffrage, that benefited women. The male-dominated economy hired more and more women. Men have steadily increased their willingness to pay for their daughters' education. Since the 1930s, the decline of male opposition to women's advances seems to have accelerated. Male unions have adopted policies against sexual discrimination. Attitude polls over the past fifty years have shown a progressive rise in men's acceptance of gender equality. Government policies and judicial decisions have interceded more directly and consistently in favor of women's interests. In short, as fathers, husbands, employers, fellow workers, and government officials, men now exhibit much less interest in keeping women down than did their counterparts a century ago.

Men have increasingly withdrawn their opposition to improvements in women's status because the uncontrolled, unanticipated development of the economic and political orders has diminished both their motives and their capacities. Over the years, ordinary men got declining benefits from keeping women subordinate, they received decreasing ideological support for opposing women trying to improve their status, and their capacity to enforce the subordination of women in their personal lives progressively fell. Powerful men, in complementary fashion, found themselves increasingly insulated from having to defend the gender dominance of ordinary men. Moreover, they found that their personal interests, associated with the accumulation and protection of institutional power, increasingly recommended policies that favored the interests of ordinary women. The shift of powerful men's interests gradually eroded the organized or collective defense of men's common interests in preserving sex inequality.

Exploring men's part in the history of gender inequality is a sensitive and potentially unnerving task. Assessing men's responsibility is not the issue before us. Responsibility is a moral category. Causal analysis is a broader concern. The issue is how men's actions have helped preserve gender inequality and how men's actions helped diminish gender inequality. Explaining men's actions does not give us an estimation of their moral responsibility for the outcomes. Generally, we exempt people from responsibility when they could not choose differently, they could not foresee the effects of their actions, or they could not grasp the moral rules at stake. Discovering the causes of people's actions alleviates their responsibility only if it shows one of these conditions occurred. If, for example, we show that people engaged in some behavior to further their interests, then we have explained their actions but left their responsibility intact.

To explain how and why men's actions preserved gender inequality, we must assume that the behavior and ideas of men were as socially determined as those of women. We cannot assume that men were free to do whatever they wished. We also cannot assume that men were seeking to preserve sex inequality whenever their actions reinforced gender advantages. Undoubtedly, most men did long prefer preserving their sex's privileges, and most men would knowingly defend those privileges under some circumstances. Still, circumstances, not primordial needs, shaped men's actions.

While men collectively sustained sex inequality, each man was personally constrained by the structure of sex inequality. Men did not individually choose sexual dominance. It was thrust on them. They were born into a society where men ruled. They were taught the identity of dominance. The opportunities denied women were not simply open to men; they often became obligations. The actions with which men sustained their privileged status seemed to them to be normal, legitimate, and often unavoidable. Because dominant groups control social institutions and social policies, their actions have more impact. Conditions that alter the actions of dominant groups more often affect other groups and redirect social change than conditions that alter the actions of subordinate groups. If the actions preserving a dominant group's common interests lose consistency, intensity, or strategic effectiveness, a subordinate group becomes increasingly likely to improve its members' circumstances.

Certain changes in social conditions can reduce the defense of inequality. The dominant group's resources or organization may diminish. Its rewards due to inequality may wane. Its members' belief in the justice and necessity of its dominance may fail. If any of these changes occur, then people in the dominant group may become unable or unwilling to deny the aspirations of the subordinate group. One hundred fifty years ago, most men could not conceive a way to act in the world that did not defend gender inequality. Men's superior status and differing opportunities seemed unquestionably natural, immutable, and just. Women held no positions of economic and political power. Neither women nor men knew how such circumstances could differ. For most men, experience suggested that men just did what men were supposed to do. Still, by the early nineteenth century cracks had begun to form in this picture, and they have widened ever since.

Men's historical retreat from the defense of inequality appears as an unacknowledged anomaly in the literature on women's rising status. Theories about gender inequality have not developed precise or subtle models of male actions, and the new literature on men and masculinity concentrates mainly on the sources and consequences of the masculine personality. This perspective shows us how men experience sex roles, but it neglects explaining why and how men act to sustain inequality. Thus, while this literature has investigated how culture determines norms of masculinity, it has not systematically addressed the causes, consequences, and organization of men's actions that preserve male dominance.[1]

MEN IN OPPOSITION TO GENDER EQUALITY

In industrial societies, men have probably sustained their gender advantages more through competition with other men than through efforts to keep women from enjoying similar opportunities or status. In particular, men sought education, they needed employment, and they tried to better their income and social standing. Men felt compelled to pursue these advantageous positions. Men did not follow this quest because their actions would sustain male dominance. Their standing in relation to other men, not their ascendancy over women, motivated these efforts. This distribution of effort and effects may seem peculiar, yet it really is commonplace in systems of inequality that achieve stability and legitimacy. For example, capitalists must sometimes concern themselves with the possibility of worker rebellion. But capitalists, particularly successful capitalists, usually have concentrated their energies on defeating other capitalists.

This pattern is one indicator of a successful system of inequality. Only when the fundamental supports of inequality have begun to fail do members of a dominant group regularly have to adopt conscious strategies to protect inequality. The more complete its dominance, the less the members of any dominant group need respond to rebellious acts by members of a subordinate group. When dominance is secure, each suppression of a rebellious act carries great weight, because it establishes precedents and denies rebellion the room for growth.

When men did defend their dominance directly, they commonly believed their actions just and necessary. Men usually believed their opposition to sexual equality was a response to injustice rather than a simple drive to retain power. In the nineteenth century, for example, male workers repeatedly opposed the employment of women, male physicians proclaimed women inferior, male educators denied women's right to knowledge, government officials denied women legal or political equality, and husbands demanded deference from their wives. In each case, the men proclaimed their actions and their motives openly, even proudly. These men were confident that right was on their side. They might be outraged, but they were not morally defensive.

Men rarely conceived their actions as an effort to defend sex inequality by preserving its links to economic and political inequality. Instead, men resisting women's advance understood themselves to be fulfilling their obligations or protecting well-earned rights. In all likelihood, the conditions under which most men pursued their individual interests hid their gender advantages from them. As individuals, most men believed the ideology of male superiority. They assumed that their abilities and efforts explained their successes. They stayed blind to women's unrealized talents. Throughout their lives, men's personal advantages accumulated slowly and built upon each other. It appeared to such men that each particular opportunity evaded women because they were not good or aspiring enough.

In day-to-day life, men's gender advantages led them to believe that women's deference was a right that they had earned. Men experienced their economic advantages as a responsibility, and they resented the effort and discipline required to fulfill that responsibility. Most jobs placed men under the authority of another man. Positions that did not involve a boss usually exposed a man to risks from competition (with other men). Women's subordination ameliorated men's sense that they were subjugated by the whims of the economy. Since men bore the major responsibility for providing income, they believed women owed them the compensatory advantage of male domination as a just right. The right to deference applied most strongly to a man's wife, but it could be generalized to all women.

Men usually experienced increases in equality not as an improvement for women but as an erosion of their own rights. In the midst of change, men did not weigh their position against women's position in society. Rather, they compared their position to the norms of male superiority and their own past expectations. Because resources, privileges, and status in society were limited, redistributing these goods would diminish the amount available to those in the previously privileged group. Men feared such changes threatened their expectations. They felt they were being deprived.

Recently, men who have tried to start a men's rights movement in response to modern feminism have explicitly interpreted their advantages as burdensome responsibilities.[2] They have given us some perceptive descriptions of this experience. They complain that men have got a raw deal for shouldering a heavy load without getting just rewards. They argue that men suffer as much misuse by society as do women. A man must constantly hold a job, support his family, and strive to get ahead, no matter how awful the work. "If men are so powerful, why do they spend a lifetime supporting themselves and other people? Why aren't women supporting them, the way kings are supported by their subjects?"[3] Why, these men ask, do we always have to keep a stiff upper lip? Why do we have to offer our bodies when there is war? Why do we have to protect women from other men but get no protection ourselves?

Behind these pained cries lies at least a century and a half of shared experience. Most men most of the time have faced recurring conditions that could result in their doing an inadequate job at filling their male responsibilities. Whatever success men had seemed transient and insecure. Only a small minority could tell themselves that they had achieved economic and social success. Everywhere, most men saw others who were doing better than they. Facing constant threats to their worthiness, men saw women as the recipients of the spoils produced by men's efforts. They felt women had a privilege being sheltered from the activity and responsibility of producing income. Thus, men who opposed women's efforts to improve their status commonly believed they were protecting themselves from an unjust deprivation. While we might now apply a different moral interpretation to their actions, in the past men have believed themselves to be fighting their own victimization. Our modern moral perspective may lead us to condemn such behavior by men, but that is irrelevant to explaining their actions in the past. The issue here is how men thought of their actions, because that will help us understand men's opposition to gender equality.

So long as most men adopted the beliefs and motives that defined and defended their dominance, the rest had little choice but to conform to the expectations of the majority. The expectations of the majority determined the content of culture and the shape of institutions. The mutually reinforcing consistency of this environment made it difficult for men to think contrary to the prevailing ideology and even harder to express any doubts or discrepant thoughts. As long as most men felt unjustly deprived by social changes favoring women, they regarded men supporting the changes as traitors. This attitude gave the majority a strong moral defense for shunning and belittling the men who deviated. These sanctions made it costly for men to support gender equality in visible ways while the ideology of male dominance was prevalent. This deviance controlling process had two contrary implications. While women's subordination was stable, the men who willingly opposed greater equality, a majority, induced the support of most other men.

Yet a reversal someday of the deviance-controlling process always had the potential to produce a rapid drop in the support for inequality. When the social conditions supporting inequality changed so as to reduce the proportion of men voluntarily committed to male dominance, the deviance-controlling processes could hide the depth of this change for a while. Eventually, the proportion of men voluntarily committed to inequality's defense would somewhere pass a threshold after which they could not induce other men to resist women's advances. The probable result would be a rapid, self-reinforcing collapse of effective male opposition to increasing equality.

The threshold effect concerning the control of deviance from a dominant ideology somewhat resembles the tokenism threshold effect analyzed by Rosabeth Kanter.[4] According to Kanter, when the first women gained employment in a formerly all-male position, the other employees saw them as odd. This perception ceased only after women constituted a significant proportion of the employees in the position. The decisive proportion would vary considerably by circumstances, with perhaps 15 percent being the minimum threshold. Before this threshold was reached, every employed woman was viewed as a token female, subject to constant scrutiny, judgment, and criticism linked to this special status. After the threshold was passed, others came to see women as normal occupants of the position. This transition did not mean that women gained the same treatment as men, but that they were accepted and judged much more as individuals rather than as representatives of their gender. Each woman's actions became evidence of how good an employee (albeit a female employee) she was rather than evidence of how good females were. The same transition characterizing paid jobs followed women's entry into politics and other organizational positions.

The parallel analysis of deviance control considers what happens if the number of men with interests substantially opposed to women's advancement declines. At some point the process of mutual reinforcement collapses, undermining sanctions inducing conformity. The opposition to women's advancement then falls rapidly. When the deviance-controlling processes lose their grip, men stop resisting women's advances if their personal interests are not at stake. This process could help to explain the acceleration of declining inequality since World War II and especially during the past two decades. Between the Great Depression and the 1970s, changing conditions seem to have reduced the number of men committed to inequality below a critical threshold. Men who did not believe in inequality became freer to act accordingly. This transition would have rapidly increased the number of men who tolerated improvements in women's status. The critical implication of this analysis does not concern the mood of men's acceptance, but a process that can help explain how resistance could decline faster than the circumstances provoking change. Men's direct opposition to women who sought higher status has not been an absolute and unchangeable attribute of membership in a dominant group or masculine culture. Men's resistance has reflected the prevalent conditions of dominance. These conditions not only gave men the means for successful opposition; they made men's opposition appear a just and worthwhile effort to protect the rights they had earned.

Men's conscious opposition to increased equality has been most consistent and effective when men have believed themselves subject to injustice and foreseen deprivations if women's actions went unchecked. Any changes in society that reduced men's sense of right or altered their assessment of gains and losses owing to women's behavior threatened to reduce men's opposition.

THE DECLINE IN MEN'S COMMITMENT TO THE SUBORDINATION OF WOMEN

Men sustained sex inequality through two kinds of actions: incidental and purposeful. Many of men's actions indirectly reinforced sex inequality even though they were not directed at women or motivated by concern with gender inequality. Still, when threatened, men often intentionally resisted women's efforts to better themselves. Both types of actions declined over time, but the initial problem is to show why men have progressively abandoned conscious opposition to greater gender equality. The answer to this problem, however, depends on some reasons for the decline in men's actions indirectly reinforcing gender inequality.

While men of all sorts opposed women's advances for varied reasons, the distinction between the actions of ordinary and powerful men is particularly important. Men who had economic or political power have had a different relationship to gender inequality from ordinary men. As a result, while both ordinary men and powerful men reduced their resistance to women's rising status, they followed different strategies, pursued different motives, and had different effects.

The acts of an ordinary man generally only directly affected his own relations to women and indirectly added to the weight of all men's similar efforts. In contrast, powerful men could influence the circumstances of many common women and men. For example, when common men opposed their wives' employment, their actions had a far more restricted range of effects than corporate directors' decisions about female employment or government officials' decisions about the legality of discriminatory hiring practices.

Before industry exploded in the nineteenth century, men had an immediate and self-evident interest in excluding women from their economic and political roles. When male-headed households controlled access to the means of livelihood and to political participation, the men's defense of their economic and political status coincided with their defense of sex inequality. To sustain their position in the male status system, men had to gain whatever property and social position they could from their parents and to provide as much property and social position as possible when their own sons repeated this competition in the next generation. Similarly, legal and political processes, controlled by small local or national elites whose own positions were at issue, reserved most citizenship rights to male heads of households. Men's status in the household and in the public realm were linked. Male household authority and men's exclusive membership in the public realm sustained each other.

Increasingly, the absorption of economic activity by firms reduced most men to employees, and large-scale, representative government reduced most men's political participation to voting during elections. Previously, a woman could personally gain economic or political status only at the expense of her husband, father, or brother. Some man had to be losing control of the family estate if a woman was gaining it. Once jobs and political participation were gained through ties between individuals and large organizations, no direct link between a woman's gain and some man's loss remained.

Men could still identify their interests with resisting women's economic and political advancement. Men could perceive their personal interests as threatened if women entered their occupation or if their wives pursued new opportunities. Born into a system where women deferred to men and protected men from low-status domestic responsibilities, men easily experienced women's efforts to improve their status as unjust attacks. These threats were, however, mild compared to earlier circumstances that had forced men to contemplate losing their family capital or their political status. Now, men's interests in preserving their status relative to other men did not stand directly in the way of women's aspirations.

As economic expansion and related changes in the family have progressively reduced the value to husbands of wives who stay at home, more and more men have discovered that the employment of their wives will, on balance, increase their standard of living. Men once commonly opposed their wives' employment, insisting that their wives spend all their time caring for their children and household.[5] When a woman did take a job, her husband usually demanded that his job and his plans continue to take precedence and that she continue to assume most responsibility for the household. Men's interest in their wives' domestic subordination was not absolute, however. Men's interests depended on social conditions. For those interests to clearly favor wives' continued domesticity, men had to believe they got a better life through their wives' personal service than they would gain by their wives' employment. Employers' interests in hiring women have meant that women have had increased opportunity to find permanent, full-time jobs. Men learned that their wives' additional income had more value than the lost domestic labor.[6] Magnifying this effect in the last two decades, men increasingly stood to gain more social respect if their wives had successful careers than if their wives stayed at home.

Moreover, however unhappily men might have greeted each new experiment of more women entering into activities previously monopolized by men, they repeatedly discovered that their anticipatory anxieties were groundless. This recurring experience also diminished the value of women's subordination.

The history of men's opposition to sexual equality teems with false prophecies of imminent disaster. Men predicted doom when women gained legal equality, won the vote, entered the labor force, or took positions in government. While these fears arose from a need to justify inequality, both historical and recent data suggest that men really believed them. When believed, these fears increased the apparent value of opposing any changes that would have improved the status of women. Although some theoretical analyses grant credence to these predictions by attributing gender inequality to the better lives men gained through women's subjection, historical experience did not support them. Men's lives have changed as women's status has risen, and some of these changes were experienced as losses. The losses were balanced by gains, however, as women provided new income to their families.

Each advance by women that left men's lives undamaged gave further evidence that such fears were dubious motives for resisting women's advances. As more women defied convention out of need or drive or circumstance, an ever wider circle of people experienced such fears as groundless. The more that women proved such fears false by broadening their social position without dire effects for men, the less commitment men had to resisting women's further advancement.[7]

The same changing circumstances that reduced the benefits men could expect from preserving sex inequality also diminished men's capacity to restrain women. The concentration of economic and political power outside the family gradually reduced men's capability to individually enforce the subordination of their wives, their daughters, and other women in their lives. This declining capacity held back even those men who did not recognize, or wished to ignore, the reduced value and legitimacy of women's subordination.

Every increase in women's options improved their standing in marriages and reduced men's capacity to control them. Once more jobs were available to women, they could conceive of living without husbands or be less dependent on their husbands' control over money. With a declining birth rate and increased government services for children, particularly schools, children functioned less as a handicap to women's independence. The increasing ease of divorce changed husbands' and wives' expectations. Both saw continued marriage less as their unavoidable fate and more as a possible future contingent on mutual acceptance. Men derived their family authority from their wives' dependence, and that dependence was due to women's constrained alternatives. As those constraints loosened, men's capacity to impose compliance on their wives dwindled.

Simultaneously, ordinary men lost their collective capacity to induce large economic and political organizations to deny women equal access or equal status in these spheres. As power migrated to these institutions, their interests gradually favored abandoning differential concern for women and men. Ordinary men could not combine effectively against this institutional momentum. The power wielded by these large organizations and the social distance between the top and bottom tiers made the organizations impervious to the concerns of ordinary men. These institutions listened to ordinary men only when their concerns were backed by widely organized efforts. As men's interests became increasingly fragmented and as the reasons for resisting women's assimilation lost their importance, such organized resistance became implausible. Ordinary men could and did still make difficulties for women entering their occupations or violating their expectations that women should defer to men. But these efforts could only slow, not substantially change, the societal movement toward less gender inequality.

With each successive generation, men also were less forceful and less successful when they resisted women working in their occupations and competing for jobs. Male opposition did not disappear, but its location and intensity changed. A century ago, men rarely worked with women. Today, men have women co-workers in most occupations and work settings. Cashiers, assembly-line workers, doctors, teachers, police officers, and managers are examples of occupations in which men now normally have female colleagues but seldom did a century ago. While many women in male-dominated occupations have had to contend with poor treatment from their male co-workers, most men now seem to abide women's presence. Sometimes this acceptance may be mere resignation, but even reluctant acceptance has allowed women much greater opportunity than the active opposition of the past.

Men in low-status blue-collar jobs or low-status white-collar jobs faced the greatest threat from competition with women, but they also had the least power to resist. They had no influence over hiring, promotion, or training, and they were often poorly organized. If the organization of the industry or labor process sometimes allowed male workers to organize lasting unions, as in some parts of the textile industry, then the male unions were apt to organize women for self-protection. If the labor process demanded cooperation among workers, then men could try to withhold cooperation from female workers. However, employers could, and often did, defeat this last strategy by segregating women from men. Not surprisingly, these low-status jobs offered employers the greatest opportunities to replace men with women. This substitution happened repeatedly, for example, to sales clerks and to many machine operators in factories. Until the 1960s, women's progressively increasing employment occurred mostly in low-status positions. The relative weakness of male worker opposition helped to concentrate women at the bottom.

The formal, organized opposition of male unions to women's entering male-identified, working-class jobs began its conclusive decline after the rapid rise of large industrial unions in the 1930s, but it had never been effective. When employers had strong economic incentives for hiring women, they usually did so even if opposed by male labor. Over time, unions switched their emphasis to organizing women rather than excluding them. This strategy extended the same logic that American unions applied to other kinds of marginal workers. Sometimes a group of workers became a competitive threat that the union could not hope to eliminate. Sometimes organizing a new group of workers promised to increase the union's power. In either circumstance, organization became union policy.[8] Even in the nineteenth century, male unions organized women when they decided this strategy was more effective than trying to prevent their employment.[9]

Self-interest drove male labor organizations to support women workers, albeit in a roundabout way. The final occasion for widespread union opposition to working women occurred during the Great Depression of the 1930s. This opposition took a special form, however. The arguments focused on married women with employed husbands. They claimed that in such hard times jobs should be rationed to families, justifying restrictions on female employment. Implicitly, these arguments accepted women's employment if it did not lead to many families' getting no jobs in a time of high unemployment. During World War II, male labor organization in the United States had to respond to a rapid increase in female employment. War transformed the leading employment issue from finding enough jobs to finding enough workers. As women replaced men in many jobs, the unions that assumed male control of occupations or industries faced a grave threat to their organizations. This threat forced them to adopt a strategy that had been evolving and applied selectively since the nineteenth century. They would demand that women entering an occupation had to receive the same wages and benefits as men. They usually did not make a general issue of discrimination against women. They mainly opposed discrimination against women when it gave employers incentives to adopt strategies that would harm male workers. Through such policies, male union strategies largely reflected their organization interests. They resisted women's entry to an occupation until women employees seemed inevitable, then they demanded equal treatment for women. Both strategies aimed to protect labor organization by protecting the position of male employees, although the first strategy also gave outlet to men's prejudices against women.

The history of informal, on-the-job opposition to women's employment (and training) is harder to evaluate. Numerous personal accounts depicting the experiences of women entering male-identified jobs during the 1960s and 1970s provide explicit testimony that such opposition still persisted. When compared to similar accounts from early in the century, however, these stories have a different impact. They commonly suggest that the informal male opposition had become significantly weaker and shorter-lived. In recent years, the women who pioneered entry into modern male occupations still needed considerable courage and tenacity. Those that followed have much for which to thank these trailblazers. While the information available is scanty, it seems likely that at some time in the past, courage would not have been enough to gain success against male resistance. However, in lower-status occupations, both blue-collar and white-collar, once employers became committed to hiring women, men's resistance could no longer hold back them back. With only a weak capacity to oppose women's employment, these men's interests shifted toward accommodating women co-workers. While men's informal on-the-job opposition once effectively prevented women's entry to a job or an occupation, this resistance is now like a decaying dam bursting before a flood.

Men in high-status blue-collar or high-status white-collar jobs encountered less threat from women and had more power to resist them. To enter the occupational world of managers, professionals, supervisors, and skilled craftsmen, a person usually needed training and promotion by people already in that occupation. Employers were much less able and less motivated to place women directly in these positions. The men in these higher-status occupations had less reason than men with lower-status jobs to fear loss of jobs or salary reductions from the general competition of women. Yet, while they may have had less inherent interest in resisting women's advancement, they also had no reason to support it. Instead, the self-interest of such men usually favored training and supporting men. This strategy would avoid any possible recriminations from other prejudiced men, and it promised much more likely future benefits than did supporting women. Because employers had considerably less leverage, because employers had fewer reasons to impose women on these occupations, and because women found it hard to get the needed skills, credentials, or experience, men in high-status occupations could effectively bar women with little apparent effort.

In middle-class occupations, professional organizations largely avoided women's entry into the prestigious professions through the 1950s. They achieved women's absence with little conscious strategy and little effort. In the prestigious professions—medicine and law were the prototypes—members of the profession, subject to professional sanctions, controlled admission to professional schools, licensing to practice, and hiring for most professional jobs. Faced with these surrounding fortifications, which seemed impregnable, most women gave up any aspirations without challenging the gatekeepers. Once the equal opportunity legislation of the 1960s gave women a battering ram, they found that these gatekeepers' flimsy bars gave way surprisingly easily. As the doors flew open to women, some of the more prejudiced and outspoken men in these professions made a lot of noise to express their despair. But the new state policies decreed women's assimilation. The modern feminist movement and fervently ambitious young women actively demanded women's assimilation. Against this pressure, the prestigious professions made little organized effort to challenge or oppose women's entry.[10]

Laws against discrimination shifted the balance of interests for men in higher-status positions. These men had a greater stranglehold on entry and promotion, but they also had less direct interest in resisting women's entry. Their influence over recruitment and training deprived employers of a sufficient incentive to force the employment of women. Women were left with no means to gain the skills and experience that would make them seem a valuable commodity that employers should exploit. Yet laws against sex discrimination altered the costs and risks enough to change the balance of interests guiding men in high-status occupations and those of their employers. The penalties attached to flagrant discrimination were more costly than the reduced likelihood of profiting from advancing the careers of men. Moreover, once the state made sex discrimination illegal, women became a better risk than in the past. One could assume that they would do better than women in the past because the same laws against discrimination would influence their future.

Ultimately, the residues of male resistance to women have fallen in one occupation after another through the sheer weight of resignation. Opposing the first women entering an occupation or workplace seemed both a plausibly practical strategy and a good outlet for resentments. As men saw the number of women employed rise, and also often experienced their own wives' taking jobs in other occupations, these motives lost their power. Women's presence became ordinary and inevitable. People rarely resist the ordinary and the inevitable, however much they may wish it were otherwise.

Every step in women's economic and political assimilation reduced ordinary men's means to oppose those women seeking the next step. As employers offered more jobs to women, ever more women either had their own income or could foresee getting an income. When income opportunities, even at low-status jobs, combined with increasingly liberal divorce laws, women gained alternatives to marriage. Simultaneously, the state increasingly denied men the right to use violence against women. The state also reduced men's legal hold over their wives and daughters. While female suffrage did not propel women into political power, it did make the female electorate a growing concern of politicians. Losing the ability to intimidate women with threats of economic deprivation or violence, and faced with women's greater ability to support themselves, men had less capacity to maintain dominance.

As it became less practical, opposing women's access to opportunities enjoyed by men has gradually lost social legitimacy. This moral shift has magnified men's response to the falling value of women's subordination. Over the past hundred years, the legitimacy of suppressing women's efforts to better themselves dwindled. Belief in such actions fell victim to meritocratic ideals expanding within society's major institutions and women's partial assimilation by those institutions.

The meritocratic and individualistic ideas developed by the educational, economic, and political systems did not eliminate men's belief in dominance, but they eroded its justification. In consequence, men had a shrinking supply of symbols to use in public claims against women. They also had a declining capacity to motivate their dominance through moral outrage. Meanwhile, mounting evidence discredited the belief that women were unable to fill men's jobs or political roles. Education gained more and more recognition as the measure of an individual's employability. Women's performance in school matched men's. Moreover, the experiments of employers tempted by the low cost of female labor belied beliefs that they were unable to perform well. When given skilled jobs with responsibility and authority, women did fine.

The evidence for these changes can be found by comparing men's statements about gender inequality issues over time. These statements appear in legislative debates, judicial decisions, social studies, popular press reports, and literature. In the early nineteenth century, the idea of women holding male positions was generally regarded as so obviously ludicrous that it could be used to make fun of other proposals. Anything as silly as women holding political office and running firms was silly indeed. By the early twentieth century, men's comments on women's place seem much more measured. Women should not be like men, but the differences in their rights and responsibilities must be weighed carefully and expressed thoughtfully. As the twentieth century progresses, men's comments favoring higher women's status become more frequent and more assured, while those supporting sex inequality become more strained and defensive. The men speaking against women's advances in the 1970s display bitterness and fear rather than the humor and confidence characteristic of men speaking against women's advances in the 1870s. Thus, uncontrollable changes in ideology made it harder for men to convince themselves or others that actions to keep women down were necessary or just. Even so, many men clung to their beliefs in male superiority, refused to apply meritocratic norms to women, and resisted giving women credit for their performance at work or in schools. These defensive efforts to sustain an ideology of female inferiority, however, became increasingly shrill and less compelling.

Over the past 150 years, ordinary men's interests have been shifting. Each generation has got less value, found fewer means, and faced less legitimacy for subordinating women than did the preceding generation. Not surprisingly, these changing circumstances dampened their opposition to women's improving status. Over time, men's generalized or abstracted opposition to women's advancement also declined. In this form, men opposed the advancement of women with whom they had no direct relationship. This included, for example, men opposing the entry of women into male occupations other than their own or men opposing the increasing political participation of all women.

How much did men oppose the advancement of women when the change they resisted would have no known, direct effect on their own lives? Theoretical work on gender inequality sometimes refers to generalized resistance by men, but concrete evidence that would allow us to compare such resistance over time and place is hard to find.

The idea that men act to protect their common interests also raises conceptual problems. Does this mean that all men's immediate self-interests consistently equal the collective interests of men? Does it mean that a common identity produced through ideology or socialization produces common action despite men's divergent self-interests? Neither seems compelling, as we know that men did not consistently defend the interests of their gender.

The many referenda on woman suffrage show this emphatically. All across America, these referenda occurred from the Civil War until woman suffrage finally realized success after World War I. In the state referenda, from one-third to three-quarters of the men who voted supported woman suffrage.[11] These men could vote any way they pleased without concern for repercussions. So, why did many men seemingly vote against men's collective interests by supporting woman suffrage? No sensible answer is possible unless we accept that *men did not possess a universal commitment to oppose general improvements in women's status.* When men did not see their own self-interests at stake, they were likely to respond mainly to the symbolic aspects of issues concerning women's status. While the proper place of women and men was one symbolic concern men would consider, it did not have an inherent priority over other symbolic concerns such as democracy, justice, or the defense of class identity.

POWERFUL MEN'S DECLINING OPPOSITION

The actions of men in positions of power embody the collective force of male dominance. These men's capacity to defend male dominance probably did not suffer significant reductions comparable to those of the average individual male. Their interests, however, were more responsive than ordinary men's when the value and legitimacy of subordinating women declined.

Powerful men could and did take actions that reduced the subordination of women in general. The conditions of power made such men responsive to practical considerations of policy effectiveness and administrative rationality. Social power also detached such men's personal interests from their actions' consequences for gender inequality. Their policies affecting women followed an erratic path. Powerful men were usually more knowledgeable than other men. Nonetheless, prejudice and ignorance often blinded them to the reality of their situation.

For a manager or a government official, objectivity was usually, at most, a possible ingredient in practical strategies. Even when managers tried to be objective, they had to resolve the inherent ambiguity involved in assessing how well people administer, cooperate, lead, or innovate. These men were not rational robots, springing to maximize their returns. However, profitability, political stability, and administrative rationality consistently commended policies that would reduce gender inequality. Over time, powerful men gradually accepted the logic of their situation to bring such policies into being.

As the power of the state and the economy over individual lives grew, so did the power of the men who controlled these institutions. This power was not without restraints. Market, organizational, and political processes imposed requirements on those in power. Men who exercised their power arbitrarily within these systems jeopardized that power. Still, no evidence suggests that the men in power lacked the capacity to continue, or even expand, policies of economic, political, and legal discrimination against women. They could have continued, *if* they had had a collective commitment to such policies.

The men who ran the state and the economy—bureaucratic officials, elected officeholders, and property owners—had, however, no inherent interests in using their power to sustain men's common advantages over women. Proven adherence to the norms of male dominance was not a significant criteria affecting their capacity to gain or hold positions of power. The same processes that reduced most men's personal capacity to dominate women also helped to insulate influential men from the concerns of the ordinary. Most of influential men's power came from their positions in the economy or the political order. They did not depend on women's general subordination for their personal capacity to dominate women (and men). Therefore, for such men, preserving the health of the institutions that gave them power was considerably more important than perpetuating male dominance. Competition for economic and political advantage and a concern for strength of their organizations gave powerful men opportunities to serve their interests through strategies that benefited women.

Men exercising institutional power saw women through an interpretive lens molded by their institutions' interests. Employers saw women as potential employees who might add profits to their firms. Politicians saw women as voters, contributors, and election workers. Organizations and the judiciary increasingly viewed women as people, the objects of rules and rationalization, who could not be usefully distinguished from men. These alternative perceptions of women gradually gained control of influential men's actions.

In special circumstances such as wars, labor shortages, or election battles, influential men often found greater opportunities to increase their power by advocating policies advantageous to women. Such policies would either give them an edge over other influential men who were their competitors or they would fortify the institutions on which their power was based. Repeatedly, men used their political or economic power to discipline ordinary men into accepting these policies. Firms forced their lower-status male employees to accept female employees. The state forced men to accept women's expanding legal and political status.

Powerful men's desire to protect their personal positions did not generate an interest in opposing women's movement into positions of power. Of course, powerful men were unlikely to contemplate women overrunning their own positions with the same detachment they could apply to a similar fate for ordinary men's positions. The historical record does not, however, show powerful men exhibiting much concern that women would displace them. Men with power had little real vulnerability to competition from women. Powerful men were not a cohesive, permanent status group. Instead, the main result of granting women equal access would be to stop the entry of men in the next generation who would otherwise have climbed to power. As these men would never achieve power, they could not defend it against women. The men who pursued power would not actually experience more competition; they would merely find that the competition now included a mix of women and men. The number of men competing for power at any specified level was not an independent constant, but was a socially constructed condition dependent on the way in which the competition was organized. Of course, men's concern for their immediate self-interest and their ignorance might still cause them to fear competition from women, however irrationally. Still, powerful men's fears about women competing over power never realistically concerned a reduction in the positions available to men.

More important to powerful men was the possibility that women could not fit into men's networks of power and therefore would develop or facilitate alternative ones. Because men in power saw no ready way (and had no desire) to integrate women, they had reason to fear that advancing women might undercut the network of support on which they depended. Also, powerful men rarely had reason to invest their resources and reputations to support women seeking power. Women seeking power could seldom offer anything special that powerful men could not get from other aspirants seeking to rise. Even the popular fantasy of women offering sex to get ahead belies these men's ready access to sex from preferable alternatives.

Assessments, recommendations, and promotion decisions involve considerable discretion. Relying on people's judgments allows considerations irrelevant to job performance to influence people's movement up a job hierarchy. As one common strategy to reduce this ambiguity, people often favor those who seem similar. While trying to explain managerial promotions within a corporation, Rosabeth Kanter called the resulting masculine bias *homosocial reproduction*.[12] Simply put, if all managers are men in an ambiguous, risky environment, they will favor other men over women just as they will favor men who think like themselves over men who think differently. Indeed, they will usually believe that men like themselves are truly superior.

Two conditions must prevail for homosocial reproduction of managers to be widespread and stable. In most circumstances, either the skill of managers must have limited practical significance or social conditions must assure that the occasional outstanding women who are allowed to advance up the hierarchy do not do well. Firms stress profits and competitiveness. If the quality of individual managers significantly and noticeably affected profits and if homosocial reproduction were the only impediment to women's advancement, then we would expect a significant minority of unusually qualified women to have worked their way up managerial ranks. The most likely reason that this rarely occurred was the presence of the other impediments to women's success. In other words, when prejudiced discrimination is widespread, even those who are not prejudiced usually find that their rational self-interests direct them to discriminate as well.

On balance, these concerns meant that powerful men's circumstances inherently gave them a mild interest in excluding women from power and no interest in aiding women into power. Also, few women were in any position to compete for powerful positions. Powerful men, therefore, had neither much opportunity nor much incentive for helping women achieve positions of power.

The general political and economic assimilation of women—partially supported by the strategies of powerful men pursuing their self-interests—ultimately caused powerful men to accept women into power in order to preserve their own power. Political and legal actions against discrimination were needed to achieve women's assimilation into high-status positions. The processes that caused women's assimilation into low-status positions—such as labor shortages, women's lower wage rates, and the drive toward rationalization—had proportionately less impact as women rose higher up the status ladder.

The political process showed a similar pattern of assimilating women into low-status positions as campaign workers or local officials but rarely promoting women to the more influential positions. The processes differed somewhat in the political realm as, for example, political actors competed for votes rather than profits and sought campaign workers rather than employees. Again, however, established politicians eschewed supporting women more because it conflicted with their personal interests for maintaining and enhancing their political power than because they wanted to keep women from political power to defend the dominance of men.

Women's general economic and political assimilation gave them the potential to exercise a political voice and made their economic activity a vital concern for men with power. Their political organization altered powerful men's interests in favor of supporting women's ascent to power.[13] Neither the assimilation of women into lower positions nor the political organization of women would have had this effect without the other. Together, they created a specter of alternative political organization with enough power to alter the outcomes of the political process. They did not have and did not need enough power to oust men. They did accumulate enough potential influence that men and (male-dominated) political parties competing for power felt that they must attract the women to compete with their male opponents.

Women's ascent into positions of power occurred less because women's political organization and institutional assimilation gave them the collective power to exact their demands than because these new conditions altered the interests of powerful men in favor of conceding these demands. Thus, the interests generated by men competing for power had changed dramatically over the long term. Once, helping women advance was a risky violation of interests. Ultimately, men found that resisting women's advancement had become a personally and organizationally risky violation of interests.

MALE REBELLION

If men experienced their position of dominance not only as a right but also a responsibility, and if the right lost its value while the responsibility remained, did some men then find it all too much of a burden? If the beliefs legitimating male dominance were losing credibility, might some men have begun to chafe at the constrictions of their identity? Since World War II, according to Barbara Ehrenreich, middle-class men have increasingly rejected their stereotyped role. They have defied the cultural expectation that they must marry and support a family to be judged mature, responsible, and worthy of public esteem. Focusing exclusively on the affluent, she portrays young, educated men starting a promising career in the 1950s as pummeled on all sides—family, work, professionals, and the media—by the message that they must marry and have children. Yet, according to Ehrenreich, these men increasingly found their wives—dedicated to childrearing and suburban domesticity—to be tiresome bores.[14] Numerous alienated men greeted and supported cultural alternatives that rejected the cult of the family. These alternatives included *Playboy* magazine's message of sexual freedom and personal consumption, the male centeredness of the "beat" literature, the self-indulgence proclaimed by the new individual-growth psychologies, and the rejection of male responsibilities characteristic of hippies.[15] Each of these cultural phenomena reflected and reinforced middle-class men's dissatisfaction with family life, which motivated increasing numbers to avoid or flee marriage.

The most plausible reasons for the possible decline in men's commitment to families are the same circumstances and processes that reduced men's opposition to greater gender equality. As the subordination of women became progressively less valuable to them, men were increasingly likely to perceive all family life as a burden. The same rising affluence and improved availability of goods and services that reduced the amount of necessary domestic work for women meant that men could replace a wife's domestic services through the marketplace. The liberalization of sexuality that accompanied the improvements in women's status also made sex more easily available to men outside marriage.

Men's rebellion against the male role has resembled women's rebellion against the cultural definitions of women's place, symbolized by feminism. Ehrenreich suggests that men's rebellion really has been an accommodation to changing circumstances that contrasts with women's revolt against prevailing conditions. She also suggests that men have been fleeing personal commitment while women have been seeking it. Beyond women's continued greater dependence on marriage for income, however, no dependable evidence shows significant differences between men's and women's capacities or desires for commitment. More important, women's efforts at change can be interpreted as an accommodation to their changing circumstances just as accurately as can men's efforts. The crucial difference between men's and women's reactions to the changes in gender relations is simpler than Ehrenreich supposed. Women were responding from a position of subordination while men reacted to changes in their dominance. While men who have rebelled may have wanted to evade burdensome demands placed on their sex, dominance per se and gender advantages were not among those disadvantages. Women were rebelling against inequality. Men were not.

More recently, Kathleen Gerson has studied how men currently respond to the demands and opportunities of families and jobs. She suggests that we can usefully categorize men into three groups. *Breadwinners,* who pursue what we now call a traditional family ideal, sought to provide a good income for their families and expected their wives to raise their children and keep up their households. *Involved fathers* were men committed to raising their children at least as much as to their work life and generally expected their wives to balance employment and home. *Autonomous* men had little interest in either providing for a family or participating in one. Gerson's research was not designed to discover the relative proportions of these three types either today or in the past (although we obviously know that the number of divorces and the number of working women have both grown steadily). While limited to the present, Gerson's research reinforces the impression that men have been rebelling against a prescribed role for some time. She concludes:

> Those who have rejected breadwinning hold different stances toward male dominance. Whether they have moved away from parenthood or become involved fathers, nonbreadwinners see less advantage and much

disadvantage to authoritarian control over wives and girlfriends. Not only does it produce economically dependent women; it also subverts the chances for an emotionally satisfying relationship.[16]

Some of these men were sympathetic to women's quest for equality; some were not. All, however, found the obligations of a traditional male breadwinner role distressing and unattractive.

These speculative ideas suggest that men have increasingly abandoned the family as a means of dominating women because it simply was not worth the effort. Because this pattern began before the rise of modern feminism, it may even have affected movements among women.[17] Ehrenreich argues intriguingly that the antifeminist movements of women opposing the Equal Rights Amendment and abortion have been a response not to feminism but to male flight from familial responsibility.[18] Equally, the women's movement could have been, in part, a response to the discovery that women could no longer expect men to dependably supply a family income, the support that women had previously accepted as the price of their consent to their subordination.

THE SURRENDER OF DOMINANCE

In the past, men have acted individually and collectively, both informally and formally through legal and economic institutions, to keep women in their place. Even when men thought only of competing with other men and fulfilling their sex-role obligations, they reinforced sex inequality by using their advantages. When women directly threatened to violate sex-role expectations, however, men typically resisted with concerted efforts to control these threats. Even then men usually perceived themselves as just, protecting rights they had earned and preserving a pattern of life that benefited all. Within-class cooperation among men against women was as common as coordinated actions by dominant classes against subordinate classes. In both cases, cooperation to control the subordinate group was intermittent and often disguised.

Some people have found it difficult to accept that men cooperatively defended their status while enjoying intimate relations in and out of families with women who were lovers, wives, daughters, and mothers. Sexuality and kinship did create very special bonds. Still, in other forms of stratification, people in dominant groups also were closely associated, and shared a common fate, with specific members of subordinate groups—for example, slave owners and slaves, lords and their peasants, businessmen and their employees. While the ties may not have been as strong or as emotionally compelling as sexuality and kinship, members of dominant and subordinate groups often had close relations. Intimacy and common fate conditioned inequality; they were not inconsistent with it.

Men once held their advantages over women with moral and practical security. They accepted women's subordination as necessary and just. They experienced unquestioned benefits from it. They had the capacity as individuals to dominate women in their families. They could depend on men in power to follow policies that would sustain gender inequality. Men's interests in actions preserving sex inequality were unequivocal.

Since the beginning of the nineteenth century, these conditions have all been changing. Men have got less from women's dependent status, men's capacity to keep women in a secondary status has diminished, and men have had less belief in the value or justice of female subordination. These altered circumstances have gradually reduced ordinary men's efforts to forestall changes that improved women's status and reduced sex inequality. Simultaneously, the interests of economic and political organizations, and of other social institutions outside the home, increasingly favored assimilating women. Men in power have commonly chosen to further the interests of the institutions they control, which they identify with their personal interests, over the interests of their sex.

Ordinary men's declining opposition to women's self-improvement and influential men's adoption of progressive policies have been decisive for improving women's social standing. However self-interested and structurally determined the changes in men's behavior, they nonetheless paved the way for the improvements in women's social position. While men's joint interests in preserving sex inequality were losing influence over their actions, women's joint interests in reducing sex inequality were gaining increasing influence over their actions. Women were better able to pursue their common interests through social movements, while men were less able to defend their common interests through the apparatus of economic and political power. Simply put, the defense of men's common interests waned as the defense of women's common interests waxed.

These accumulating changes in men's behavior were due to changes in men's self-interests rather than to a moral concern with women's plight. The subordination of women has been increasingly inconsistent with the developing logic of the evolving market economy, large organizations, and the liberal democratic political order. By withdrawing their opposition to greater equality, ordinary men have adjusted pragmatically to changing circumstances that increased the costs and reduced the rewards of continuing women's subordination. By adopting policies that benefited women, men holding economic and political power have implemented the developmental logic of the systems that gave them power.

None of these changes has been complete, and male opposition continues to trouble the adoption of gender equality. Nonetheless, the long-term trend has been a decline in the opposition of ordinary men and a rise in the support of powerful men. All this grew from the economic and political restructuring of society. Many men have continued to resist women's rising status, but their efforts have resembled a rearguard action by an army already acknowledging defeat. This resistance has none of the sureness, commitment, and universality that greeted any hopes for gender equality two centuries ago. The bitter complaints of diehards about what they see as a decline of manhood have accurately penetrated a fundamental change in modern times. Men are progressively ceding women more ground.

CHAPTER SEVEN

THE END OF INEQUALITY?

Gender inequality has been fated for extinction since the emergence of modern economic and political organization. For a long time it tried to adapt to the changing social environment and sometimes appeared to thrive. But it slowly lost its vitality while its defenders grew weak and its enemies grew strong. Gender inequality does not fit the needs, the distribution of power, the organizational logic, or the moral perspectives of modern society. It cannot survive.

In the United States, gender inequality has been on the defensive since the nation's birth two centuries ago. In each of the three historical periods that comprise the past 150 years, women have experienced significant improvements in their legal and political status, economic opportunities, access to higher education, freedom to leave marriages through divorce, cultural image, and control over their sexuality and reproductive capacity. The rights, resources, and opportunities of women were once dramatically different from those of men. Since the early nineteenth century, these differences have diminished markedly. They will keep declining until they disappear.

Modern bureaucratic organizations such as businesses, political parties, and schools have little or no vested interest in preserving gender domination, so the general drift of social power from the patriarchal family to these faceless bureaucracies gives women the opening they need to battle successfully for more equal treatment. Patriarchy depends on the preeminence of patriarchal families. Modern societies continually erode the power of the patriarchal family, as power seeps from the family into large, impersonal bureaucratic organizations. Modern bureaucrats have little or no stake in maintaining male dominance. They may do so, but they may also benefit in particular ways from policies that open some doors for women. The growing domination of modern life by organizations provides an irresistible force that slowly and steadily expands women's rights and opportunities in modern society. The specific operative principles vary across political, economic, legal, and educational organizations, but the general lack of interests in preserving gender inequality appears in all.

Full equality is women's destiny because gender inequality is inherently inconsistent with modern economic and political organization. This inconsistency is not a simple, direct one. Gender inequality can and does coexist with modern economic and political organization. Status inequality does not persist from simple momentum, however. It must be reproduced across generations and across repeated transformations of the economic and political landscape. In modern society, the processes sustaining gender inequality have become increasingly fragile and vulnerable.

To say that continued progress toward equality is inevitable is not to imply that our future path is predictable. The causal processes driving society toward greater gender equality have been decentralized and loosely coupled. They create an ever-increasing potential that people and organizations will act in ways contradictory to gender inequality's requirements. Nevertheless, they do not directly decide which people will act on this potential, or when, or how. Concrete historical conditions and the interrelations between diverse developments determine the specific historical path taken by inequality's decline.

Admittedly, although modern social institutions have an intrinsic developmental pattern that promises to keep reducing inequality, we cannot determine conclusively how far this process will go or how it will seem at its end. Unforeseeable circumstances could impede the continued development of societies' fundamental institutions. Conditions still little understood may make full equality an elusive goal. Such conditions could emerge or become more severe as economic and political organization develop beyond the limits of our present understanding. Some unanticipated events could push our economic and political systems off the developmental path they have been following. Barring these unlikely possibilities, however, gender inequality will continue to decline because it is fundamentally at odds with the organization of modern social life, particularly the distribution of power and interests.

GENDER INEQUALITY'S INEVITABLE FALL

From the writing of the Declaration of Independence, through the preparation of the Seneca Falls Declaration of Sentiments, through the victory of the woman suffrage amendment, through the tumultuous rise of modern feminist movements in the 1960s—through all these landmark events women's status has slowly improved. What has been the driving force? What has given direction to changes in women's social roles and opportunities? What has brought us from there to here?

Some well-known social theories have formulated vital ideas that provide a sound starting point to solving these problems, although the ideas were formulated for other purposes. Women's status has risen as men's resistance to women's advance has fallen. Male resistance fell because the logic of modern economic and political institutions shifted power toward interests indifferent to gender inequality. This shift and its consequences appear in various forms in social theory. Max Weber, a towering figure in the history of social thought, contended that rationalization and bureaucratization were fundamental trends in modern societies, and that they evoked the creation of standard rules applied similarly to all people. Rational bureaucratic action has little concern with personal characteristics such as sex. Talcott Parsons, the central figure of American functionalist sociology, argued that the increasing differentiation of modern social organization caused universalistic rules and actions to displace particularist ones. Universalism contradicts sexism and gender discrimination. T. H. Marshall, a key influence on theories of the modern state, argued that the development of the state occurred through the elaboration of citizenship rights in successive, progressive stages. Women's status rose through their incremental acquisition of citizenship. Neoclassical economics suggests that competitive market forces make prejudiced discrimination insecure because it creates opportunities to garner exceptional profits by those who ignore it. Karl Marx's theory of capitalism argued essentially the same thing. Both the neoclassical and Marxist economic principles suggest that employers will eventually abandon women's economic exclusion. Each of these significant, influential social theories contained ideas that could explain and predict the decline of gender inequality. Interpreted this way, these general theoretical perspectives suggest that in modern societies bureaucratic rationalization, universalistic individualism, political dependence on the extension of citizenship, and the discipline of economic competition would combine to undermine gender inequality, just as we have discovered. Apparently, however, the pervasiveness and cultural legitimacy of gender inequality were so extensive that even outstanding minds failed to see clearly their implications for women's status (although, to be fair, this was not their goal). Equally, most contemporary analyses of gender inequality, even when they rely on these theoretical traditions, have largely neglected their potential starting points for explaining inequality's decline, probably because most were more concerned with explaining inequality's existence.

The arguments now used most often to explain the decline of gender inequality can be categorized into three basic analytic strategies, each stressing different causal processes. The first strategy stresses the proximate causes of the varied events that have reduced inequality. By treating these events independently, this approach implies that the decline of gender inequality was due to a fortuitous combination of historical conditions. A second approach emphasizes women's role as agents of change. This perspective attributes inequality's decline to the success of women who rebelled against their disadvantages. A third strategy emphasizes changes in popular beliefs about justice and about the nature of women and men. It implies that gender inequality declined because beliefs about the justice of equality drove out beliefs that women's secondary status was necessary, desirable, or just.

The first analytic strategy implicitly attributes women's improving status to an adventitious confluence of events that favored women by the strategy stressing proximate causes. This approach is common in studies that focus on one event or period, studies focusing on one facet of inequality, and in historical overviews that try to summarize the varied changes of the past two centuries. Examples include studies that try to explain women's rising employment as a function of the wage rate,[1] studies that attribute legal changes affecting women to concurrent historical conditions,[2] and most studies that stress models built from many variables, especially studies that try to explain the varying degree of gender inequality across societies.[3]

This approach suggests that the coalescence of events or conditions that progressively reduced gender inequality was indeterminate, coincidental, contingent, and serendipitous. To be fair, many authors whose ideas seem to fit into this mold probably would not defend or even accept this vision of gender inequality's decline. Nonetheless, by ignoring (or bracketing) the need to explain why diverse events and conditions had a consistent impact, they do theoretically imply that such consistency was accidental or did not occur.

Work in this vein has produced a large body of research about particular aspects of gender inequality and the many events that constitute inequality's modern history. This approach has given us extensive knowledge about the proximate causes of many historical processes linked to women's rising status. Among other things, it has shown that the invention of better contraceptive methods freed women from vulnerability to pregnancy. Declining fertility reduced women's household responsibilities. Higher production of consumption goods lowered domestic labor needs. Industrial development created jobs that did not depend on strength. Labor shortages caused employers to hire women. Wars encouraged social policies that favored women. The availability of higher education increased women's ability and readiness to organize. Competition for votes caused politicians to heed women's interests. When trying to clarify specific historical issues such as these, much of this work is compelling.

The variety of events and processes identified through this perspective also suggests some limits to its theoretical power. While linking each social change benefiting women to immediately preceding or concurrent conditions, processes, and structures is valuable, it is not enough. Coincidence cannot explain the continuity of women's rising status in different places under different conditions through highly varied events over the past 200 years. A series of disconnected and arbitrary developments did not just happen to point in a common direction of reducing inequality. Some enduring and pervasive influences had to induce the diverse events that all helped reduce sex inequality.

The second analytic strategy solves the problem of integrating causal influences by associating declining gender inequality with women's expanding triumphs over their oppression by men. Studies of feminism and women's organization,[4] studies documenting male domination,[5] and journalistic accounts often stress this perspective.

Implicitly, this analytic approach suggests that gender inequality represents the state of collective struggle between women and men, and that women's collective action caused women's rising status. It assumes that men have an inherent interest in preserving gender inequality and commonly accept a collective commitment to keeping women down. Because men have an organized defense of their dominance, only a collective rebellion can unseat it. If asked directly, many authors whose work relies on this analytic strategy might agree that other causes contributed significantly to inequality's decline. Nonetheless, their exclusive focus on women's collective actions or male oppression implies that women's collective action is decisive.

Women's movements have obviously played a highly visible role fighting against gender inequality, and studies focusing on these movements have accumulated much valuable information. They have shown that an adequate model of gender inequality's decline must incorporate the historical agency of women's organizations. They have also raised some important subsidiary questions. The history of women's movements shows that women's capacity to organize in their own defense and the effectiveness of women's insurrections varied greatly. Discovering what conditions decided when women could rebel effectively is crucial for explaining gender inequality's decline. The history of women's improving status also shows that some kinds of beneficial changes occurred without any collective action from women while others seemed highly dependent on women's organizing. Discovering what distinguishes these two categories of changes is critical.

A third analytic strategy attributes gender inequality's decline to changing attitudes and beliefs. This implicitly assumes that ideas and beliefs guide actions, suggesting that we can understand changes in social organization if we can understand changes in beliefs.

This analytic strategy has two complementary variants, one stressing conciliation and the other stressing conflict. The conciliatory variant suggests that changing ideas transformed gender inequality by diffusing conflict. In time, according to the declining-conflict interpretation, new beliefs in greater gender equality won more adherents among both men and women. These beliefs caused both sexes to see people differently and to change their behavior accordingly. Both sexes sought more egalitarian companionship in marriage, adopted more similar relationships to daughters and sons, and withdrew from expectations of distinctive roles for women and men. The conflict-oriented variant suggests that changing beliefs became effective by enlarging conflict. According to this interpretation, changing beliefs influenced the content, frequency, and effectiveness of women's rebellions. Women's status rose because new beliefs incited ambition and rebellion among women and depleted men's willingness to resist women's efforts.

Writers stressing this perspective have produced a rich literature on people's ideas about sex roles and the differences between women's and men's ideas. Undoubtedly, these changing ideas played an important role in inequality's decline, both by easing conciliation and by inciting conflict. However, an analytic strategy attributing causal primacy to moral and cultural shifts invariably creates difficulty interpreting causal sequences, making the analysis of long-term change tentative and unconvincing.

A comprehensive theoretical analysis of gender inequality's decline can build on the insights present in each of these analytical strategies while trying to overcome their limitations. The historically specialized accounts and multivariate models meaningfully attribute each change in women's status to an array of historically specific conditions. However, to understand why highly varied specific causal conditions consistently favored reductions in gender inequality over time, it is necessary to discover their linkages to systematic long-term transformations inhospitable to gender inequality. Studies of women's movements and male oppression show that women's rebellion has been a dynamic, integral mechanism that fueled change. Such studies, however, commonly link women's rising status only to women's occasional conspicuous public rebellions. Women's continual individual acts of resistance and occasional collective rebellions both contributed to gender inequality's historic decline. Their influence needs to be situated in the changing structural circumstances that allowed women's rebellion, both individual and collective, to take new forms and gain new effectiveness. The cultural and moral approaches show that prevailing ideas about the necessity and justice of gender roles contribute to inequality. Yet morality and ideology developed through their links with interests and the practices of inequality. In particular, crucial ideas—including those that stress merit as the criteria for rewards and opportunities and those that reject the necessity of women's subordination—depended on the reconstruction of economic and political interests.

While building on these three existing analytic strategies, the analysis developed here differs with them in some key ways. While accepting many concrete claims of the historically particularistic and multivariate accounts, this analysis stresses that a unified underlying social process caused gender inequality's decline. While it treats women's resistance to inequality as an essential ingredient to change, this analysis emphasizes the reasons that men withdrew from the defense of inequality. While acknowledging the role of changing beliefs, this analysis places much more causal weight on the role of institutional change, the reorganization of interests, and the redistribution of power.

This book advances the theory that a nonlinear but relatively deterministic historical process has significantly eroded gender inequality over the past 150 years and will continue to do so. The transition to modern political and economic structures has driven this process by shifting social power into impersonal organizations and by redefining interests. The inherent logic of organizational interests gradually separates strategies preserving economic and political inequality from those needed to preserve gender inequality. Individuals and organizations reflect these changing circumstances through diverse, seemingly unrelated actions and events that cumulatively reduce gender inequality. Although these processes ensure gender inequality's ultimate decline, they are not tightly linked to the actions that precipitate women's rising status, so that the concrete historical path to equality varies considerably across nations.

Two forces worked against sex inequality. First, women individually contested their lower status and sometimes collectively rebelled against it. Second, the transition to modern institutions slowly depleted the interests supporting gender inequality. While each force was significant, they were most effective together because they complemented each other.

Women rebelled against the constraints that limited their activities and circumscribed their status. While most women did as expected most of the time, all women sometimes balked and some women constantly fought against the fetters confining their sex.

The force of women's resistance, however, was like gravity pulling on a building or tree. The building and tree were fashioned to withstand gravity. The gravitational pull brings them down only when some other process erodes the building's foundations or the tree's roots. Similarly, women's resistance became effective only when social processes eroded crucial structural supports for gender inequality.

These structural supports lost their stability when the interests generated by economic and political power separated from the interests generated by gender inequality. The development of modern economic and political organization produced this separation of interests. Gender inequality gradually dissociated from economic and political inequality. This separation allowed women's resistance to become more effective. Simultaneously, as organizations accumulated ever more social power, their interests and actions became increasingly indifferent to people's gender.

Once the organization of production moved out of the household, the goal of preserving male economic advantages could not be reconciled permanently or consistently with the goal of advancing the economic interests of firms. Once social power drifted from families to firms and organizations, the goal of preserving male political ascendancy could not be reconciled consistently with the goals of winning political offices and advancing the state's power and legitimacy.

The movement of power into economic and political organizations made it increasingly impractical to sustain gender inequality's congruence with positional inequality, rendering it unstable. For most of recorded history, gender inequality was securely embedded in economic and political inequality. This embeddedness coincided with family organization. Families controlled productive resources and were the fundamental units of political organization. The internal politics of family life governed the relations between women and men and were directly linked to the structures of economic and political inequality. Over the past two centuries, the emerging modern economic and political systems ended this easy coexistence. These systems gradually eroded conditions necessary for gender inequality's continuance, because their organizational forms obstructed the fit between status inequality by sex and positional inequality now existing largely through organizations. Initially, men gained control over all the new economic and political positions, but their monopoly proved transitory.

To be effective, all systems of status inequality, including gender inequality, must be embedded in positional inequality. A system of status inequality is embedded in a system of positional inequality to the degree that a person's rank or circumstances in the status inequality system gives her or him differential access to locations in the system of positional inequality. When status inequality is embedded in positional inequality, the degree of inequality between status groups is determined by the resultant aggregate discrepancy between their locations in the systems of positional inequality. For one status group, such as men, to retain a superior social standing over another status group, such as women, the higher-status group *must* sustain preferential access to high-ranking economic and political positions.

Gender inequality has been embedded in economic and political inequality in several ways. Women have been absent from positions of power and influence within both the political and economic structures. Therefore, they could not bend policy toward their collective interests. The state, directly representing only male interests, has typically also held women to inferior legal and political standing. State power has helped to give ordinary men greater liberty and more opportunities than women and helped to preserve women's dependence on men. In the economy, discriminatory processes have restricted women's job opportunities, denying them positions with high social standing and income. These cumulative disadvantages have manifested, sustained, and reinforced women's dependence on men, keeping the two sexes in structurally unequal positions in society.

Economic and political systems alleviated women's disabilities mainly by improving their access to positions. The positions remained the same,[6] but women's access to those positions gradually came to resemble more closely men's access. To achieve women's assimilation, the men who ran businesses and government had to make their organizations treat women the same as men, both internally (for example, by promoting women and men equally) and externally (for example, by applying the same criteria and giving the same services to women and men). Complex processes caused this transformation, but adaptive organizations did not have to change the structures of inequality among positions. The structures of economic and political positional inequality remained largely unaltered, but gender became progressively disembedded from them.

While the paths by which women gained greater access differed between high-status and low-status positions, in both cases organizations needed to change the hiring, training, evaluation, and promotion processes but they did not need to transform the structure of their organizations. The assimilation of women occurred first and most completely in low-status economic and political positions. High-ranking positions were less responsive to the changing interests promoting women's incremental assimilation. Women gained wide access to most high-status positions only after political intervention augmented other trends. Still, adaptation through assimilation rather than through restructuring was the rule. At all levels of positional inequality, undoing political and economic inequality between the sexes, once these were organized outside families, has mainly required that organizations treat women the same as men.

Gender inequality also has been embedded in family role differentiation, a unique structure of positional inequality. Gender-identified family roles have helped to sustain women's greater responsibility for childrearing and men's greater opportunities for personal advancement outside the family. Family role differentiation assigns distinctive responsibilities, rights, and activities to husbands and wives. Although these roles have many minor variations, they typically have differentiated a *provider and leader* role from a *childrearer and follower* role. Because these roles create inherently unequal positions (which, in theory, either men or women could occupy), family role differentiation is an instance of positional inequality. However, this form of positional inequality has considerably less durability and influence than economic or political inequality. With a much smaller scale of organization and far fewer resources, modern family role differentiation has only a limited capacity to sustain itself against outside influences.

As gender inequality has become disembedded from political and economic processes, so has family role differentiation. Before modern institutions arose, family role differentiation was directly embedded in economic and political inequality, which were then organized within families. As economic and political power shifted into institutions and processes remote from families, gender inequality became the crucial link between family role differentiation and social power. Women deferred to men and depended on husbands because they had no practical alternatives outside the family. By shouldering the burden of sole economic responsibility, men gained deference and superiority within their families. As the structures of economic and political inequality gradually disengaged from gender inequality, the structure of family role differentiation faced increasing pressures.

Thus, the family role differentiation associated with the so-called *traditional* family of industrial societies was produced interactively by *gender inequality* and the *transition to an industrial economy*. This argument partially reverses some famous ideas associated with the functionalist theories of Talcott Parsons. Parsons suggested that family role differentiation had a special functional fit to industrial society. Actually, if this family form fitted something, it was not the permanent, inherent needs of industrial society but the transitional imbalance between the long-term egalitarian implications of modern society and the momentum that sustained gender inequality. The role-differentiated family—with an employed husband and a homemaker wife—was a transitory family form that bridged the transition between a family economy and a modern industrial economy.

The decline of family role differentiation has lagged behind the improvements in women's economic and political status. This lag represents the distinct causes behind the two changes, not differences in the difficulty of the two processes or resistance to them.[7] Lacking an integral engine of change, family roles change as they adapt to external shifts in the status inequality between women and men. This process has been slowly but persistently changing patterns in the United States for some time, but is still distant from equality.[8]

As social power became concentrated in economic and political organizations, everyone became subject to the rules of large-scale organizations. Simultaneously, families lost control over social resources, and people lost influence over their children's destinies. Increasingly powerful organizations fostered interests indifferent to the group distinctions essential to status inequality. Organizational interests promoted an institutional individualism in which people were judged by their actions and achievements, not by their personal characteristics or links to status groups. This institutional individualism gradually subordinated status-group interests to organizational interests.

As the economy and state increasingly treated all individuals in the same impersonal way, institutional individualism diffused to other social contexts. Schools are prototypical examples. Schools substituted training within organizations for much of family childrearing, becoming a powerful force for individualism. Schools inevitably promoted achievement norms even as they tried to preserve allegiance to family ties and personal status characteristics. Institutional individualism gradually produced an ideology that stressed meritocratic ideals and expectations. Meritocratic ideas linked performance, rewards, and rights, changing people's thoughts both about what was fair and about what was effective. People retained many of their status-group prejudices about gender-appropriate roles even while they adopted meritocratic ideas. Nonetheless, these meritocratic ideas promoted women's aspirations, undermined the moral defense of inequality, and encouraged organizational policies that neglected gender distinctions.

Ever-increasing institutional indifference to gender inequality was a principal cause of women's rising status. This influence was often overlooked, in part because women seeking to improve their circumstances focused on the resistance they endured from employers, politicians, bureaucrats, husbands, and men in general. Looking backward, however, we can more readily see the progressive erosion of interests attached to gender inequality. As interests eroded, resistance to women's efforts at self-improvement also declined with each successive generation.

The institutions that undermined sex inequality did not start down this road intending to alleviate gender inequality (or any other kind of inequality). If anything, their leaders sought the reverse, aiming to preserve powerful groups' privileged statuses.

History, however, has little respect for human motives. People's goals and understandings exercise only a limited control. The economy and the political order had to respond to social imperatives dictated by markets, organizational constraints, and political processes. Both industrial capitalism and liberal democracy needed administrative rationality and an ideological justification for their authority. To those guiding economic and political organizations, women and men posed equal issues of control, exploitation, and legitimacy.

While the evolution of economic and political institutions eroded the support for gender inequality, it did not generate interests opposed to all inequality. The issue was what kind of inequality. The institutions valued some forms of inequality, were indifferent to some other kinds, and found some forms of inequality problematic. These institutions, or more precisely the men who ran them, remained dedicated to sustaining and enhancing their power and stability. They refined and defended economic, political, and organizational inequalities linked to their well-being. Inequality between women and men was not so linked.

Even so, powerful men did tolerate and often openly supported male dominance. Because men were ascendant throughout society, the powerful men who ran institutions shared many of ordinary men's ideas. More important, men with power stressed ordinary men's wishes over women's interests because the exercise of power depended much more on the goodwill of ordinary men than on that of ordinary women.

Yet when their institutional needs conflicted with the preservation of gender inequality, powerful men took actions that eventually undermined male ascendancy. Over the long term, consistent organizational interests prevailed over powerful men's irrational prejudices. They hired women, took in female students, and embraced female voters.

The people who initiated and adopted these structural changes rarely foresaw how much they might someday improve women's status. Indeed, the abstract question of women's status was probably far from their minds. Obviously, some political issues such as voting rights for women or laws against discrimination made women's status a self-evident focus. Even then, however, government officials and politicians generally aimed at moderate adaptations to existing changes in women's circumstances, not at policies intended to significantly alter women's future social role. Usually, the men making policy changes were hunting for short-term solutions to problems in the economy or political order. They were not trying to decide the future of gender inequality. Instead, they worried about administration, profit making, sustaining order, and limiting conflict.

Nonetheless, the changes they introduced progressively eroded women's subordination. Women's gains included jobs, legal rights, voting power, and education. Often, those enacting new policies had no idea of their consequences for gender inequality, both because they were almost impossible to foresee and because the issue was usually not salient. Even when they could see such effects were possible, they were unlikely to stress the defense of men's abstract group interests over their concrete personal and political interests.

The structural evolution of society that eroded gender inequality changed both men's and women's circumstances and their attitudes. Men's advantages over women declined. They had less to gain through women's domination. And they found it harder to believe in the justice and necessity of women's subordination. Women's circumstances moved in the opposite direction. Women enjoyed greater opportunities. Their aspirations rose. The justifications of their subordination grew ever more suspect. And their dependence on men lessened.

Men's shifting interests gradually translated into a withdrawal from actions that preserved inequality. Men did not universally or suddenly alter their behavior or embrace the idea of gender equality. Men's interests changed slowly and unevenly. They responded to these changing interests in diverse and often unpredictable ways. Nonetheless, men's shrinking interests in preserving the constraints on women's roles increasingly guided men's actions.

Over time, ordinary men's behavior became less of an obstruction to women's rising status. Changing circumstances reduced men's resources, diminished the value of gender inequality to men, and eroded beliefs that inequality was just or necessary. Men's actions still limited women, because men retained competitive advantages and their use of these advantages reinforced them. Still, as economic and political organizations increasingly dominated people's lives, these advantages waned, and ordinary men's simple pursuit of schooling, jobs, or respectability was less detrimental to women's efforts. Ordinary men also reduced both their indirect and direct opposition to women's rising status. Simply put, men lost both the will and the means to restrain women.

A typical man apparently adapted to changing gender relations by adopting different expectations for different generations. He probably resisted some efforts by his wife and other women in his generation who wanted to expand their roles. Yet he also probably accepted and even expected his wife to have more modern and more egalitarian roles than did his mother. Moreover, he probably also expected and wanted his daughters to do things he resented and resisted with women his own age. For example, many men who raised children in the decades following World War II were likely to have a mother who never held a job after she married, a wife he felt could hold lesser jobs part of the time, and a daughter whom he wanted to have a significant career. Ordinary men encapsulated historical change by adopting standards for each generation that reflected the historical state of gender inequality into which each cohort was born.

Powerful men's actions reflected the widening gap between positional inequality and gender inequality even more vividly than those of ordinary men. Over time, economic and political developments eroded the links between powerful men's interests and male dominance while gradually increasing their interests in policies that benefited women's status. The interests of powerful men were unavoidably linked to the source of their power. Events that could directly or indirectly alter their power had the greatest potential for altering their lives.

Powerful men's political and economic influence freed them from personal dependence on gender inequality for their well-being. Economic and political resources allowed powerful men to dominate both women and men. They could not enhance their power through gender inequality, because they could not accumulate women like slaves under a plantation system. While powerful men commonly shared patriarchal attitudes, accepting the prevalent beliefs about the justice and necessity of male superiority, those attitudes did not supply a compelling set of interests to rule their actions. Powerful men had long supported gender inequality, and some of their actions helped keep all men ascendant, but their primary interest was to safeguard their personal power among other men.

Powerful men slowly altered economic and political organization policies so that they increasingly treated ordinary women and ordinary men similarly. Organizations became more powerful at the same time that ordinary men's opposition to women's advances declined. The men controlling these organizations became increasingly unconcerned with ordinary men's objections to policies that might benefit women. Generally indifferent to sex, organizational interests slowly favored assimilating women. From an organizational perspective, women and men offered similar opportunities for exploitation or support and similar risks. Competition for profit and power, reinforced by a rationalized search for control, gradually and intermittently increased the organizational interests favoring women's assimilation. From time to time, men running businesses and governments would face an opportunity or a need that caused them to adopt policies that eventually helped women's status to improve. Usually, these men did not want or aim to help women. Nevertheless, it suited their institutional or private interests to exploit or appease women.

Men still resist. Nevertheless, men trying to ensure that wives accept more responsibility in the care of small children or men resisting women's access to top management jobs are acting in ways that seem pale reflections of past times, when men refused to let women have any decent job, denied women any voice in government, withheld education from women, and blocked women's efforts to live independently from men. While men's resistance to women's rising status might seem stable or even on the rise over short periods, the long-term perspective reveals a clear retreat.

As men's resistance to women's advance declined, women's rebellion against the constraints of inequality rose, both individually and collectively. The continual pressure of individuals wanting better lives fueled the expansion of opportunities resulting from the organizational realignment of interests. Collective action occurred when individual efforts were frustrated after considerable individual progress had already occurred.

As individuals, women tried to break out of the traditional bounds of female role expectations. Many women followed a well-worn path toward a life of domestic labor, caring for children and a household, always dependent on and obedient to a man. Other women, however, sought education, jobs, and more autonomous lifestyles. Even the women who seemed entirely conventional commonly pushed at the boundaries of the role obligations between women and men.

Women typically pursued individual strategies when they could and adopted collective approaches when individual efforts produced excessive frustration. Ambitious women used the gradually expanding opportunities for individual advancement whenever possible. When opportunities appeared, women were quick to enter schools at all levels, to take jobs of all kinds, and to enter diverse organizations. Through these individual efforts, women gained a public good, for every increase in women's assimilation made it easier for the women who followed.

Throughout the past 150 years, some women were advocating collective action for women, but effective, widespread organization occurred mainly in two phases: the women's suffrage movement and the modern feminist movement. The first invoked collective strategies to gain the vote, an inherently collective good that was not forthcoming. The second used collective strategies to combat discriminatory practices that directly limited women's ability to advance individually. Both movements aimed at changes that proved unreachable through individual effort.

The imbalance between their experience of progress and rebuff was the catalyst prompting women's disenchantment to culminate in effective collective protest. The long-term trends widening women's opportunities had uneven effects. Economic and political processes gradually, if unevenly, assimilated women into ordinary positions but gave them no dependable access to high-status positions. This dissymmetry occurred because the processes governing access to high-level and low-level positions differed. Neither organizational nor personal interests gave men who ran economic and political organizations a strong incentive for promoting or hiring women in high-status positions. Labor shortages, cost concerns, and organizational rationalization—which induced employers to hire women for low-status jobs—were minor considerations for most high-status jobs. Against this, more important considerations such as predictability and conformity gave those running organizations an interest in promoting men. In combination with the prevalent bias against women, this array of interests impeded the gradual assimilation of women into high-status positions. Analogous considerations limited women's assimilation by the political process.

The male resistance to women's assimilation into high-status positions was not much higher than the resistance to women's movement into lower-status male positions. It was, however, more effective. Most of the time, men kept women out simply by inaction. They endured no effort or cost.

Thus, widespread, cumulative improvements in women's general status and opportunities ran into rigidly unyielding constraints when women sought access to collective power or the high-status positions. The resulting strain between the diffuse improvements in women's status and the barriers protecting power and high-status positions led almost inexorably to political confrontations.

Women's movements had to overcome two main barriers. First, they had to supply some leverage to open high-level positions to women. While gradual structural changes eroded men's, particularly powerful men's, interests in opposing gender equality, they did not create interests that induced men to promote women. Second, they had to overcome transition impediments. Politicians, businessmen, and bureaucrats resisted women's efforts to enter positions of power because they feared risks inherent in change.

The women's suffrage movement and modern women's movements provided the critical force needed to accelerate the transition toward equality. On one side, the conjunction of women's rising resources and increasing frustration was certain to induce impassioned reactions against the status quo eventually. On the other side, the progress of structural transformation reduced men's, particularly powerful men's, interests in resisting women's assimilation.

Historical opportunity, not moral worthiness or the balance of forces, gave direction to both women's and men's actions. Over time, women pushed against the limits on their roles, and men gradually conceded ground. When acting as individuals, the most common occurrence, women and men thought mainly about their private aims, not the wider issues of gender inequality. When women and men contested gender inequality through collective actions, they pursued a muddled mix of moral claims and self-interests. Indifferent to both sexes' ideas and efforts, the emerging forms of economic and political organization gradually disembedded gender inequality from positional inequality. Both women and men were forced to adapt to their new constraints and opportunities.

In this transition, women's general interests have coincided with history's demands. The two major occasions when women engaged in sustained collective organization and action might seem exceptions to this generalization. Here women seem most emphatically to have commandeered control of history. Yet it was not the women's movements but the resistance of men in the state and economy that was out of step with history. Both the movement for women's political incorporation at the turn of the century and the movement to end general discrimination against women in recent decades suggest a similar picture. Each blended smoothly into the trajectory of history. The primary goals of these movements did not declare a moral rebellion against their times. Instead, they were a logical extension of surrounding circumstances.

In short, as social conditions became progressively more hospitable to gender equality, women's and men's actions followed suit. The new, expansive economic and political orders diminished men's advantages. They increased men's subjection to labor markets and the state while expanding women's access to jobs and citizenship rights. Structural changes altered both the plausibility and the value of women's subordination. Men's and women's social resources grew more alike while inequality lost its aura of fairness. As a result, women strove more effectively as time passed, and men's defense of their prerogatives lost both verve and punch.

Gender inequality has had great momentum, despite the forces imperiling it. Since economic and political institutions evolved in a piecemeal way over a long period, the shift of power from families to external institutions transformed interests and curtailed gender inequality slowly. Even as economic and political changes weakened the foundations of gender inequality, other social conditions sustained it. Because most institutions and social arrangements assumed gender inequality, their organization and their actions reinforced it. Because men experienced reductions in gender inequality as attacks on their status, they dug in their heels against change. Gender inequality has also diminished unevenly and unpredictably because its primary causes worked indirectly.

The social transformations that fostered the decline usually created the opportunity for change rather than forcing it. As they unfolded, the interests of people and organizations shifted. How and when people responded to these changes in interests was not strictly determined. The specific timing and form of the actions that transformed this rising potential into manifest reductions of inequality depended on varied, unpredictable historical conditions.

The pervasiveness of gender inequality caused the ordinary practice of life to confirm and reinforce inequality. The activities of most institutions and the actions of both women and men implicitly favored conformity. The organization of all social life assumed men's superior status and women's domestic obligations. The movement toward equality faced hurdles as diverse as school curricula, work schedules, the absence of child-care services, and religious imagery. The need to adjust so many aspects of social life to permit equality slowed change considerably.

When the ordinary conduct of life was not enough to restrain women's efforts to better themselves, men commonly adopted an embattled attitude. Experiencing the direction of change as an unfair attack on their social standing and just rights, they resisted women's efforts. As politicians, officials, employers, workers, voters, fathers, husbands, and anonymous acquaintances, men adopted policies and pursued patterns of behavior that slowed women's progress.

Because the economic and political changes that threatened gender inequality accumulated slowly, the processes resisting gender inequality's decline have had considerable influence. As a result, while movement toward equality has been inexorable, it has also been incremental and uneven, occurring through countless individual actions and occasional collective actions.

Women's resulting economic and political assimilation ensued gradually and assuredly but unpredictably over a long period. The primary processes and circumstances that caused women's subordination to decline did not determine why changes occurred when they did, rather than earlier or later. The long-term institutional evolution and short-term contingent historical conditions together decided when gender inequality changed. Over the long term, gender inequality's decline was as inevitable as any major historical transformation can be. The developmental pattern awaiting industrial capitalism and liberal democracy was intrinsic to these institutions even in the early nineteenth century. Intrinsic does not mean known. No one could have known enough from the past to predict where these institutions would lead. While these institutions followed the developmental logic inherent in their structure, historical circumstances greatly influenced the pace of development. Wars, depressions, the ebb and flow of political conflicts, the supply of natural resources, the rate of invention, and many other circumstances influenced the speed of change. Undoubtedly, varied snowball and threshold effects also made change uneven and unpredictable.[9] Still, the direction of development was inevitable and intrinsic to the organization of society.

While trying to show why and how shifting interests caused gender inequality to disembed from positional inequality, this study straddles the divide between determinist and antideterminist approaches. It rejects both all-embracing, indiscriminate determinist assumptions and historicist, atheoretical assumptions made in the name of human agency. For the kind of problem being studied here, these competing assumptions seem to reflect a superfluous opposition. To reconcile these approaches, this analysis distinguishes the social causality of long-term structural change from the historical causality of short-term events.

A wish to give due weight to people's part in making history has repeatedly raised serious reservations about the search for social causes. Theories that appear to challenge our sense of control and responsibility—such as Freudian, behaviorist, Marxist, and functionalist theories—have always prompted critiques calling them overly determinist. Some critics have completely rejected the theories, substituting interpretive approaches that eschew causal language, claiming that human action transcends the causal paradigms used in other fields. Others have tried to pursue a moderate course, offering variants of the determinist theories that try to leave greater room for human agency, the idea that people's choices have historical effects.

This analysis assumes that all events are determined, but not exhaustively determined through the long-term causal processes stressed here. It does not slight the influence of human agency, because people create events and make history. All events have been caused by those that preceded them, and each event is uniquely determined by its preceding conditions and history. In the short term, however, people respond to many conditions other than those affecting the long-term outcomes. An event emerges from the interaction between all relevant actors, each guided by a singular biography.

My theoretical approach accords people and organizations high levels of self-determination. The theoretical model achieves this flexibility by building long-term deterministic causal processes on highly variable and unpredictable short-term actions and events. In explaining long-term social change, this analysis assumes that the timing of specific changes often depends on historical contingencies independent of the social causes that propel and guide the long-term process. It does not require that these short-term events operate outside the long-term processes as some kind of uncoupled epiphenomena. Instead, these varied demonstrations of human agency enable, implement, pace, and give concrete form to long-term transformations.

For example, changes in social practices benefiting women have commonly occurred through three realms of social action: dispersed individual efforts (of women, men, and organizations), collective agitation by women's interest groups, and government initiative. For many kinds of changes, the relative contribution of these three realms could vary, depending on historical circumstances. Much of gender inequality's gradual decline has occurred through individual actions. With each generation more people individually adapted to the emerging pattern of interests. Women sought education, jobs, promotions, and more egalitarian lifestyles. Powerful men sought competitive advantages for their organizations or themselves; to these ends they used women in roles such as students, employees, clients, or voters. Ordinary men somewhat begrudgingly conceded women's expanding claims in their own generation, and often encouraged their daughters to do more. At times, however, even as interests and conditions changed, individual action was ineffective or implausible. The resulting pressures of unfulfilled interests increased the likelihood of collective agitation or government actions. Sometimes the state seems to have taken the initiative, as when it passed the Married Women's Property Acts in the nineteenth century or when it passed equal pay legislation in the mid-twentieth century. At other times the state seems to have resisted acting until pressured by women's organized agitation, as when the state granted women suffrage and when it outlawed various kinds of discrimination against women. Theoretically, these two sequences are functionally equivalent alternatives selected by historically specific conditions. Shifting interests increased the likelihood of *both* sequences whenever decentralized adaptations were obstructed. The parallel rise in the potential for these two sequences suggests, for example, that if women had not achieved organizations and collective action, eventually the state would have taken the initiative to extend the vote to women and proscribe discrimination. Similarly, if the state had not autonomously adopted laws giving married women property rights or requiring equal wages, eventually women would have organized and agitated until the state became responsive. Around issues such as these, both autonomous state action and collective action by women become ever more likely as the economic and political transformations continue to shift interests but fulfillment of the realigned interests remains blocked to individual actions. Which is triggered into action depends on the way interests change and on the existing distribution of power. It also depends on incidental historical conditions. In this way, the broad changes eroding gender inequality were unavoidable but not predictable.

The gradual realignment of institutional and gender interests decisively undermined gender inequality, but these structural processes did not strongly restrict the behavior of individuals or narrowly determine the outcomes of specific historical events. Rather, shifting interests decided that actions with egalitarian effects were increasingly more likely than actions preserving the unequal arrangements of the past. By this means, a highly determinist theory stressing structures and processes rather than events and actors can accommodate human agency, even granting people more freedom than approaches that try to build explanations on the assumption of human agency.

Disembedding gender inequality from economic and political structures did not directly reduce inequality. Gender inequality declined because both men and women pursued new interests and opportunities that encouraged greater equality. The emerging economic and political orders produced the new interests and opportunities. Still, men and women had to pursue these new interests and use the new opportunities before they could affect inequality.

Interests link structural circumstances and people's behavior. As power shifted from families to economic and political organizations, it became the servant of specialized interests distinct from men's shared interest in male ascendancy. Both power and productive economic activity moved from families to large and impersonal organizations, oriented toward profit, organizational expansion, bureaucratic control, and efficiency. As households lost control over economic productivity and family capital shrank, ordinary men's interest in preserving male dominance gradually diminished. As gender inequality weakened and women's opportunities grew, women's interests in attempting strategies to improve their social standing rose and men's interests in resisting those efforts fell.

As used in this analysis, the role of interests mirrors our ordinary understandings of human action and our commonplace expectations of reasonable behavior.[10] *Normally, people will not, without good reason, knowingly and repeatedly make choices that will worsen their lives.* In any particular instance, other considerations may influence behavior more than interests do. These other considerations include, for example, anger, personal obsessions, or stupidity. Thus, self-interest is assumed to be one of the competing motives guiding action. We focus on interests rather than on other motives because they play a more important role in the explanation of social phenomena.

Interests gain their special significance not because they are psychologically more compelling than other motives but because they represent the relationship between the social environment and people's values. Outcomes disproportionately reinforce actions consistent with interests even when interests do not motivate actions. Those interests that are widespread and stable will exercise a broader, more consistent influence than most other motives. Whether interests are widespread and stable is determined by the social environment, not by people's psychological constitutions. The analytic concept of interests encapsulates the idea that social circumstances determine the likelihood that alternative actions will bring about more or less desirable outcomes, where the desirability of outcomes depends on cultural definitions for groups and biographical adaptations for individuals. People have similar interests if they have similar preferences and face similar social conditions. Because people in the same cultural milieu commonly share many basic goals, such as peace, prosperity, good housing, personal autonomy, prestige, and leisure, those with a common group identity will have common interests.

How far must interests change to produce a significant shift in people's actions? The characteristics of the interests largely decide how much interests control behavior. The important characteristics include homogeneity across people; severity, or the significance of different outcomes; consistency over time, or predictability; and transparency, as it affects people's ability to connect actions and outcomes. A group's typical actions will change faster and more completely when more members experience changing interests and when the changes in their interests are large, stable, and transparent.

In the historical decline of gender inequality, interests have been paramount because the driving force behind women's rising status has been the transformation of the economic and political orders, which affect people mainly through their interests. Because realigned interests have had a consistent, enduring influence that gradually increased the likelihood of actions inconsistent with gender inequality's persistence, they have had a decisive cumulative impact.

As one expression of interests, women have always resisted their subordination. No one can show that gender inequality has produced resistance by women everywhere, but all the evidence we have is consistent with this assertion. Women's constant pressure against their subordinate status was not a distinguishing characteristic of gender inequality. All inequality seems to breed resistance from people in the disadvantaged group. Even enduring systems, like the Indian castes or the Roman Catholic hierarchy, produce resistance. In subordinate groups, no matter how docile their appearance, some people always struggle against their constraints, and many people will occasionally resent and question some specific order, ruling, event, or other circumstance.

Because it was contingent on interests, men's defense of inequality was no surer than women's submission to it. Men's interest in sustaining inequality has been neither automatic nor constant. This interest has depended on trade-offs between the gains and costs involved in preserving inequality. These gains and costs depended in part on men's values or goals, but they also depended on the resources and the opportunities of both sexes. Accordingly, men's interests have varied by group and by period because these trade-offs varied.

Although sexual bigotry ruled many men's thoughts, over the long run the scope of men's efforts to resist women's bids to improve themselves subsided as the balance of men's interests changed. Over the past 150 years, changing circumstances gradually lessened the conflict between men's interests and women's advances. Successive generations of men have had smaller resource advantages and less to gain from deterring women's advance. This declining conflict of interests gradually moderated men's resistance. (Men who suffer an apparent loss of prestige might lash back more in the short run. Successive generations, however, experience the outcomes of the previous generation as a starting point, a benchmark for their assessments of what is possible and just.)

The interests of powerful men are a crucial special case. These men have controlled government and business. They also have created and enforced the laws, employment practices, and varied social policies that favored men. Through these actions, they have reinforced ordinary men's ascendance. But powerful men eventually pursued strategies that benefited women and eroded ordinary men's privileges. They adopted policies that gave women education, employment, and expanded legal rights. Powerful men were rarely ruled by some inherent, enduring interest in preserving male dominance simply because they enjoyed its privileges. Instead, powerful men's interests were most firmly tied to the sources of their power, whether business or government.

The gender-related interests of powerful men have significantly changed over the past 150 years. First, powerful men became gradually less dependent on ordinary men's responses to policies that benefited women. In part, powerful men became more distant from ordinary men and less dependent on their goodwill as government and business grew large. In part, ordinary men's potential opposition to improvements in women's status declined because their interests and resources changed. Second, powerful men's personal interests became more attached to the interests of the organizations giving them power. Third, economic and political transformations created opportunities for powerful men to exploit women as employees or political party workers, indirectly increasing women's opportunities. Fourth, after women's status started to rise, they became economic and political actors whose responses to policies had increasing weight.

As the links between powerful men's personal interests and the source of their power were changed by economic and political development, they increasingly induced powerful men to adopt policies that benefited women's status. In the modern era, it is not that men lack sexist motives or that they have no interests in preserving male dominance; rather, other interests have greater social and historical effect. Men's interests in preserving patriarchal privileges are now much less than in the premodern family. In the modern world, organizational interests are indifferent to gender, power becomes attached to organizational interests, and the interests and actions of men who wield power become subject to the interests of the organizations that provide their power. The social significance of interests always depends on the distribution of power relative to those interests. That is why there is little explanatory value in saying it was as much in women's interests as in men's to monopolize family power or good jobs. The statement is accurate, but it is not meaningful, because women did not have the resources to realize such preferences. To be theoretically useful, interests usually must refer not simply to preferences but to the relative value of practically possible actions, taking into account their costs and the variability of outcomes. In the modern world, economic and political power, concentrated in organizations with no interests in gender inequality, eroded men's interests in preserving women's collective disadvantages and reduced men's capacity to act on what residual interests they experienced. Men's attachment to their gender advantages have gradually changed from sustainable interests toward nominal preferences.

The emergence of modern economic and political organization has been the engine of change that slowly disengaged positional inequality from gender inequality. It severed the power needed to preserve male dominance from the interests linked to it. The economic and political transformations did not directly oppose sex inequality, but they sufficiently separated the interests produced by positional inequality from the interests generated by sex inequality that the two sets of interests lost their capacity to consistently reinforce each other.

The more disembedded gender inequality became from economic and political structures, the more vulnerable it became. This separation rearranged the interests of women, men, and organizations, giving ever more people priorities that no longer fitted the actions needed to preserve gender inequality. Treating the sexes differently increasingly became more a burden than an advantage to institutions and people with power. Although men remained in control, economic and political organizations gradually adapted policies to suit their institutional interests, even when those policies favored women's collective interests over those of men. For example, employers would hire women if they believed this would substantially increase profits even if they personally believed women should stay at home. Similarly, politicians would support women's political participation if they thought that doing so would enhance their party's power, even if they personally disliked having women in politics. As social power became ruled by institutional interests, women's interests in reducing sex inequality became more effective than men's interests in preserving it. Because of their inherent interests in bettering themselves, women continually resisted inequality and responded quickly to new opportunities. Women's constant pressure required men to maintain an equally constant defense of inequality. Ordinary men's defense of inequality, however, depended on the value they got from it and faltered as such value diminished. Powerful men's actions went even further. Their interests in stabilizing and expanding their power, economic or political, increasingly fostered policies that coincided more with women's interests than with those of men.

GENERALIZATION FROM AN ANALYSIS BASED ON ONE NATION

Women's status has risen similarly in many countries, though at different rates and with different historical contours.[11] Gender inequality has declined in many nations because they have experienced comparable but independent causal conditions. International influence has played a lesser role.

Although the history of gender inequality's decline may differ in many ways across nations, the driving causal processes have been the same. In each case, power migrated into bureaucratic organizations, gender inequality became disembedded from economic and political positional inequality, and interests concerning gender inequality gradually realigned.

If this argument is correct, the crucial causes of gender inequality's decline have been conditions and processes characteristic of modern nations. To the degree that I have accurately identified these causes in the United States, the analysis is generalizable to other countries.

While women's progress toward equality everywhere has similar causes, it has followed diverse paths. Women's status has changed greatly in some countries and much less in others. The transition began long ago in some places and only recently in others. Women's movements have sometimes played a major role and sometimes a minor role. Political parties have led the change in some places and largely resisted it elsewhere.

The theory presented here about long-term causes common to all countries does not address and cannot readily predict cross-country variations. Indeed, the model of social change developed here suggests that narrow hypotheses of the form "more industrialized nations will display less gender inequality" are theoretically weak. Such hypotheses would be valid only in an extreme, simplistic, and generally uninteresting form. Nonetheless, from its portrayal of the long-term dynamics, this analysis could help identify the conditions and processes that account for each country's unique path to greater equality. This theory suggests that explanations of international variation focus on historical and cultural differences that alter the strength and impact of the primary causal processes which the theory claims are everywhere decisive.

Stressing the causal processes within a society, this theoretical analysis has neglected international influences. Advocates of world system analysis suggest that we can understand a nation only in the context of its economic, political, and historical relationships to other nations. Capitalism, representative democracy, technology, and contending ideologies all develop through competition, alliances, and exchanges between nations. As far as international dynamics influence the pace of economic and political transformation, they also influence the movement toward gender equality. International dynamics also have a more direct, but even more incalculable impact. Policymakers, women's advocates, and the public may have their interests and expectations influenced by knowledge of historical currents in other countries. Usually, this should accelerate the shift toward greater equality, by reducing the need for experimentation and hastening acceptance of changes as workable, desirable, and inevitable. Only comparative research can accurately specify how international dynamics have influenced the decline of gender inequality.

The United States provides a good case for developing a generalizable analysis. It has been a leading nation during most phases of women's rising status for the past two centuries. It has not always been first to experience the crucial turning points, but it has been among the front runners. In the birth of the suffrage movement, the rise of modern feminism, the passage of laws granting married women equal legal status, woman suffrage laws (at the state and the national levels), laws prohibiting sex discrimination, the rising employment of women, and the rising education of women, the United States was among the international leaders. This leading role makes the American case useful for investigating the fundamental social processes gradually reducing gender inequality across the world. In America's history, we can observe processes that are sometimes more difficult to see in other nations, where the same processes occur but sometimes have not yet matured sufficiently and where residues from earlier periods have obscured them.

While the theoretical model developed here should apply to other nations, its roots in the history of the American case define some limits. This analysis cannot substitute for comparative analyses that examine gender inequality's history in many countries. Undoubtedly, future studies will reveal errors in the line I have drawn between what was unique to the American case and what was integral to modern economic and political organization wherever it appeared. Nonetheless, this analysis *should* explain why gender inequality declines in all countries undergoing a transition to modern economic and political organization.

AN EGALITARIAN AGE?

Our age cares passionately about equality and freedom. We take great pride in the advances we have made and often experience dismay over shortcomings that persist. We proudly teach our children about leaders, revolts, wars, inventions, and laws that have expanded equality and liberty. Popular images of evil commonly stress ideas, such as totalitarianism, that would deny people equality or freedom. In varied forms, social inequality has been a prominent public issue for two centuries. The ideals of legal and political equality first gained wide visibility through their prominence in the American and French Revolutions. The ideal of equal opportunity grew more slowly and diffusely, apparently as a response to wage labor and universal education. These ideals mark our age.

How these ideals will withstand the test of time is difficult to judge. Future generations will discard the details of our history and judge us by standards we cannot predict. Several hundred years from now, our greatest technological achievements will be museum artifacts. Our most cherished new ideas will be distilled into a few short comments in intellectual histories. Many of our most passionate causes will become curiosities, associated with a backward civilization and increasingly alien to more modern sensibilities. People will disparage some of our most respected ideas and proudest achievements as embarrassing symbols of our ignorance and barbarism.

As future historians throw aside the details of our history, they will emphasize some theme salient to their perspective, as we now treat the Renaissance or the Enlightenment. They could stress some amoral facet so that we become, for example, the Bureaucratic Age or the Electronic Era. They may see us as one of the dark periods in history, identified perhaps as the Era of Environmental Decay, the Age of World Wars, or the Era of Cultural Genocide. If we are lucky, they may remember more about the ways we nurtured and refined civilization, for example as the Age of Representative Government or the Period of Universal Education.

One hopeful contender for such a title will be the Egalitarian Age. We have not gained universal equality in the world. Far from it. Nonetheless, the past several centuries have witnessed an extraordinary leveling. For the first time since large, complex societies emerged thousands of years ago, the ideals of equal opportunity for all and universal citizenship became prominent throughout the world. The practices implied by these ideas have an uneasy relationship both with the residues of traditional inequalities and with modern society's new patterns of unequal authority and rewards. Still, a reign of merit, rationality, and rights has supplanted a considerable part of the former inequality based on personal characteristics such as race, age, and sex. What inequality remains is constantly on the defensive. Women's rising status has been a crucial part of this worldwide pattern. Recall Charles Fourier's claim that "the extension of women's privileges is the general principle for all social progress."[12] For an era proud of its egalitarian achievements, it is fitting that women's rising status has proved a defining characteristic of modern societies.

If sex equality is our inevitable destiny, what does this imply for social policy or political action? Should we abandon efforts to increase equality? No! In truth, the analysis developed here suggests exactly the opposite.

Continued efforts to improve women's status are still valuable. They can hasten movement toward equality and can help shape the meaning of that equality. While we have made great strides toward equality over the past two centuries, considerable differences still separate women and men. The structure of modern political and economic institutions makes continued movement toward equality almost unavoidable. Yet structural imperatives do not directly determine either the rate of change or the form taken by equality.

Inherent institutional developments of modern societies create an ever-enlarging potential for people to act in ways inconsistent with gender inequality. These structural conditions do not normally force greater equality into being. Instead, they alter people's interests and change the opportunities that face individuals and groups. The varied rates of women's rising status across nations reflect this causal pattern. Over the long term, most nations have moved toward greater equality, but they have followed diverse paths. Political efforts to raise women's status can significantly accelerate the movement toward equality.

Political efforts also can influence the meaning of equality. Commentators often forget that people can be rendered equal by all being made impoverished subjects of a domineering authority just as they can be rendered equal by all being made affluent, independent citizens. Equality implies the erasure of differences, but it does not say at what level the leveling occurs. Structural developments induce a gradual erosion of the differences between women and men, but they leave considerable room for political efforts to influence the destination of the leveling. How much childrearing will occur in families and how much in other institutions? How much leave from jobs will parents receive when children are born? How long will the work week be? How will we adapt childrearing and other arrangements to the pattern of serial monogamy (commonly serial marriage) that appears likely to become one norm for adult relationships? These and many other questions must face a historical reckoning. Whether we guide that process or merely accept the outcome is our choice.

Political efforts to forestall movement toward gender equality are inherently futile. Occasionally, such efforts might temporarily slow the progress toward equality, but they cannot hope to alter the long-term momentum toward equality. People discomfited by the atrophy of sex-role differences would use their energy much more effectively if they accepted the inescapable triumph of equality. In future generations, our granddaughters and grandsons will be living similar lives, no matter what those who dislike that prospect might do today. What those grandchildren's lives will look like is not certain, however. Here is where those disquieted by change could best aim their energy after accepting their inability to deter equality's triumph. Defining a good way for both women and men to live in the future would contribute far more to their descendants than would a doomed struggle against equality.

The political implications of this analysis, then, are surprisingly similar for feminists committed to the goal of gender equality and conservatives committed to preserving traditional sex-role differences. Gender equality is coming, regardless of either side's wishes. Advocates on both sides would do well to accept this as our inevitable future and to focus on making it a good one. Those fighting for equality would be making a mistake to assume that conservatives' rhetoric about families, intimacy, commitment, and similar values does not merit close attention and concern. Those unsettled by the prospect that sex-role differences will disappear would be making a mistake to waste their energies on a fruitless attachment to the past, when they could be working to preserve their most important values in an egalitarian future.

We are going to continue moving toward gender equality. We should try to make it the best form of equality we can imagine and to achieve it as fast as possible. Perhaps then we can truly claim to be an egalitarian age.

NOTES

Sources are cited by author and main title. For complete publication data, see the Bibliography.

1. THE EGALITARIAN IMPULSE

1. Mirra Komarovsky, "Cultural Contradictions and Sex Roles," pp. 184, 189. Cf. Helen Hacker, "Women as a Minority Group."
2. For studies of these various groups see, e.g., Paula Giddings, *When and Where I Enter;* Alfredo Mirande and Evangelina Enriquez, *La Chicana;* Evelyn Nakano Glen, *Issei, Nisei, War Bride;* Jacqueline Jones, *Labor of Love, Labor of Sorrow.*
3. Positional inequality and status inequality are theoretical constructs. They identify two distinctive kinds of social inequality with distinctive principles of organization. In practice, the inequality people experience rarely looks exactly like either of these definitions. Like Weber's *ideal types,* these theoretical models abstract from the complexity and contingency of real life, giving us a purer representation than we will ever find in human history.
4. This does not mean that inequality between structural positions is *functional.* Positional inequality need not be optimal, necessary, or desirable.
5. Absolute economic equality, implying that everyone has the same income and wealth, has never been a significant ideal in America except in the truncated form of concern with reducing poverty.
6. I am here assuming the apparent standards shared today by the majority of women and men. If women's relative status has declined in some area of life (this remains to be shown) and someone believes that this area of life is far more important than all others combined, that person could claim that, by

her or his standards, women's status has declined. I believe that this assessment is only legitimately possible if a person's values deviate greatly from those shared by most people.

7. The conditions causing some phenomenon, including a long-term social trend, to persist can differ from those that caused its origin. For example, I argue elsewhere that the processes causing gender inequality's modern historical persistence were not the conditions responsible for its primitive origins. (See Jackson, *The Subordination of Women.*) However, the empirical evidence suggests that the primary causes of women's rising status have remained the same.

8. In Arthur L. Stinchcombe's terms, the social value of gender inequality lost its significance as it lost its association with power, for "to have any appreciable effect on social functioning, the correlation [between commitment to a value and having power] has to be quite high"; *Constructing Social Theories,* p. 188.

9. While the analysis presented here considers only gender inequality, it has some application to other forms of inequality, for example, race. Other forms of inequality have distinctive institutional foundations, however, and therefore the process of change is different.

2. CITIZENSHIP

1. See, e.g., Catharine A. MacKinnon, *Toward a Feminist Theory of the State,* p. 162; Deborah L. Rhode, "Feminism and the State"; Ann Shola Orloff, "Gender and the Social Rights of Citizenship"; Kathleen Jones, "Citizenship in a Woman-Friendly Polity."

2. E.g., see Joan Hoff's suggestion that women have received rights only when they lose their value; *Law, Gender, and Injustice.*

3. For a more general definition of the state, Theda Skocpol and Edwin Amenta suggest that "states are organizations that extract resources through taxation and attempt to extend coercive control and political authority over particular territories and the people residing within them"; "States and Social Policies," p. 131.

4. Hoff, *Law, Gender, and Injustice;* Morton J. Horwitz, *The Transformation of American Law, 1780–1860;* Norma Basch, *In the Eyes of the Law;* Peggy A. Rabkin, *Fathers to Daughters.*

5. Norma Basch, *In the Eyes of the Law,* p. 125, remarks that "much of the early support for married women's [property rights] statute focused on the economic dislocations of men; considerations of women were often secondary." Rabkin, *Fathers to Daughters,* p. 154, adds that "protection of a married woman's property, more often than not, meant protection from the husband's creditors, rather than from the husband."

6. Horwitz, *The Transformation of American Law;* see also C. B. MacPherson, *The Political Theory of Possessive Individualism.*

7. Notes following the 1836 *Revised Statutes,* quoted in Rabkin, *Fathers to Daughters,* pp. 76–77.

8. Norma Basch and Peggy Rabkin, a legal historian, both discovered this while studying the married women's property rights laws in New York, which became a guide for many other states. The issues in debate and the sequence of legal changes were also typical. These two studies reach similar conclusions about the major causes, although they disagree about their relative importance. The presentation here draws extensively from these two studies. See Basch, *In the Eyes of the Law;* Rabkin, *Fathers to Daughters.* See also Elizabeth Bowles Warbasse, *The Changing Legal Rights of Married Women, 1800–1861;* Marylynn Salmon, *Women and the Law of Property in Early America.*

9. Hoff, *Law, Gender, and Injustice,* pp. 117–135, 377–382.

10. For the history of the woman suffrage issue in the United States see Elizabeth Cady Stanton, Susan B. Anthony, Matilda Joslyn Gage, and Ida Husted Harper, eds., *The History of Woman Suffrage;* Eleanor Flexnor, *Century of Struggle;* Aileen S. Kraditor, *The Ideas of the Woman Suffrage Movement, 1890–1920;* William L. O'Neill, *Everyone Was Brave;* Steven Buechler, *Women's Movements in the United States.*

11. With the exception of New Jersey, which had left out the gender restriction until the beginning of the nineteenth century, probably as a simple oversight.

12. Carrie Chapman Catt and Nettie Rogers Shuler, *Woman Suffrage and Politics,* pp. 32–73.

13. Ibid., p. 107.

14. For general treatments of suffrage and citizenship, see Reinhard Bendix, *Nation-Building and Citizenship;* and Steven Rokkan, *Citizens, Elections, and Parties.*

15. David Morgan, *Suffragists and Democrats.*

16. Catt and Schuler, *Woman Suffrage and Politics.*

17. Stanton, Anthony, Gage, and Harper, *History of Woman Suffrage,* vol. 5, pp. 205–206.

18. Robert Max Jackson and Ralph Chipman, "The Growth of Male Support for Woman Suffrage in American States."

19. Beverly Beeton, *Women Vote in the West.*

20. *New York Times,* August 22, 1892, sec. 3, p. 6.

21. U.S. Congress, Senate Committee on Woman Suffrage, 50th Cong., 2d sess., 1889, Senate Report 2543, p. 7.

22. *New York Times,* November 22, 1871, sec. 5, p. 4.

23. U.S. Congress, Senate Committee on Woman Suffrage, 47th Cong., 1st sess., 1882, Senate Report 686, p. 6.

24. These were not pure tests of support for woman suffrage, but no votes at the federal level were. Legislators raised other issues, including states' rights. Still, the extensive debate makes it clear that the legislators saw their vote centered on one crucial issue: would women become voters in national elec-

tions? See *Congressional Record,* 51st Cong., 1890, pp. 2697–2710, 6519–30, 6574–88.

25. *Congressional Record,* 63d Cong., 1915, p. 1476.

26. Jackson and Chipman, "Growth of Male Support for Woman Suffrage."

27. The experience of blacks in the American South—who were effectively denied their franchise rights for decades by discriminatory state laws and political processes—has shown that suffrage could be revoked in practice if not in law. But the original franchise for blacks grew out of Civil War politics that had little correspondence to blacks' social status. They certainly did not receive the franchise from Southern whites.

28. For examples, see Susan Lehrer, *Origins of Protective Labor Legislation for Women, 1905–1925;* Judith A. Baer, *The Chains of Protection;* Elizabeth Pleck, *Domestic Tyranny.*

29. Alice K. Leopold, "Federal Equal Pay Legislation," pp. 26–27.

30. Equal Pay Act of 1963 (29 U.S.C. §206 [1964]), quoted in Leo Kanowitz, *Women and the Law,* p. 132.

31. U. S. Department of Labor, Women's Bureau, *Case Studies in Equal Pay for Women,* p. 6.

32. Maurine Weiner Greenwald, "Women Workers and World War I."

33. Equal pay should be distinguished from the issue of women's right to work at occupations. This had a separate history, which included some significant legislation. For example, Illinois passed a law in 1872 stating: "no person shall be precluded or debarred from any occupation, profession or employment (except military) on account of sex; provided that this act shall not be construed to effect the eligibility of any person to an elective office"; *New York Times,* April 1, 1872, sec. 1, p. 5. In the opposite direction, some protectionist laws, made popular during the Progressive Era, indirectly prevented women's employment in occupations.

34. Cynthia Harrison, *On Account of Sex.*

35. U.S. Congress, House Committee on Education and Labor, *Equal Pay for Equal Work,* pp. 44–57.

36. Harrison, *On Account of Sex,* pp. 176–182; Hoff-Wilson, "The Unfinished Revolution."

37. Title VII of the Civil Rights Act of 1964 (78 Stat. 253, 42 U.S.C. §2000 et seq. [1964]), reprinted in Kanowitz, *Women and the Law,* pp. 207–221; quotes from §703.

38. Kanowitz, *Women and the Law,* pp. 103–106.

39. Jo Freeman, *The Politics of Women's Liberation;* Harrison, *On Account of Sex,* pp. 192–209.

40. See Caroline Bird, *Born Female,* chap. 1; and Jo Freeman, "Women, Law, and Public Policy."

41. Deborah L. Rhode, *Justice and Gender,* esp. pp. 81–107.

42. For opposition to affirmative action, see Nathan Glazer, *Affirmative Discrimination;* and William Beer, "Sociology and the Effects of Affirmative Action."

43. Frederick R. Lynch, *Invisible Victims,* p. 144.

44. For example, the *1995 Women's Equality Poll,* prepared for the Feminist Majority Foundation in April 1995 by Louis Harris and the Peter Harris Research Group.

45. On the rise and consequences of rationalism, see Wolfgang Schluchter, *The Rise of Western Rationalism;* Bryan R. Wilson, ed., *Rationality;* Shaun Hargreaves Heap, *Rationality in Economics;* Charles Edward Lindblom, *Politics and Markets;* Michael Hechter, ed., *Social Institutions;* James Samuel Coleman, *Foundations of Social Theory;* Edward O. Laumann and David Knoke, *The Organizational State;* William Edward Nelson, *The Roots of American Bureaucracy, 1830-1900;* Stephen Skowronek, *Building a New American State.*

46. Joyce Gelb and Marian Lief Palley, *Women and Public Policies.*

47. Data from Naomi B. Lynn, "Women and Politics"; and *New York Times,* August 14, 1988, sec. 1, p. 32.

48. Emmy E. Werner, "Women in the State Legislatures"; Peggy Simpson, "Politics"; National Women's Political Caucus, *National Directory of Women Elected Officials,* p. 12; and *New York Times,* May 24, 1992, sec. 4, p. 5; Center for the American Woman and Politics, Eagleton Institute of Politics, Rutgers University.

49. National Women's Political Caucus, *National Directory of Women Elected Officials;* and *Municipal Year Book 1989,* pp. 12, 249.

50. *Municipal Year Book 1989.* For cities with more than 2,500 in population, 34.4 percent (1,787) had a woman as the chief financial officer; for counties, 50 percent (1,245) had women.

51. Alvin P. Sanoff, "The Mixed Legacy of Women's Liberation," p. 61.

52. Scott Brown, Melissa Ludtke, and Martha Smilgis, "Onward Women," p. 82.

53. Karen O. Mason, J. L. Czajka, and S. Arber, "Change in U.S. Women's Sex-Role Attitudes, 1964-1974"; Andrew Cherlin and Pamela Barnhouse Walters, "Trends in U.S. Men's and Women's Sex-Role Attitudes."

54. Gelb and Palley, *Women and Public Policies,* pp. 5, 7-8.

55. Ibid., esp. pp. 1-13, 167-182.

56. For instrumental or social-pressure models, Marxist and elite theory examples assuming a narrow distribution of effective power include Ralph Miliband, *The State in Capitalist Society;* and G. William Domhoff, *The Higher Circles.* Pluralist examples assuming complex, uneven patters of power include Robert A. Dahl, *Pluralist Democracy in the United States;* and Nelson W. Polsby, *Community Power and Political Theory.* For examples of functionalist models assuming highly concentrated social power, see, e.g., Nicos Poulantzas, *Political Power and Social Classes;* or Fred L. Block, *Revising State Theory.* For examples assuming widely distributed and disputed power, see Talcott Parsons, "A Revised Analytical Approach to the Theory of Social Stratification"; or Harold L. Wilensky, *The Welfare State and Equality.* For examples of institutional or state-centered models, see James March and Johan P. Olsen, "The New Institutionalism"; Theda Skocpol, "Bringing the State Back In."

3. EMPLOYMENT

1. Claudia Goldin, *Understanding the Gender Gap;* Clarence D. Long, *The Labor Force under Changing Income and Employment;* Valerie Kincade Oppenheimer, *The Female Labor Force in the United States;* Julie A. Matthaei, *An Economic History of Women in America;* Barbara R. Bergmann, *The Economic Emergence of Women;* Alice Kessler-Harris, *Out to Work;* John D. Durand, *The Labor Force in the United States, 1890–1960;* and Lynn Y. Weiner, *From Working Girl to Working Mother.*
2. Bergmann, *Economic Emergence of Women.*
3. Oppenheimer, *Female Labor Force.*
4. Goldin, *Understanding the Gender Gap.*
5. Ibid., pp. 160–179; Oppenheimer, *Female Labor Force;* Samuel Cohn, *The Process of Occupational Sex-Typing.*
6. J. D. B. DeBow, *Statistical View of the United States.*
7. Kessler-Harris, *Out to Work,* pp. 70–71. For a fine study of urban women's employment, see Christine Stansell, *City of Women.*
8. The population census data from the nineteenth century are not accurate, but they offer a reasonable estimate. Data gathered separately through the Censuses of Manufactures also suggest that women must have held between one-fifth and one-quarter of jobs outside agriculture during the second half of the nineteenth century; Robert Max Jackson, *The Formation of Craft Labor Markets,* p. 148 n. 26.
9. The data do not let us distinguish between new and old jobs, but they do show what proportion of the increase in total jobs is accounted for by women's employment.
10. For more economic and demographic data on women in recent decades, consult Suzanne M. Bianchi and Daphne Spain, *American Women in Transition.*
11. Data (in Figure 3.1) are for women aged 10 and over, 1870–1880; 15 and over, 1890–1930; 14 and older, 1940–1960; 16 and older, 1970–1984. Data for 1920 do not distinguish single from divorced or widowed. Data for 1910 probably enumerated women's employment rates more completely than those for surrounding years; most likely the rates only increased between 1900 and 1930 rather than moving up and then down as the numbers make it appear. The earlier the data, the more likely that they are inaccurate and the more likely that they underestimate women's labor force participation. Many sources erroneously include all adult women in estimates of women's labor force participation over time. This confuses the picture because the number of elderly women, who rarely hold jobs, accounted for a steadily increasing proportion of the female population.
12. Tamara K. Hareven, *Family Time and Industrial Time;* Elizabeth H. Pleck, "A Mother's Wages"; Karen Oppenheim Mason and Barbara Laslett, "Women's Work in the American West"; Matthaei, *Economic History of Women in America.*

13. Goldin, *Understanding the Gender Gap.*

14. U.S. Bureau of the Census, *Historical Statistics of the United States* (hereafter *Historical Statistics*), vol. 1, p. 20.

15. Ibid., p. 132.

16. Ibid., p. 133. Married women constituted more than half of the women employed in only a small number of occupations in 1940, including various textile and needle-trades industries and laundries; charwomen; cooks; and owners or managers of "eating and drinking" places, lodging places, in miscellaneous wholesale or retail trades, and shops offering "personal services" (like hair cutting); Hooks, *Women's Occupations through Seven Decades*, p. 42. While they did not employ the largest number of married women, these occupations allowed working-class women to work after marriage, either because they paid low wages to both sexes or because they involved family enterprises.

17. For a study of the new, urban working woman, see Joanne J. Meyerowitz, *Women Adrift.*

18. Hooks, *Women's Occupations through Seven Decades*, p. 38.

19. *Historical Statistics*, vol. 1, pp. 11–12.

20. U.S. Bureau of the Census, *Statistical Abstract of the United States*, pp. 15, 399–400.

21. *Historical Statistics*, vol. 1, pp. 139–140; U.S. Bureau of the Census, *Statistical Abstract of the United States*, p. 405; Debra Renee Kaufman, "Professional Women," p. 355; U.S. Department of Labor, *Handbook of Labor Statistics: 1985*, p. 49.

22. *New York Times*, August 18, 1986, sec. D, pp. 1, 3.

23. Compare Long, *Labor Force under Changing Income and Employment*, pp. 135–136; Oppenheimer, *Female Labor Force*; Kessler-Harris, *Out to Work*; Samuel Cohn, *The Process of Occupational Sex-Typing*; Jacob Mincer, "Labor Force Participation of Married Women"; James P. Smith and Michael P. Ward, *Women's Wages and Work in the Twentieth Century*; Goldin, *Understanding the Gender Gap*, especially pp. 131–138.

24. Data are compiled from *Historical Statistics*, vol. 1, pp. 20–21, 129, 132, 133, 139–140; Hooks, *Women's Occupations through Seven Decades*, pp. 34, 222, 238; U.S. Department of Labor, Women's Bureau, *Time of Change*, pp. 12, 14, 55, 56; *Employment and Earnings* 36 (September 1989): 7; Alba M. Edwards, *Comparative Occupational Statistics for the United States, 1870 to 1940*, pp. 113–129; U.S. Department of Labor, Bureau of Labor Statistics, *Handbook of Labor Statistics: 1985*, pp. 7, 19, 115–122; U.S. Bureau of the Census, *Statistical Abstract of the United States: 1989*, pp. 385 (tables 637, 638), 428; idem, *Current Population Reports*, p. 3, table 1, "Marital Status and Living Arrangements: March 1988."

25. On immigration see William S. Bernard, "Immigration"; Leonard Dinnerstein and David M. Reimers, *Ethnic Americans*; Oscar Handlin, *The Uprooted*; Oscar Handlin, ed., *Immigration as a Factor in American History.*

26. *Historical Statistics*, vol. 1, pp. 105–106, 116.

27. Ibid., pp. 11–12, 96. The census defines places with fewer than 2,500 people as rural and those with more as urban.

28. Robert Max Jackson, *The Formation of Craft Labor Markets;* David R. Roediger and Philip S. Foner, *Our Own Time.*

29. Nathan Rosenberg, *Technology and American Economic Growth.*

30. Oppenheimer, *Female Labor Force;* Barbara F. Reskin and Patricia A. Roos, *Job Queues, Gender Queues.*

31. Carol A. Heimer, *Reactive Risk and Rational Action.*

32. Joseph H. Pleck, "The Work-Family Role System"; Elizabeth Pleck and Joseph H. Pleck, eds., *The American Man.*

33. However, another process could also have caused the various types of women to join the labor market in the same order. Family burdens could have dictated *women's* interest in taking jobs rather than employers' interest in hiring them. We will return to this alternative possibility shortly.

34. Data are from *Historical Statistics*, vol. 1, pp. 20–21, 133; Hooks, *Women's Occupations through Seven Decades*, p. 34; U.S. Department of Labor, Bureau of Labor Statistics, *Handbook of Labor Statistics: 1985*, pp. 7, 19, 115–122; U.S. Bureau of the Census, *Statistical Abstract of the United States: 1989*, tables 637, 638, p. 385; idem, *Current Population Reports*, p. 3, table 1, "Marital Status and Living Arrangements: March 1988."

35. Jerry A. Jacobs, *Revolving Doors;* Goldin, *Understanding the Gender Gap*, pp. 75–82. The index of dissimilarity used in these studies is not reliable because it depends on the categorization of occupations being used, and this is rather arbitrary.

36. Barbara F. Reskin, ed., *Sex Segregation in the Workplace;* Cohn, *The Process of Occupational Sex-Typing;* Oppenheimer, *Female Labor Force;* Ruth Milkman, *Gender at Work;* Jacobs, *Revolving Doors;* Reskin and Roos, *Job Queues, Gender Queues;* Harriet Bradley, *Men's Work, Women's Work;* Karen Oppenheim Mason, "Commentary"; Rosemary Crompton and Kay Sanderson, *Gendered Jobs and Social Change;* James N. Baron and William T. Bielby, "Organizational Barriers to Gender Equality"; Heidi Hartmann, "Capitalism, Patriarchy, and Job Segregation by Sex"; Solomon W. Polachek, "Occupational Segregation among Women."

37. Matthaei, *Economic History of Women in America.*

38. For examples, see Susan Porter Benson, *Counter Cultures;* Lisa M. Fine, *The Souls of the Skyscrapers;* Frances Gottfried, *The Merit System and Municipal Civil Service.*

39. Graham S. Lowe, *Women in the Administrative Revolution*, pp. 4–5; see also pp. 63–85.

40. Cf. Margery Davies, *Woman's Place Is at the Typewriter;* Ronald Gordon Walton, *Women in Social Work;* Lori D. Ginzberg, *Women and the Work of Benevolence;* David B. Tyack, *The One Best System;* Lynn D. Gordon, *Gender and Higher Education in the Progressive Era.*

41. Reskin and Roos, *Job Queues, Gender Queues.*

42. Oppenheimer, *Female Labor Force,* p. 120.

43. This contrasts with other secondary causes, such as women's lower rates of higher education, that had a consistent long-term secondary effect of reinforcing gender inequality.

44. Victor R. Fuchs's analysis of persisting sex differences in occupations, wages, and participation rates shows these theoretical concerns in a clear, thoughtful overview; *Women's Quest for Economic Equality,* pp. 33–57.

45. Benson, *Counter Cultures.*

46. Elyce J. Rotella, *From Home to Office,* esp. pp. 151–169. Cf. Fine, *The Souls of the Skyscrapers;* Anita J. Rapone, "Clerical Labor Force Formation"; Lowe, *Women in the Administrative Revolution;* Paul Attewell, "The Clerk Deskilled"; Davies, *Woman's Place Is at the Typewriter;* David B. Tyack and Myra H. Strober, "Jobs and Gender"; and Kessler-Harris, *Out to Work.*

47. U.S. Department of Labor, *Eleventh Annual Report of the Commissioner of Labor, 1895–6,* pp. 30–31.

48. E.g., D'Ann Campbell, *Women at War with America.*

49. Goldin, *Understanding the Gender Gap,* pp. 34, 235 n. 27.

50. Ibid., pp. 33–46.

51. *Historical Statistics,* vol. 1, pp. 128–129.

52. Some studies of women's employment in the early twentieth century have also suggested little responsiveness to wage rates (although this is not quite the same as the number of jobs offered). See Martha Norby Fraundorf, "The Labor Force Participation of Turn-of-the-Century Married Women"; Rotella, *From Home to Office,* esp. pp. 56–60.

53. Leslie Woodcock Tentler, *Wage Earning-Women,* pp. 1, 8.

54. U.S. Department of Labor, *Dual Careers,* pp. 21, 196.

55. Richard A. Berk, "The New Home Economics"; Gary Becker, "Human Capital, Effort, and the Sexual Division of Labor"; Sarah Fenstermaker Berk, *The Gender Factory;* Heidi Hartmann, "The Family as the Locus of Gender, Class, and Political Struggle."

56. For an overview of the relevant changes, see Steven Mintz and Susan Kellogg, *Domestic Revolutions.*

57. E. A. Wrigley, *Population and History;* Carlo Cipolla, *The Economic History of World Population;* Susan Householder Van Horn, *Women, Work, and Fertility, 1900–1986;* William J. Goode, *World Revolution and Family Patterns;* Ronald R. Rindfuss, S. Philip Morgan, and C. Gray Swicegood, *First Births in America.*

58. Maxine L. Margolis, *Mothers and Such;* Susan Strasser, *Never Done;* Ruth Schwartz Cowan, *More Work for Mother.*

59. Oppenheimer, *Female Labor Force,* pp. 25–63; Cowan, *More Work for Mother;* Margolis, *Mothers and Such,* pp. 108–109.

60. Joann Vanek, "Time Spent in Housework."

61. Hartmann, "The Family as the Locus of Gender, Class, and Political Strug-

gle;" Berk, *The Gender Factory;* Joseph H. Pleck, *Working Wives, Working Husbands.*

62. Vanek, "Time Spent in Housework."

63. Because the data ignore the *intensity* of labor, they show the time devoted to domestic work, not the amount of work accomplished. The amount of work should be measured as the product of time spent working and the intensity of effort.

64. Betty Friedan, *The Feminine Mystique.*

65. Jacob Mincer and Solomon Polachek, "Family Investments in Human Capital"; Mary Corcoran and Greg J. Duncan, "Work History, Labor Force Attachment, and Earnings Differences between the Races and Sexes." For some criticism and doubts about these effects see Mary Corcoran, Greg J. Duncan, and Michael Ponza, "Work Experience, Job Segregation, and Wages."

66. The value of this improved competitiveness was, however, restricted within the bounds set by the sex segregation of occupations. See Chapter 5.

67. On the relationship between divorce and women's employment, see Richard Peterson, *Women, Work, and Divorce.*

68. Bergmann's *Economic Emergence of Women* explicitly argues this, but diverse other economists have agreed.

69. For direct evidence on the influence of domestic circumstances, see Jennifer Glass, "Job Quits and Job Changes."

70. Gary Becker, *The Economics of Discrimination.*

71. Edmund S. Phelps, "The Statistical Theory of Racism and Sexism."

72. For a strong historical argument, see Hartmann, "Capitalism, Patriarchy, and Job Segregation by Sex."

73. Kenneth Arrow, "The Theory of Discrimination."

74. Max Weber, *Economy and Society;* Wolfgang Schluchter, *The Rise of Western Rationalism;* Jürgen Habermas, *The Theory of Communicative Action.*

75. See, e.g., Reinhard Bendix, *Work and Authority in Industry.*

76. For a parallel argument see Thomas A. DiPrete and David B. Grusky, "Structure and Trend in the Process of Stratification for American Men and Women."

77. James E. Rosenbaum, *Career Mobility in a Corporate Hierarchy,* shows how affirmative action policy in a firm caused significant reductions in sex segregation.

78. See Michael J. Carter and Susan Boslego Carter, "Women's Recent Progress in the Professions."

79. Bregger, "Self-Employment in the United States, 1948–62."

80. This is the reverse of conditions that made it difficult for employers to hire women for jobs associated with male labor markets.

4. INSTITUTIONAL INDIVIDUALISM

1. Steven Lukes, *Individualism.* For examples of alternative treatments see Alan Macfarlane, *The Origins of English Individualism;* W. Richard Scott and

John W. Meyer, *Institutional Environments and Organizations;* Daniel Shanahan, *Toward a Genealogy of Individualism.*

2. For thoughtful discussions see Talcott Parsons, *The Structure of Social Action;* and Marvin Harris, *Cultural Materialism.* Alexis de Tocqueville's *Democracy in America* appeared in 1835, Henry Sumner Maine published *Ancient Law* in 1861, Ferdinand Tönnies presented his ideas in *Gemeinschaft und Gesellschaft* in 1887, and Emile Durkheim introduced his ideas about solidarity in *The Division of Labor in Society* in 1893.

3. Talcott Parsons, *The Social System.*

4. David B. Tyack, *The One Best System;* Mabel Newcomer, *A Century of Higher Education for American Women;* David B. Tyack and Elisabeth Hansot, *Learning Together;* Nancy F. Cott, *The Bonds of Womanhood.*

5. Tyack and Hansot, *Learning Together;* and John L. Rury, *Education and Women's Work,* document America's widespread and rapid acceptance of coeducation. Unfortunately, although they describe it well, they do not explain it successfully.

6. *Historical Statistics,* vol. 1, pp. 375, 379. The share of all youths receiving high school degrees increased from about 6 percent in 1900 to about 75 percent in 1970.

7. Data are from *Historical Statistics,* vol. 1, pp. 379–380, 385–386; U.S. Department of Education, *The Condition of Education: 1984,* pp. 58, 88, 98; idem, *Digest of Education Statistics, 1996,* pp. 253, 281.

8. See Rury, *Education and Women's Work.*

9. *Historical Statistics,* vol. 1, p. 375.

10. Barbara Miller Solomon, *In the Company of Educated Women.*

11. Newcomer, *Century of Higher Education,* p. 37. On coeducation see Newcomer, pp. 35–51; Solomon, *In the Company of Educated Women,* pp. 43–61; Sheila M. Rothman, *Woman's Proper Place;* Patricia A. Graham, "Expansion and Exclusion"; Thomas Woody, *A History of Women's Education in the United States;* Cynthia Fuchs Epstein, *Woman's Place.*

12. Solomon, *In the Company of Educated Women,* pp. 62–77.

13. Susan Ware, *Beyond Suffrage,* pp. 21–23.

14. The evidence on changing inheritance is not precise. See, e.g., Carole Shammas, Marylynn Salmon, and Michel Dahlin, *Inheritance in America;* Susan Grigg, "Women and Family Property."

15. The first generation of college-educated women is well known to have experienced a relatively low rate of marriage. Exceptional and unusual women chose to be among the first attending college, and it is difficult to say if their college experience had any effect on their marriage experiences. This does not controvert the observation that some middle-class families hoped daughters might find a better husband by going to college.

16. Newcomer, *Century of Higher Education,* p. 49.

17. Angell quoted in Annie Nathan Meyer, *Woman's Work in America,* pp. 78–79.

18. Elizabeth Cady Stanton, Susan B. Anthony, Matilda Joslyn Gage, and Ida Husted Harper, eds., *The History of Woman Suffrage,* vol. 4, p. 966.

19. Newcomer, *Century of Higher Education*, pp. 72–103; Jerry A. Jacobs, *Revolving Doors*.

20. Some evidence supports the claim that medical schools began applying the same admissions standards to women and men before modern affirmative action policies or modern feminist beliefs had any effects (Stephen Cole, "Sex Discrimination and Admission to Medical School, 1929–1984"), so that women's low representation reflects a lack of interest. While this evidence probably accurately represents a surface truth, it neglects widespread discriminatory processes that allowed medical schools to achieve the appearance of impartiality while still avoiding the assimilation of women. Cf. Judith Lorber, *Women Physicians*. See also Robert Fiorentine and Stephen Cole, "Why Fewer Women Become Physicians."

21. On the determinants of curricula, see Randall Collins, *The Credential Society*; Margaret Scotford Archer, *Social Origins of Educational Systems*; Ivor Goodson, *School Subjects and Curriculum Change*; Herbert M. Kliebard, *The Struggle for the American Curriculum, 1893–1958*; John Boli, Francisco O. Ramirez, and John W. Meyer, "Explaining the Origins and Expansion of Mass Education."

22. Tyack, *The One Best System*; Tyack and Hansot, *Learning Together*.

23. Edward T. James, Janet Wilson James, and Paul S. Boyer, eds., *Notable American Women, 1607–1950*.

24. Collins, *The Credential Society*.

25. Michael Young, *The Rise of the Meritocracy, 1870–2033*.

26. Reinhard Bendix, *Work and Authority in Industry*; Carl N. Degler, *In Search of Human Nature*; Richard Hofstadter, *Social Darwinism in American Thought, 1860–1915*. For a recent example of derivative thinking, see Robert Wright, *The Moral Animal*.

27. Max Weber, *Economy and Society*; Richard Edwards, *Contested Terrain*.

28. Max Weber, *Max Weber on Law in Economy and Society*. On Weber's conceptions of rationality see Stephen Kalberg, "Max Weber's Types of Rationality."

29. But for an analysis of the public civil service's direct effects on women's employment, see Frances Gottfried, *The Merit System and Municipal Civil Service*.

30. John Meyer and his students show a strong similarity in the curriculum coverage of primary education across nations in Aaron Benavot et al., "Knowledge for the Masses."

31. C. James Quann, "Grades and Grading"; Mark W. Durm, "An A Is Not an A"; Tyack, *The One Best System*.

32. Tyack and Hansot, *Learning Together*; Rury, *Education and Women's Work*.

33. See, e.g., Deborah Rhode's comments on the judiciary in *Justice and Gender*, pp. 19–28.

34. Cf. Christopher Lasch, *Haven in a Heartless World*.

35. Carl N. Degler, *At Odds*; J. E. Goldthorpe, *Family Life in Western Societies*;

Jack Goody, Joan Thirsk, and E. P. Thompson, eds., *Family and Inheritance;* Edward Shorter, *The Making of the Modern Family.*

36. While some societies have applied their kinship terminology to fairly extensive clans and the like, these commonly are forms of political organization imposed on the family institution. A large clan is not a family. How we should assess the family as an institution in these cases is open to debate, but need not concern us here.

37. E.g., David Popenoe, *Disturbing the Nest.*

38. Talcott Parsons and Robert F. Bales, *Family Socialization and Interaction Process.* A good, brief review of criticism received by the isolated family idea appears in Steven Ruggles, "The Transformation of American Family Structure," pp. 104–105.

39. William J. Goode, "Why Men Resist."

40. This idea is consistent with Barbara Ehrenreich's contention, in *The Hearts of Men,* that middle-class men began to rebel against family life and to abandon it well before modern feminism sprang to life. See Chapter 6 for further discussion.

41. Andrew J. Cherlin, *Marriage, Divorce, Remarriage;* Paul H. Jacobson, *American Marriage and Divorce;* Kingsley Davis, "The American Family in Relation to Demographic Change."

42. Roderick Phillips, *Putting Asunder;* Elaine Tyler May, *Great Expectations* and "The Pressure to Provide"; William O'Neill, *Divorce in the Progressive Era;* George E. Howard, *A History of Matrimonial Institutions;* Nelson M. Blake, *The Road to Reno;* Degler, *At Odds;* Robert L. Griswold, *Family and Divorce in California, 1850–1890.*

43. On power relations between spouses see Dair L. Gillespie, "Who Has the Power?"; Rebecca L. Warner, Gary R. Lee, and Janet Lee, "Social Organization, Spousal Resources, and Marital Power"; Carolyn Vogler and Jan Pahl, "Money, Power and Inequality within Marriage"; Sara Arber and Jay Ginn, "The Marriage of Gender Equality"; Karen D. Pyke, "Women's Employment as a Gift or Burden?"; Janeen Baxter, "Power Attitudes and Time."

44. Willard Walter Waller, *The Family.*

45. Waller's idea may be properly interpreted as one elegant, nonmathematical precursor to modern game theory.

46. Goody, Thirsk, and Thompson, *Family and Inheritance;* Grigg, "Women and Family Property"; Ann R. Tickamyer, "Wealth and Power"; Marylynn Salmon, *Women and the Law of Property in Early America;* Shammas, Salmon, and Dahlin, *Inheritance in America.*

47. For simplicity, I ignore here the wide range of patterns between impartible and partible inheritance, e.g., the classic presentation in H. J. Habakkuk, "Family Structure and Economic Change in Nineteenth-Century Europe."

48. John H. Langbein, "The Inheritance Revolution."

49. These numbers represent the predicted distribution assuming male and female births were equally likely.

50. These estimates are derived from birth cohort data, *Historical Statistics,* vol. 1, pp. 53–54. The actual number of families with only daughters is difficult to estimate accurately. Reproduction rates varied considerably by class and location (particularly rural versus urban). Also, several generations with divergent histories coexist at any time. This means that one must have precise data about specific groups to achieve accurate and thorough estimates. The average number of children born to white urban women (including all classes), for example, was probably about 3.5 in 1800 and declined to about 2.5 by 1900; during the 1800s, the proportion of the population living in urban areas rose from 5 percent to 40 percent.

5. WOMEN'S REJECTION OF SUBORDINATION

1. For full bibliographic information on these and other books, see Duane R. Bogenschneider, ed., *The Gerritsen Collection of Women's History, 1543–1945.*
2. Andrew J. Cherlin and Pamela Barnhouse Walters, "Trends in U.S. Men's and Women's Sex-Role Attitudes"; Karen O. Mason, J. L. Czajka, and S. Arber, "Change in U.S. Women's Sex-Role Attitudes, 1964–1974"; Janeen Baxter, "Is Husband's Class Enough?"
3. For a recent assessment, see Scott J. South and Glenna Spitze, "Housework in Marital and Nonmarital Households."
4. See, e.g., Nancy Cott, *The Grounding of Modern Feminism.*
5. Neil Smelser, *Theory of Collective Behavior;* John D. McCarthy and Mayer N. Zald, "Resource Mobilization and Social Movements"; Doug McAdam, *Political Process and the Development of Black Insurgency, 1930–1970;* William A. Gamson, *The Strategy of Social Protest;* Russell Hardin, *Collective Action;* Charles Tilly, *From Mobilization to Revolution;* Jean L. Cohen, "Strategy or Identity"; Anthony Oberschall, *Social Movements;* Sidney G. Tarrow, *Power in Movement.*
6. It is possible to phrase these questions in terms of severity rather than in terms of numbers of women, for example, by asking if women were more dissatisfied. But there have always been some women at every level of satisfaction with their circumstances, from delighted to distraught. And it is better to avoid the ambiguity created by discussing dissatisfaction, freedom, or other attributes of individuals as if they increased or decreased for all women.
7. For a much more detailed examination of these questions and other related ones, see Steven M. Buechler, *Women's Movements in the United States.* Buechler's interpretations differ in some cases from those offered here.
8. Anita J. Rapone, "Clerical Labor Force Formation."
9. Mabel Newcomer, *A Century of Higher Education for American Women;* Barbara Miller Solomon, *In the Company of Educated Women.*
10. See Chapters 1 and 3 for more details on women's employment. Based on data in *Historical Statistics,* vol. 1, pp. 139–140; Alba M. Edwards, *Com-*

parative Occupational Statistics for the United States, 1870 to 1940, pp. 113–129; U.S. Department of Labor, Women's Bureau, *Time of Change,* pp. 55–56.

11. Leslie Woodcock Tentler, *Wage-Earning Women.*

12. Theodora Penny Martin, *The Sound of Our Own Voices.*

13. Ibid.; Lori D. Ginzberg, *Women and the Work of Benevolence;* Jack S. Blocker, "Separate Paths."

14. Elizabeth Cady Stanton, Susan B. Anthony, Matilda Joslyn Gage, and Ida Husted Harper, eds., *The History of Woman Suffrage,* vol. 4, pp. 1042–73.

15. Ibid.; Eleanor Flexner, *Century of Struggle;* Aileen S. Kraditor, *The Ideas of the Woman Suffrage Movement, 1890–1920;* William L. O'Neill, *Everyone Was Brave;* Buechler, *Women's Movements in the United States;* Ellen Carol DuBois, *Feminism and Suffrage.* Richard J. Evans, *The Feminists,* provides comparisons with other countries.

16. Janet Saltzman Chafetz and and Anthony Gary Dworkin, *Female Revolt.*

17. See Evans, *The Feminists;* and Chafetz and Dworkin, *Female Revolt.* For suffrage dates see Ruth Leger Sivard, *Women: A World Survey;* and Elise Boulding et al., *Handbook of International Data on Women.* Chafetz and Dworkin, for example, conclude that the countries named in the text (among others) never had more than incipient women's movements when they achieved suffrage (pp. 105–162).

18. Myra Marx Ferree and Beth Hess, *Controversy and Coalition;* Jo Freeman, *The Politics of Women's Liberation;* Judith Hole and Ellen Levine, *Rebirth of Feminism;* Ethel Klein, *Gender Politics;* Leila J. Rupp and Verta Taylor, *Survival in the Doldrums;* and Cynthia Ellen Harrison, *On Account of Sex.*

19. See, e.g., Freeman, *The Politics of Women's Liberation.*

20. *Historical Statistics,* vol. 1, pp. 383, 140.

21. This experience is comparable to that of labor unions, which rarely become effective unless they achieve the organizational conditions necessary to compel, or at least induce, conformity to their policy decisions. See Mancur Olson, *The Logic of Collective Action;* Robert Max Jackson, *The Formation of Craft Labor Markets.*

22. Joyce Gelb and Marian Lief Palley, *Women and Public Policies.*

23. Viola Klein, *The Feminine Character.*

24. See, e.g., Jessie Bernard's argument that feminism serves society by forcing it to properly accommodate structural changes; "Foreword," in Ferree and Hess, *Controversy and Coalition.*

25. Barbara Ehrenreich, *The Hearts of Men;* Mirra Komarovsky, "Cultural Contradictions and Sex Roles."

26. On antifeminism see Margaret Hobbs, "Rethinking Antifeminism in the 1930s"; Susan E. Marshall, "In Defense of Separate Spheres" and "Who Speaks for American Women?"; Erin Steuter, "Women against Feminism"; Anne M. Benjamin, *A History of the Anti-Suffrage Movement in the United States from 1895 to 1920.*

27. Cynthia Fuchs Epstein, *Woman's Place*, p. 129.
28. Jane Mansbridge, *Why We Lost the ERA*; Mary Frances Berry, *Why ERA Failed*; Susan E. Marshall, "Keep Us on the Pedestal"; Carole J. Sheffield, "Sexual Terrorism."
29. Quoted in Marshall, "Keep Us on the Pedestal," p. 574.
30. Kristin Luker, *Abortion and the Politics of Motherhood*.
31. Luker (ibid., p. 196) found that anti-abortion activists were three times as likely to have been raised as Catholics. Although sampling deficiencies make these numbers unreliable, they suggest the importance of early cultural milieus for determining the life choices that result in adult commitments. More interesting, Luker also found that one-fifth of the anti-abortionists had converted to Catholicism, while an equivalent one-fifth of pro-choice activists had abandoned the Catholicism of their childhoods. This result suggests the willingness of adults to adopt new ideologies and associations that are suited to their interests.

6. SURRENDERING THE HERITAGE OF MALE DOMINANCE

1. Joseph Pleck, *The Myth of Masculinity*; Elizabeth H. Pleck and Joseph H. Pleck, eds., *The American Man*; Michael S. Kimmel and Michael A. Messner, *Men's Lives*; Kenneth C. Clatterbaugh, *Contemporary Perspectives on Masculinity*.
2. See, e.g., Herb Goldberg, *The Hazards of Being Male*; Richard Haddad, "The Men's Liberation Movement"; and Warren Farrell, *Why Men Are the Way They Are*.
3. Richard Haddad, "Concepts and Overview of the Men's Liberation Movement," p. 285.
4. Rosabeth Moss Kanter, *Men and Women of the Corporation*.
5. Harriet Bradley, *Men's Work, Women's Work*.
6. Lynn Y. Weiner, *From Working Girl to Working Mother*.
7. This argument assumes that men have no greater inherent lust for dominance than do women. I cannot perceive any strategy to measure the value of subservience per se. While there are many who seem to believe that wielding power over other people is innately pleasing (including people of all political and theoretical leanings), I remain doubtful. I suspect that people must learn to enjoy the subservience of others, or they must be placed in difficult positions where power gives compensatory advantages.
8. Robert Max Jackson, *The Formation of Craft Labor Markets*.
9. Susan Lehrer, *Origins of Protective Labor Legislation for Women, 1905–1925*; Joy Parr, *The Gender of Breadwinners*; Joan Acker, *Doing Comparable Worth*; Diane Balser, *Sisterhood and Solidarity*; Sonya O. Rose, *Limited Livelihoods*.
10. Penina Migdal Glazer and Miriam Slater, *Unequal Colleagues*; Cynthia Fuchs

Epstein, *Woman's Place;* Patricia A. Graham, "Expansion and Exclusion"; Joyce Antler, *Educated Women;* Bradley, *Men's Work, Women's Work.*

11. Robert Max Jackson and Ralph Chipman, "The Growth of Male Support for Woman Suffrage in American States."

12. Kanter, *Men and Women of the Corporation,* pp. 47–49, 59–63.

13. Cf. Susan M. Hartmann, *From Margin to Mainstream;* Virginia Sapiro, *The Political Integration of Women;* Ethel Klein, *Gender Politics.*

14. Barbara Ehrenreich and Deirdre English, *For Her Own Good,* made this point clearly in a discussion of Helen Gurley Brown, author of *Sex and the Single Girl* (1962) and longtime editor of *Cosmopolitan.* They suggest that Brown's message praising the life of the sexy, active single women succeeded because "she grasped the appalling fact . . . that men didn't like the suburban ideal . . . Men resented their domestication, and hated the company of sexless 'Moms'" (p. 287).

15. Barbara Ehrenreich, *The Hearts of Men.*

16. Kathleen Gerson, *No Man's Land,* pp. 266–267.

17. Ehrenreich's work provides no evidence that the period following World War II should be singled out as she has done. The nineteenth-century temperance movement (to which Ehrenreich refers in another context) was also aimed at a fear of male irresponsibility. The divorce rate has been rising for a full century. Examples of male literature that complained about marriage are hardly a recent phenomenon. And men still have not yet engaged in a mass exodus from the institution of marriage. Thus it remains to be shown that the changes since World War II have been as unprecedented as Ehrenreich suggests.

18. Cf. Kristin Luker, *Abortion and the Politics of Motherhood.*

7. THE END OF INEQUALITY?

1. E.g., Barbara Bergmann, *Economic Emergence of Women;* Victor R. Fuchs, *Women's Quest for Economic Equality.*

2. E.g., Susan Lehrer, *Origins of Protective Labor Legislation for Women, 1905–1925.*

3. E.g., Janet Saltzman Chafetz, *Gender Equity;* Randall Collins et al., "Toward an Integrated Theory of Gender Stratification"; Joan Huber, "A Theory of Gender Stratification."

4. E.g., Steven E. Buechler, *Women's Movements in the United States;* Ellen Carol DuBois, *Feminism and Suffrage;* Olive Banks, *Faces of Feminism;* Richard J. Evans, *The Feminists;* Myra Marx Ferree and Beth Hess, *Controversy and Coalition;* William L. O'Neill, *Everyone Was Brave;* Eleanor Flexner, *Century of Struggle.*

5. Examples of these are legion. Notable are Catharine A. MacKinnon, *Toward a Feminist Theory of the State;* Susan Brownmiller, *Against Our Will.*

6. Occupations changed considerably over time, of course, as a result of general economic and technological changes. The assimilation of women, however, had little influence on these changes.

7. We seem unable to determine if *separating* gender from the structures of public inequality is simpler or harder than *dismantling* the structure of family inequality. Disembedding status inequality and undoing positional family role differentiation are extremely complex and interdependent processes. Both happen gradually over many decades. We have no way to measure the difficulty of either process. The time needed for either process will depend greatly on historical conditions. We must conclude that we cannot compare the difficulty of these two processes.

8. Kathleen Gerson, *No Man's Land.*

9. A snowball effect happens when the frequency of some event is an increasing function of previous occurrences. A threshold effect happens when the recurrence or accumulation of some events at some point results in a discontinuous change or a new event greater than the simple sum of the preceding events.

10. This circumvents controversies about rationality assumptions in theoretical models. See, e.g., Barry Hindess, *Choice, Rationality, and Social Theory;* and Pierre Birnbaum and Jean Leca, eds., *Individualism.*

11. Some theorists have forcefully argued that the intrusion of market economies and Western political systems into *simpler* societies has worsened women's status. In essence, gender statuses in these societies get dragged down toward the pattern of inequality that was common in Europe on the brink of industrialization. Often only after this decline do the opposite tendencies of modern societies begin to reduce gender inequality.

12. Quoted in Susan Groag Bell and Karen M. Offen, *Women, the Family, and Freedom,* vol. 1, pp. 38, 41.

BIBLIOGRAPHY

Acker, Joan. *Doing Comparable Worth: Gender, Class, and Pay Equity.* Philadelphia: Temple University Press, 1989.

Antler, Joyce. *The Educated Woman and Professionalization: The Struggle for a New Feminine Identity, 1890–1920.* New York: Garland, 1987.

Arber, Sara, and Jay Ginn. "The Marriage of Gender Equality: Occupational Success in the Labour Market and within Marriage." *British Journal of Sociology* 46 (1995): 21–43.

Archer, Margaret Scotford. *Social Origins of Educational Systems.* London: Sage, 1979.

Arrow, Kenneth. "The Theory of Discrimination." In *Discrimination in Labor Markets,* ed. Orley Ashenfelter and Albert Rees. Princeton: Princeton University Press, 1973.

Attewell, Paul. "The Clerk Deskilled: A Study in False Nostalgia." *Journal of Historical Sociology* 2 (1989): 357–388.

Baer, Judith A. *The Chains of Protection: The Judicial Response to Women's Labor Legislation.* Westport, Conn.: Greenwood Press, 1978.

Balser, Diane. *Sisterhood and Solidarity: Feminism and Labor in Modern Times.* Boston: South End Press, 1987.

Banks, Olive. *Faces of Feminism.* Oxford: Martin Robertson, 1981.

Baron, James N., and William T. Bielby. "Organizational Barriers to Gender Equality: Sex Segregation of Jobs and Opportunities." In *Gender and the Life Course,* ed. Alice Rossi. New York: Aldine, 1985.

Basch, Norma. *In the Eyes of the Law: Women, Marriage, and Property in Nineteenth-Century New York.* Ithaca: Cornell University Press, 1982.

Baxter, Janeen. "Is Husband's Class Enough? Class Location and Class Identity in the United States, Sweden, Norway, and Australia." *American Sociological Review* 59 (1994): 220–235.

——— "Power Attitudes and Time: The Domestic Division of Labour." *Journal of Comparative Family Studies* 23 (1992): 165–182.

Becker, Gary. *The Economics of Discrimination.* Chicago: University of Chicago Press, 1957.

——— "Human Capital, Effort, and the Sexual Division of Labor." *Journal of Labor Economics,* suppl. 3 (1985): S33–S58.

Beer, William. "Sociology and the Effects of Affirmative Action: A Case of Neglect." *American Sociologist,* Fall 1988: 218–231.

Beeton, Beverly. *Women Vote in the West: The Woman Suffrage Movement, 1869–1896.* New York: Garland, 1986.

Bell, Spurgeon. *Productivity, Wages, and National Income.* Washington, D.C.: Brookings Institution, 1940.

Bell, Susan Groag, and Karen M. Offen, eds. *Women, the Family, and Freedom: The Debate in Documents.* 2 vols. Stanford: Stanford University Press, 1983.

Benavot, Aaron, Yun-Kyung Cha, David Kamens, John W. Meyer, and Suk-Ying Wong. "Knowledge for the Masses: World Models and National Curricula, 1920–1986." *American Sociological Review* 56 (1991): 85–100.

Bendix, Reinhard. *Nation-Building and Citizenship.* New York: John Wiley, 1964.

——— *Work and Authority in Industry: Ideologies of Management in the Course of Industrialization.* New York: John Wiley, 1956.

Benjamin, Anne M. *A History of the Anti-Suffrage Movement in the United States from 1895 to 1920: Women against Equality.* Lewiston, N.Y.: Edwin Mellen Press, 1991.

Benson, Susan Porter. *Counter Cultures: Saleswomen, Managers, and Customers in American Department Stores, 1890–1940.* Urbana: University of Illinois Press, 1986.

Bergmann, Barbara R. *The Economic Emergence of Women.* New York: Basic Books, 1986.

Berk, Richard A. "The New Home Economics: An Agenda for Sociological Research." In *Women and Household Labor,* ed. Sarah Fenstermaker Berk. Beverly Hills: Sage, 1980.

Berk, Sarah Fenstermaker. *The Gender Factory: The Apportionment of Work in American Households.* New York: Plenum, 1985.

Bernard, William S. "Immigration: History of U.S. Policy." In *The Harvard Encyclopedia of American Ethnic Groups,* ed. Stephan Thernstrom. Cambridge, Mass.: The Belknap Press of Harvard University Press, 1980.

Berry, Mary Frances. *Why ERA Failed.* Bloomington: Indiana University Press, 1986.

Bianchi, Suzanne M., and Daphne Spain. *American Women in Transition.* New York: Russell Sage, 1986.

Birnbaum, Pierre, and Jean Leca, eds. *Individualism: Theories and Methods.* Oxford: Clarendon Press, 1990.

Block, Fred L. *Revising State Theory: Essays in Politics and Postindustrialism.* Philadelphia: Temple University Press, 1987.

Blocker, Jack S. "Separate Paths: Suffragists and the Women's Temperance Crusade." *Signs* 10 (1985): 460–476.

Bogenschneider, Duane R., ed. *The Gerritsen Collection of Women's History, 1543–1945: A Bibliographic Guide to the Microform Collection.* Sanford, N.C.: Microfilming Corporation of America, 1983.

Boli, John, Francisco O. Ramirez, and John W. Meyer. "Explaining the Origins and Expansion of Mass Education." *Comparative Education Review* 29 (1985): 145–170.

Boulding, Elise, et al. *Handbook of International Data on Women.* New York: Sage, 1976.

Bradley, Harriet. *Men's Work, Women's Work.* Minneapolis: University of Minnesota Press, 1989.

Bregger, John E. "Self-Employment in the United States, 1948–62." *Monthly Labor Review* 76 (January 1963): 37–43.

Brownmiller, Susan. *Against Our Will: Men, Women, and Rape.* New York: Simon and Schuster, 1975.

Buechler, Steven. *Women's Movements in the United States: Woman Suffrage, Equal Rights, and Beyond.* New Brunswick, N.J.: Rutgers University Press, 1990.

Campbell, D'Ann. *Women at War with America: Private Lives in a Patriotic Era.* Cambridge, Mass.: Harvard University Press, 1984.

Carnes, Mark Christopher. *Secret Ritual and Manhood in Victorian America.* New Haven: Yale University Press, 1989.

Carter, Michael J., and Susan Boslego Carter. "Women's Recent Progress in the Professions; or, Women Get a Ticket to Ride after the Gravy Train Has Left the Station." *Feminist Studies* 7 (1981): 477–504.

Catt, Carrie Chapman, and Nettie Rogers Shuler. *Woman Suffrage and Politics.* New York: Charles Scribner's Sons, 1923.

Chafetz, Janet Saltzman. *Gender Equity: An Integrated Theory of Stability and Change.* Newbury Park, Calif.: Sage, 1990.

Chafetz, Janet Saltzman, and Anthony Gary Dworkin. *Female Revolt: Women's Movements in World and Historical Perspective.* Totowa, N.J.: Rowman and Allanheld, 1986.

Cherlin, Andrew J. *Marriage, Divorce, Remarriage.* Cambridge, Mass.: Harvard University Press, 1981.

Cherlin, Andrew J., and Pamela Barnhouse Walters. "Trends in U.S. Men's and Women's Sex Role Attitudes: 1972–1978." *American Sociological Review* 46 (1981): 453–460.

Cipolla, Carlo. *The Economic History of World Population.* Rev. ed. Baltimore: Penguin, 1964.

Clatterbaugh, Kenneth C. *Contemporary Perspectives on Masculinity: Men, Women, and Politics.* Boulder: Westview Press, 1990.

Cohen, Jean L. "Strategy or Identity: New Theoretical Paradigms and Contemporary Social Movements." *Social Research* 52 (1985): 663–716.

Cohn, Samuel. *The Process of Occupational Sex-Typing: The Feminization of*

Clerical Labor in Great Britain, 1870–1936. Philadelphia: Temple University Press, 1986.

Cole, Stephen. "Sex Discrimination and Admission to Medical School, 1929–1984." *American Journal of Sociology* 92 (1986): 549–567.

Coleman, James Samuel. *Foundations of Social Theory.* Cambridge, Mass.: Harvard University Press, 1990.

Collins, Randall. "A Conflict Theory of Sexual Stratification." *Social Problems* 19 (1971): 3–21.

——— *The Credential Society: An Historical Sociology of Education and Stratification.* Orlando, Fla.: Academic Press, 1979.

Collins, Randall, Janet Saltzman Chafetz, Rae Lesser Blumberg, Scott Coltrane, and Jonathan H. Turner. "Toward an Integrated Theory of Gender Stratification." *Sociological Perspectives* 36 (1993): 185–216.

Corcoran, Mary, and Greg J. Duncan. "Work History, Labor Force Attachment, and Earnings Differences between the Races and Sexes." *Journal of Human Resources* 14 (1979): 3–20.

Corcoran, Mary, Greg J. Duncan, and Michael Ponza. "Work Experience, Job Segregation, and Wages." In *Sex Segregation in the Workplace: Trends, Explanations, Remedies,* ed. Barbara F. Reskin. Washington, D.C.: National Academy Press, 1984.

Cott, Nancy F. *The Bonds of Womanhood: "Woman's Sphere" in New England, 1780–1835.* New Haven: Yale University Press, 1977.

——— *The Grounding of Modern Feminism.* New Haven: Yale University Press, 1987.

Cowan, Ruth Schwartz. *More Work for Mother: The Ironies of Household Technology from the Open Hearth to the Microwave.* New York: Basic Books, 1983.

Crompton, Rosemary, and Kay Sanderson. *Gendered Jobs and Social Change.* London: Unwin Hyman, 1990.

Dahl, Robert A. *Pluralist Democracy in the United States: Conflict and Consent.* Chicago: Rand McNally, 1967.

Davies, Margery W. *Woman's Place Is at the Typewriter: Office Work and Office Workers, 1870–1930.* Philadelphia: Temple University Press, 1982.

Davis, Kingsley. "The American Family in Relation to Demographic Change." In Commission on Population Growth and the American Future, *Research Reports.* Vol. 1: *Demographic and Social Aspects of Population Growth,* ed. Charles F. Westoff and Robert Parke Jr. Washington, D.C.: Government Printing Office, 1972.

DeBow, J. D. B. *Statistical View of the United States: Being a Compendium of the Seventh Census.* 1854; reprint, New York: Gordon and Breach Science Publishers, 1970.

Deckard, Barbara Sinclair. *The Women's Movement: Political, Socioeconomic, and Psychological Issues.* New York: Harper & Row, 1979.

Degler, Carl N. *At Odds: Women and the Family in America from the Revolution to the Present.* New York: Oxford University Press, 1980.

—— In Search of Human Nature: The Decline and Revival of Darwinism in American Social Thought. New York: Oxford University Press, 1991.

Dinnerstein, Leonard, and David M. Reimers. Ethnic Americans: A History of Immigration and Assimilation. New York: New York University Press, 1977.

DiPrete, Thomas A., and David B. Grusky. "Structure and Trend in the Process of Stratification for American Men and Women." American Journal of Sociology 96 (1990): 107–143.

Domhoff, G. William. The Higher Circles: The Governing Class in America. New York: Random House, 1970.

Dubbert, Joe L. A Man's Place: Masculinity in Transition. Englewood Cliffs, N.J.: Prentice-Hall, 1979.

DuBois, Ellen Carol. Feminism and Suffrage: The Emergence of an Independent Women's Movement in America, 1848–1869. Ithaca: Cornell University Press, 1978.

Duby, Georges. Rural Economy and Country Life in the Medieval West. Trans. Cynthia Postan. Columbia: University of South Carolina Press, 1976.

Durand, John D. The Labor Force in the United States, 1890–1960. New York: Social Science Research Council, 1948.

Durkheim, Emile. The Division of Labor in Society. New York: Free Press, 1933.

Durm, Mark W. "An A Is Not an A: The History of Grading." Educational Forum 57 (1993): 294–297.

Edwards, Alba M. Comparative Occupational Statistics for the United States, 1870 to 1940. In U.S. Bureau of the Census, Sixteenth Census of the United States: 1940. Washington, D.C.: Government Printing Office, 1943.

Edwards, Richard. Contested Terrain: The Transformation of the Workplace in the Twentieth Century. New York: Basic Books, 1979.

Ehrenreich, Barbara. The Hearts of Men: American Dreams and the Flight from Commitment. Garden City, N.Y.: Anchor Press/Doubleday, 1983.

Ehrenreich, Barbara, and Deirdre English. For Her Own Good: 150 Years of the Experts' Advice to Women. Garden City, N.Y.: Anchor Press/Doubleday, 1978.

Epstein, Cynthia Fuchs. Woman's Place: Options and Limits in Professional Careers. Berkeley: University of California Press, 1970.

Evans, Richard J. The Feminists: Women's Emancipation Movements in Europe, America, and Australasia, 1840–1920. New York: Barnes & Noble, 1977.

Farrell, Warren. Why Men Are the Way They Are: The Male-Female Dynamic. New York: McGraw-Hill, 1986.

Ferree, Myra Marx, and Beth Hess. Controversy and Coalition: The New Feminist Movement. Boston: Twayne, 1985.

Fine, Lisa M. The Souls of the Skyscrapers: Female Clerical Workers in Chicago, 1870–1930. Philadelphia: Temple University Press, 1990.

Fiorentine, Robert, and Stephen Cole. "Why Fewer Women Become Physicians: Explaining the Premed Persistence Gap." Sociological Forum 7 (1992): 469–496.

Flexner, Eleanor. Century of Struggle: The Woman's Rights Movement in the United States. Cambridge, Mass.: Harvard University Press, 1959.

Fraundorf, Martha Norby. "The Labor Force Participation of Turn-of-the-Century Married Women." *Journal of Economic History* 39 (1979): 401–418.

Freeman, Jo. *The Politics of Women's Liberation: A Case Study of an Emerging Social Movement and Its Relation to the Policy Process.* New York: McKay, 1975.

——— "Women, Law, and Public Policy." In *Women: A Feminist Perspective,* ed. Freeman. 3d ed. Palo Alto: Mayfield, 1984.

Friedan, Betty. *The Feminine Mystique.* New York: W. W. Norton, 1963.

Fuchs, Victor R. *Women's Quest for Economic Equality.* Cambridge, Mass.: Harvard University Press, 1988.

Gamson, William A. *The Strategy of Social Protest.* 2d ed. Belmont, Calif.: Wadsworth, 1990.

Gelb, Joyce, and Marian Lief Palley. *Women and Public Policies.* Princeton: Princeton University Press, 1982.

Gerson, Kathleen. *Hard Choices.* Berkeley: University of California Press, 1985.

——— *No Man's Land: Men's Changing Commitments to Family and Work.* New York: Basic Books, 1993.

Giddings, Paula. *When and Where I Enter: The Impact of Black Women on Race and Sex in America.* New York: William Morrow, 1984.

Gillespie, Dair L. "Who Has the Power?" *Journal of Marriage and the Family* 33 (1971): 445–478.

Ginzberg, Lori D. *Women and the Work of Benevolence: Morality, Politics, and Class in the Nineteenth-Century United States.* New Haven: Yale University Press, 1990.

Glass, Jennifer. "Job Quits and Job Changes: The Effects of Young Women's Work Conditions and Family Factors." *Gender and Society* 2 (1988): 228–240.

Glazer, Nathan. *Affirmative Discrimination.* New York: Basic Books, 1975.

Glazer, Penina Migdal, and Miriam Slater. *Unequal Colleagues: The Entrance of Women into the Professions, 1890–1940.* New Brunswick, N.J.: Rutgers University Press, 1987.

Glen, Evelyn Nakano. *Issei, Nisei, War Bride.* Philadelphia: Temple University Press, 1986.

Goldberg, Herb. *The Hazards of Being Male: Surviving the Myth of Masculine Privilege.* New York: Signet, 1976.

Goldin, Claudia. *Understanding the Gender Gap: An Economic History of American Women.* Oxford: Oxford University Press, 1990.

Goode, William J. "Why Men Resist." In *Rethinking the Family: Some Feminist Questions,* ed. Barrie Thorne. New York: Longman, 1982.

——— *World Revolution and Family Patterns.* New York: Free Press, 1963.

Goodson, Ivor. *School Subjects and Curriculum Change.* London: Croom Helm, 1983.

Goody, Jack, Joan Thirsk, and E. P. Thompson, eds. *Family and Inheritance.* Cambridge: Cambridge University Press, 1976.

Gordon, Lynn D. *Gender and Higher Education in the Progressive Era.* New Haven: Yale University Press, 1990.

Gottfried, Frances. *The Merit System and Municipal Civil Service: A Fostering of Social Inequality.* New York: Greenwood Press, 1988.

Graham, Patricia A. "Expansion and Exclusion: A History of Women in American Higher Education." *Signs* 3 (1978): 759–773.

Greenwald, Maurine Weiner. "Women Workers and World War I: The American Railroad Industry, a Case Study." *Journal of Social History* 9 (1975): 154–177.

Grigg, Susan. "Women and Family Property: A Review of U.S. Inheritance Studies." *Historical Methods* 22 (1989): 116–122.

Habakkuk, H. J. "Family Structure and Economic Change in Nineteenth-Century Europe." *Journal of Economic History* 15 (1955): 1–12.

Habermas, Jürgen. *Legitimation Crisis.* Trans. Thomas McCarthy. Boston: Beacon Press, 1975.

Hacker, Helen. "Women as a Minority Group." *Social Forces* 30 (1951): 60–69.

Haddad, Richard. "Concepts and Overview of the Men's Liberation Movement." In *Men Freeing Men,* ed. Francis Baumli. Jersey City: New Atlantis, 1985.

——— "The Men's Liberation Movement: A Perspective." *American Man* 2 (1984): 13–17.

Handlin, Oscar. *The Uprooted: The Epic Story of the Great Migrations That Made the American People.* Boston: Little, Brown, 1952.

———, ed. *Immigration as a Factor in American History.* Englewood Cliffs, N.J.: Prentice-Hall, 1959.

Hardin, Russell. *Collective Action.* Baltimore: Johns Hopkins University Press, 1982.

Hareven, Tamara K. *Family Time and Industrial Time: The Relationship between the Family and Work in a New England Industrial Community.* Cambridge: Cambridge University Press, 1982.

Harris, Marvin. *Cultural Materialism: The Struggle for a Science of Culture.* New York: Random House, 1979.

Harrison, Cynthia Ellen. *On Account of Sex: The Politics of Women's Issues, 1945–1968.* Berkeley: University of California Press, 1988.

Hartmann, Heidi. "Capitalism, Patriarchy, and Job Segregation by Sex." *Signs* 3 (1976): 137–171.

——— "The Family as the Locus of Gender, Class, and Political Struggle: The Example of Housework." *Signs* 6 (1981): 366–394.

Hartmann, Susan M. *From Margin to Mainstream: American Women and Politics since 1960.* New York: Alfred A. Knopf, 1989.

Hechter, Michael, ed. *Social Institutions: Their Emergence, Maintenance, and Effects.* New York: Aldine de Gruyter, 1990.

Heimer, Carol A. *Reactive Risk and Rational Action: Managing Moral Hazard in Insurance Contracts.* Berkeley: University of California Press, 1985.

Hill, Martha S. *The Panel Study of Income Dynamics: A User's Guide.* Newbury Park, Calif.: Sage, 1992.

Hindess, Barry. *Choice, Rationality, and Social Theory.* London: Unwin Hyman, 1988.

Hobbs, Margaret. "Rethinking Antifeminism in the 1930s: Gender Crisis or Workplace Justice? A Response to Alice Kessler-Harris." *Gender & History 5* (1993): 4.

Hoff, Joan. *Law, Gender, and Injustice: A Legal History of U.S. Women.* New York: New York University Press, 1991.

Hofstadter, Richard. *Social Darwinism in American Thought, 1860–1915.* Philadelphia: University of Pennsylvania Press, 1944.

Hole, Judith, and Ellen Levine. *Rebirth of Feminism.* New York: Quadrangle Books, 1971.

Hooks, Janet. *Women's Occupations through Seven Decades.* Women's Bureau Bulletin No. 218. Washington, D.C.: Government Printing Office, 1947.

Horwitz, Morton J. *The Transformation of American Law, 1780–1860.* Cambridge, Mass.: Harvard University Press, 1977.

Huber, Joan. "A Theory of Gender Stratification." In *Feminist Frontiers II,* ed. Laurel Richardson and Verta Taylor. New York: Random House, 1989.

Jackson, Robert Max. *The Formation of Craft Labor Markets.* New York: Academic Press, 1984.

———— *The Subordination of Women.* Forthcoming, Cambridge University Press.

Jackson, Robert Max, and Ralph Chipman. "The Growth of Male Support for Woman Suffrage in American States." Manuscript, 1995.

Jacobs, Jerry A. *Revolving Doors: Sex Segregation and Women's Careers.* Stanford: Stanford University Press, 1989.

Jacobson, Paul H. *American Marriage and Divorce.* New York: Rinehart, 1969.

James, Edward T., Janet Wilson James, and Paul S. Boyer, eds. *Notable American Women, 1607–1950: A Biographical Dictionary.* 3 vols. Cambridge, Mass.: The Belknap Press of Harvard University Press, 1971.

Jones, Jacqueline. *Labor of Love, Labor of Sorrow: Black Women, Work, and the Family from Slavery to the Present.* New York: Basic Books, 1986.

Jones, Kathleen. "Citizenship in a Woman-Friendly Polity." *Signs 15* (1990): 781–812.

Kalberg, Stephen. "Max Weber's Types of Rationality: Cornerstones for the Analysis of Rationalization Processes in History." *American Sociological Review 85* (1980): 1145–79.

Kanowitz, Leo. *Women and the Law: The Unfinished Revolution.* Albuquerque: University of New Mexico Press, 1969.

Kanter, Rosabeth Moss. *Men and Women of the Corporation.* New York: Basic Books, 1977.

Kaufman, Debra Renee. "Professional Women: How Real Are the Gains?" In *Women: A Feminist Perspective,* ed. Jo Freeman. 3d ed. Palo Alto: Mayfield, 1984.

Kessler-Harris, Alice. *Out to Work: A History of Wage-Earning Women in the United States.* Oxford: Oxford University Press, 1982.

Kimmel, Michael S., and Michael A. Messner, eds. *Men's Lives.* New York: Macmillan, 1989.

Klein, Ethel. *Gender Politics: From Consciousness to Mass Politics.* Cambridge, Mass.: Harvard University Press, 1984.

Klein, Viola. *The Feminine Character: History of an Ideology.* Urbana: University of Illinois Press, 1971.

Kliebard, Herbert M. *The Struggle for the American Curriculum, 1893–1958.* Boston: Routledge & Kegan Paul, 1986.

Komarovsky, Mirra. "Cultural Contradictions and Sex Roles." *American Journal of Sociology* 52 (1946): 184–189.

——— *The Unemployed Man and His Family.* 1940; reprint, New York: Arno Press, 1971.

Kraditor, Aileen S. *The Ideas of the Woman Suffrage Movement, 1890–1920.* New York: Columbia University Press, 1965.

Langbein, John H. "The Inheritance Revolution." *Public Interest* 102 (1991): 15–31.

Lasch, Christopher. *Haven in a Heartless World: The Family Besieged.* New York: Basic Books, 1977.

Laumann, Edward O., and David Knoke. *The Organizational State: Social Change in National Policy Domains.* Madison: University of Wisconsin Press, 1987.

Lehrer, Susan. *Origins of Protective Labor Legislation for Women, 1905–1925.* Albany: State University of New York Press, 1987.

Leopold, Alice K. "Federal Equal Pay Legislation." *Labor Law Journal* 6 (January 1955): 7–32.

Lindblom, Charles Edward. *Politics and Markets: The World's Political Economic Systems.* New York: Basic Books, 1977.

Long, Clarence D. *The Labor Force under Changing Income and Employment.* Princeton: Princeton University Press, 1958.

Lorber, Judith. *Women Physicians: Careers, Status, and Power.* New York: Tavistock, 1984.

Lowe, Graham S. *Women in the Administrative Revolution: The Feminization of Clerical Work.* Toronto: University of Toronto Press, 1987.

Luker, Kristin. *Abortion and the Politics of Motherhood.* Berkeley: University of California Press, 1984.

Lukes, Steven. *Individualism.* Oxford: Blackwell, 1973.

Lynch, Frederick R. *Invisible Victims: White Males and the Crisis of Affirmative Action.* Westport, Conn.: Greenwood Press, 1989.

Lynn, Naomi B. "Women and Politics." In *Women: A Feminist Perspective,* ed. Jo Freeman. 3d ed. Palo Alto: Mayfield, 1984.

Macfarlane, Alan. *The Origins of English Individualism: The Family, Property, and Social Transition.* Oxford: Basil Blackwell, 1979.

MacKinnon, Catharine A. *Toward a Feminist Theory of the State.* Cambridge, Mass.: Harvard University Press, 1989.

MacPherson, C. B. *The Political Theory of Possessive Individualism: Hobbes to Locke.* Oxford: Clarendon Press, 1962.

Maine, Henry Sumner. *Ancient Law.* London: J. M. Dent and Sons, 1917.

Mansbridge, Jane. *Why We Lost the ERA.* Chicago: University of Chicago Press, 1986.

March, James, and Johan P. Olsen. "The New Institutionalism: Organizational Factors in Political Life." *American Political Science Review* 78 (1984): 734–749.

Margolis, Maxine L. *Mothers and Such: Views of American Women and Why They Changed.* Berkeley: University of California Press, 1984.

Marshall, Susan E. "In Defense of Separate Spheres: Class and Status Politics in the Anti-Suffrage Movement." *Social Forces* 65 (1986): 327–351.

——— "Keep Us on the Pedestal: Women against Feminism in Twentieth-Century America." In *Women: A Feminist Perspective,* ed. Jo Freeman. 3d ed. Palo Alto: Mayfield, 1984.

——— "Who Speaks for American Women? The Future of Antifeminism." *Annals of the American Academy of Political and Social Science* 515 (1991): 50–62.

Marshall, T. H. "Citizenship and Social Class." In *Citizenship and Social Class.* Cambridge: Cambridge University Press, 1950.

Martin, Theodora Penny. *The Sound of Our Own Voices: Women's Study Clubs, 1860–1910.* Boston: Beacon Press, 1987.

Mason, Karen Oppenheim. "Commentary: Strober's Theory of Occupational Sex Segregation." In *Sex Segregation in the Workplace,* ed. Barbara F. Reskin. Washington, D.C.: National Academy Press, 1984.

Mason, Karen Oppenheim, and Barbara Laslett. "Women's Work in the American West: Los Angeles, 1880–1900, and Its Contrast with Essex County, Massachusetts, in 1880." Research Report no. 83–41. Ann Arbor: Population Studies Center, University of Michigan, 1983.

Mason, Karen Oppenheim, J. L. Czajka, and S. Arber. "Change in U.S. Women's Sex-Role Attitudes, 1964–1974." *American Sociological Review* 41 (1976): 579–596.

Matthaei, Julie A. *An Economic History of Women in America: Women's Work, the Sexual Division of Labor, and the Development of Capitalism.* New York: Schocken Books, 1982.

May, Elaine Tyler. *Great Expectations: Marriage and Divorce in Post-Victorian America.* Chicago: University of Chicago Press, 1980.

McAdam, Doug. *Political Process and the Development of Black Insurgency, 1930–1970.* Chicago: University of Chicago Press, 1982.

McCarthy, John D., and Mayer N. Zald. "Resource Mobilization and Social Movements." *American Journal of Sociology* 82 (1977): 1212–41.

Meyer, Annie Nathan. *Women's Work in America.* 1891; reprint, New York: Arno Press, 1972.

Meyerowitz, Joanne J. *Women Adrift: Independent Wage Earners in Chicago, 1880–1930.* Chicago: University of Chicago Press, 1988.

Miliband, Ralph. *The State in Capitalist Society.* New York: Basic Books, 1969.

Milkman, Ruth. *Gender at Work: The Dynamics of Job Segregation by Sex during World War II.* Urbana: University of Illinois Press, 1987.

Mill, J. S. *The Subjection of Women.* 1869; reprint, London: Everyman, 1929.

Mincer, Jacob. "Labor Force Participation of Married Women." In *Aspects of Labor Economics,* ed. H. Gregg Lewis. Princeton: Princeton University Press, 1962.

Mincer, Jacob, and Solomon Polachek. "Family Investments in Human Capital: Earnings of Women." *Journal of Political Economy* 82, suppl. (1974): S76–S108.

Mintz, Steven, and Susan Kellogg. *Domestic Revolutions: A Social History of American Family Life.* New York: Free Press, 1988.

Mirande, Alfredo, and Evangelina Enriquez. *La Chicana.* Chicago: University of Chicago Press, 1979.

Morgan, David. *Suffragists and Democrats: The Politics of Woman Suffrage in America.* East Lansing: Michigan State University Press, 1972.

Municipal Year Book 1989. Washington, D.C.: International City Management Association, 1989.

National Women's Political Caucus. *National Directory of Women Elected Officials.* Washington, D.C., 1982.

Nelson, William Edward. *The Roots of American Bureaucracy, 1830–1900.* Cambridge, Mass.: Harvard University Press, 1982.

Newcomer, Mabel. *A Century of Higher Education for American Women.* New York: Harper, 1959.

Oberschall, Anthony. *Social Movements: Ideologies, Interests, and Identities.* New Brunswick, N.J.: Transaction, 1992.

Olson, Mancur. *The Logic of Collective Action.* Cambridge, Mass.: Harvard University Press, 1971.

O'Neill, William L. *Divorce in the Progressive Era.* New Haven: Yale University Press, 1977.

—— *Everyone Was Brave: The Rise and Fall of Feminism in America.* Chicago: Quadrangle, 1969.

Oppenheimer, Valerie Kincade. *The Female Labor Force in the United States.* Berkeley: University of California, Institute of International Studies, 1970.

Orloff, Ann Shola. "Gender and the Social Rights of Citizenship: The Comparative Analysis of Gender." *American Sociological Review* 58 (1993): 303–328.

Parr, Joy. *The Gender of Breadwinners: Women, Men, and Change in Two Industrial Towns, 1880–1950.* Buffalo: University of Toronto Press, 1990.

Parsons, Talcott. "A Revised Analytical Approach to the Theory of Social Stratification." In *Essays in Sociological Theory.* Glencoe, Ill.: Free Press, 1954.

—— *The Social System.* Glencoe, Ill.: Free Press, 1951.

—— *The Structure of Social Action.* New York: McGraw-Hill, 1937.

Parsons, Talcott, and Robert F. Bales. *Family Socialization and Interaction Process.* Glencoe, Ill.: Free Press, 1954.

Peterson, Richard. *Women, Work, and Divorce.* Albany: State University of New York Press, 1989.

Phelps, Edmund S. "The Statistical Theory of Racism and Sexism." *American Economic Review* 62 (1972): 659–661.

Phillips, Roderick. *Putting Asunder: A History of Divorce in Western Society.* Cambridge: Cambridge University Press, 1988.

Pleck, Elizabeth H. *Domestic Tyranny: The Making of American Social Policy against Family Violence from Colonial Times to the Present.* Oxford: Oxford University Press, 1987.

—— "A Mother's Wages: Income Earning among Married Italian and Black Women, 1886–1911." In *The American Family in Social-Historical Perspective,* ed. Michael Gordon. 2d ed. New York: St. Martin's Press, 1978.

Pleck, Elizabeth H., and Joseph H. Pleck, eds. *The American Man.* Englewood Cliffs, N.J.: Prentice-Hall, 1980.

Pleck, Joseph H. *The Myth of Masculinity.* Cambridge, Mass.: MIT Press, 1981.

—— "The Work-Family Role System." In *Women and Work: Problems and Perspectives,* ed. Rachel Kahn-Hut, Arlene Kaplan Daniels, and Richard Colvard. New York: Oxford University Press, 1982.

—— *Working Wives, Working Husbands.* Beverly Hills: Sage, 1985.

Polachek, Solomon W. "Occupational Segregation among Women: Theory, Evidence, and a Prognosis." In *Women in the Labor Market,* ed. C. B. Lloyd, E. S. Andrews, and C. L. Gilroy. New York: Columbia University Press, 1979.

Polsby, Nelson W. *Community Power and Political Theory.* New Haven: Yale University Press, 1963.

Popenoe, David. *Disturbing the Nest: Family Change and Decline in Modern Societies.* New York: Aldine de Gruyter, 1988.

Poulantzas, Nicos. *Political Power and Social Classes.* Trans. Timothy O'Hagan. London: NLB; Sheed and Ward, 1973.

Pyke, Karen D. "Women's Employment as a Gift or Burden? Marital Power across Marriage, Divorce, and Remarriage." *Gender and Society* 8 (1994): 73–91.

Quann, C. James. "Grades and Grading." *College and University* 1984.

Rabkin, Peggy A. *Fathers to Daughters: The Legal Foundations of Female Emancipation.* Westport, Conn.: Greenwood Press, 1980.

Rapone, Anita J. "Clerical Labor Force Formation: The Office Woman in Albany, 1870–1930." Ph.D. diss., New York University, 1981.

Reskin, Barbara F., ed. *Sex Segregation in the Workplace: Trends, Explanations, Remedies.* Washington, D.C.: National Academy Press, 1984.

Reskin, Barbara F., and Patricia A. Roos. *Job Queues, Gender Queues: Explaining Women's Inroads into Male Occupations.* Philadelphia: Temple University Press, 1990.

Rhode, Deborah L. "Feminism and the State." *Harvard Law Review* 107 (1996): 1181–1208.

—— *Justice and Gender: Sex Discrimination and the Law.* Cambridge, Mass.: Harvard University Press, 1989.

Rindfuss, Ronald R., S. Philip Morgan, and C. Gray Swicegood. *First Births in America: Changes in the Timing of Parenthood.* Berkeley: University of California Press, 1988.

Roediger, David R., and Philip S. Foner. *Our Own Time: A History of American Labor and the Working Day.* Westport, Conn.: Greenwood Press, 1989.

Rokkan, Steven. *Citizens, Elections, and Parties.* New York: McKay, 1970.

Rose, Sonya O. *Limited Livelihoods: Gender and Class in Nineteenth-Century England.* Berkeley: University of California Press, 1991.

Rosenbaum, James E. *Career Mobility in a Corporate Hierarchy.* New York: Academic Press, 1984.

Rosenberg, Nathan. *Technology and American Economic Growth.* White Plains, N.Y.: M. E. Sharpe, 1972.

Rotella, Elyce J. *From Home to Office: U.S. Women at Work, 1870–1930.* Ann Arbor: UMI Research Press, 1981.

Rothman, Sheila M. *Woman's Proper Place: A History of Changing Ideals and Practices, 1870 to the Present.* New York: Basic Books, 1978.

Ruggles, Steven. "The Transformation of American Family Structure." *American Historical Review* 99 (1994): 103–128.

Rupp, Leila J., and Verta Taylor. *Survival in the Doldrums: The American Women's Rights Movement, 1945 to the 1960s.* New York: Oxford University Press, 1987.

Rury, John L. *Education and Women's Work: Female Schooling and the Division of Labor in Urban America, 1870–1930.* Albany: State University of New York Press, 1991.

Ryscavage, Paul. "More Wives in the Labor Force Have Husbands with 'Above-Average' Incomes." *Monthly Labor Review* 102 (1979): 40–42.

Salmon, Marylynn. *Women and the Law of Property in Early America.* Chapel Hill: University of North Carolina Press, 1986.

Sapiro, Virginia. *The Political Integration of Women: Roles, Socialization, and Politics.* Urbana: University of Illinois Press, 1983.

Schluchter, Wolfgang. *The Rise of Western Rationalism: Max Weber's Developmental History.* Trans. Guenther Roth. Berkeley: University of California Press, 1981.

Scott, W. Richard, and John W. Meyer. *Institutional Environments and Organizations: Structural Complexity and Individualism.* Thousand Oaks, Calif.: Sage, 1994.

Shammas, Carole, Marylynn Salmon, and Michel Dahlin. *Inheritance in America: From Colonial Times to the Present.* New Brunswick, N.J.: Rutgers University Press, 1987.

Shanahan, Daniel. *Toward a Genealogy of Individualism.* Amherst: University of Massachusetts Press, 1992.

Sheffield, Carole J. "Sexual Terrorism." In *Women: A Feminist Perspective,* ed. Jo Freeman. 3d ed. Palo Alto: Mayfield, 1984.

Shorter, Edward. *The Making of the Modern Family.* New York: Basic Books, 1975.

Simpson, Peggy. "Politics." In *The Women's Annual, 1985: The Year in Review,* ed. Barbara Haber. Boston: G. K. Hall, 1985.

Sivard, Ruth Leger. *Women: A World Survey.* Washington, D.C.: World Priorities, 1985.

Skocpol, Theda. "Bringing the State Back In: Strategies of Analysis in Current Research." In *Bringing the State Back In,* ed. Peter B. Evans, Dietrich Rueschemeyer, and Theda Skocpol. New York: Cambridge University Press, 1985.

Skocpol, Theda, and Edwin Amenta. "States and Social Policies." *Annual Review of Sociology* 12 (1986): 131–157.

Skowronek, Stephen. *Building a New American State: The Expansion of National Administrative Capacities, 1877–1920.* Cambridge: Cambridge University Press, 1982.

Smelser, Neil. *Theory of Collective Behavior.* New York: Free Press, 1963.

Smith, James P., and Michael P. Ward. *Women's Wages and Work in the Twentieth Century.* Santa Monica, Calif.: Rand Corporation, 1984.

Solomon, Barbara Miller. *In the Company of Educated Women: A History of Women and Higher Education in America.* New Haven: Yale University Press, 1985.

South, Scott J., and Glenna Spitze. "Housework in Marital and Nonmarital Households." *American Sociological Review* 59 (1994): 327–347.

Stansell, Christine. *City of Women: Sex and Class in New York, 1789–1860.* New York: Alfred A. Knopf, 1986.

Stanton, Elizabeth Cady, Susan B. Anthony, Matilda Joslyn Gage, and Ida Husted Harper, eds. *The History of Woman Suffrage.* 6 vols. Rochester, N.Y.: Fowler and Wells, 1881–1922.

Steuter, Erin. "Women against Feminism: An Examination of Feminist Social Movements and Anti-feminist Countermovements." *Canadian Review of Sociology and Anthropology* 29 (1992): 288–306.

Stinchcombe, Arthur L. *Constructing Social Worlds.* New York: Harcourt, Brace & World, 1968.

Strasser, Susan. *Never Done: A History of American Housework.* New York: Pantheon, 1982.

Tarrow, Sidney G. *Power in Movement: Social Movements, Collective Action and Politics.* Cambridge: Cambridge University Press, 1994.

Tentler, Leslie Woodcock. *Wage-Earning Women: Industrial Work and Family Life in the United States, 1900–1930.* Oxford: Oxford University Press, 1979.

Tickamyer, Ann R. "Wealth and Power: A Comparison of Men and Women in the Property Elite." *Social Forces* 60 (1981): 463–481.

Tilly, Charles. *From Mobilization to Revolution.* Reading, Mass.: Addison-Wesley, 1978.

Tocqueville, Alexis de. *Democracy in America.* 1835; reprint, New York: Modern Library, 1981.

Tönnies, Ferdinand. *Gemeinschaft und Gesellschaft: Grundbegriffe der reinen Soziologie.* Berlin: K. Curtius, 1912.

Tyack, David B. *The One Best System: A History of American Urban Education.* Cambridge, Mass.: Harvard University Press, 1974.

Tyack, David B., and Elisabeth Hansot. *Learning Together: A History of Coeducation in American Schools.* New Haven: Yale University Press and Russell Sage Foundation, 1990.

Tyack, David B., and Myra H. Strober. "Jobs and Gender: A History of the Structuring of Education Employment by Sex." In *Educational Policy and Management: Sex Differentials,* ed. Patricia Schmuck and W. W. Charters. New York: Academic Press, 1981.

U.S. Bureau of the Census. *Current Population Reports.* Population Characteristics, Series P20, No. 433. Washington, D.C.: Government Printing Office, 1988.

—— *The Eighteenth Census of the United States. Census of Population: 1960.* Vol. 1, pt. 1: "United States Summary." Washington, D.C.: Government Printing Office, 1964.

—— "Employment and Family Characteristics of Women." In *The Sixteenth Census of the United States: 1940. Population: The Labor Force (Sample Statistics).* Washington, D.C.: Government Printing Office, 1943.

—— *Historical Statistics of the United States.* 2 vols. Washington, D.C.: Government Printing Office, 1975.

—— "Occupational Characteristics." In *Census of Population: 1950. A Report of the Seventeenth Decennial Census of the United States.* Special Reports, Series P-E. Washington, D.C.: Government Printing Office, 1956.

—— *Statistical Abstract of the United States: 1996.* Washington, D.C.: Government Printing Office, 1996.

—— *U.S. Census of Population: 1970.* Subject Reports. *Employment Status and Work Experience.* Washington, D.C.: Government Printing Office, 1973.

—— *U.S. Census of Population: 1970.* Vol. 1, pt. 1: "United States Summary." Washington, D.C.: Government Printing Office, 1973.

U.S. Congress. House. Committee on Education and Labor. *Equal Pay for Equal Work.* Hearings before the Select Subcommittee on Labor. 87th Cong., 2d sess. Washington, D.C.: Government Printing Office, 1962.

U.S. Department of Education. *The Condition of Education: 1984 Edition.* Washington, D.C.: Government Printing Office, 1984.

—— *Digest of Education Statistics, 1996.* Washington, D.C.: Government Printing Office, 1996.

U.S. Department of Labor, Bureau of Labor Statistics. *Eleventh Annual Report of the Commissioner of Labor, 1895–6: Work and Wages of Men, Women and Children.* Washington, D.C.: Government Printing Office, 1897.

—— *Handbook of Labor Statistics: 1980.* Washington, D.C.: Government Printing Office, 1980.

—— *Handbook of Labor Statistics: 1985.* Washington, D.C.: Government Printing Office, 1985.

——— *Marital and Family Patterns of Workers: An Update*. Bulletin 2163. Washington, D.C.: Government Printing Office, May 1983.

U.S. Department of Labor, Manpower Administration. *Dual Careers: A Longitudinal Study of Labor Market Experience of Women*. Washington, D.C.: Government Printing Office, 1985.

U.S. Department of Labor, Women's Bureau. *Case Studies in Equal Pay for Women*. Washington, D.C.: Government Printing Office, 1951.

——— *Handbook of Facts on Women Workers*. Bulletin 225. Washington D.C.: Government Printing Office, 1948.

——— *Time of Change: 1983 Handbook on Women Workers*. Bulletin 298. Washington, D.C.: Government Printing Office, 1983.

Vanek, Joann. "Time Spent in Housework." *Scientific American* 231 (1974): 116–120.

Van Horn, Susan Householder. *Women, Work, and Fertility, 1900–1986*. New York: New York University Press, 1988.

Vogler, Carolyn, and Jan Pahl. "Money, Power, and Inequality within Marriage." *Sociological Review* 42 (1994): 263–288.

Waller, Willard Walter. *The Family: A Dynamic Interpretation*. New York: Cordon, 1938.

Walton, Ronald Gordon. *Women in Social Work*. London: Routledge and Kegan Paul, 1975.

Warbasse, Elizabeth Bowles. *The Changing Legal Rights of Married Women, 1800–1861*. New York: Garland, 1987.

Ware, Susan. *Beyond Suffrage: Women in the New Deal*. Cambridge, Mass.: Harvard University Press, 1981.

Warner, Rebecca L., Gary R. Lee, and Janet Lee. "Social Organization, Spousal Resources, and Marital Power: A Cross-Cultural Study." *Journal of Marriage and the Family* 48 (1986): 121–128.

Weber, Max. *Economy and Society,* ed. Guenther Roth and Claus Wittich. Berkeley: University of California Press, 1978.

——— *Max Weber on Law in Economy and Society,* ed. Max Rheinstein, trans. Edward Shils and Max Rheinstein. Cambridge, Mass.: Harvard University Press, 1954.

Weiner, Lynn Y. *From Working Girl to Working Mother: The Female Labor Force in the United States, 1820–1980*. Chapel Hill: University of North Carolina Press, 1985.

Werner, Emmy E. "Women in the State Legislatures." *Western Political Quarterly* 21 (1968): 40–50.

Wilensky, Harold L. *The Welfare State and Equality: Structural and Ideological Roots of Public Expenditures*. Berkeley: University of California Press, 1975.

Wilson, Bryan R., ed. *Rationality*. Oxford: Blackwell, 1970.

Woody, Thomas. *A History of Women's Education in the United States*. 2 vols. 1929; reprint, New York: Octagon Books, 1966.

Wright, Robert. *The Moral Animal: The New Science of Evolutionary Psychology.* New York: Pantheon Books, 1994.

Wrigley, E. A. *Population and History.* New York: McGraw-Hill, 1969.

Young, Michael. *The Rise of the Meritocracy, 1870–2033.* London: Thames and Hudson, 1958.

INDEX

Abortion, 207, 208

Administrative rationality. *See* Rationalization

Affirmative action, 51–54, 141; backlash, 54; causes, 59; conceded, 53–54

American Revolution, 31, 32

Anthony, Susan B., 35

Antifeminism, 202–209; causes, 204–206, 208, 211; class and, 206; motives, 207, 208; women's interests and, 208–210

Assimilation (women's), 61–70; effects, 210, 235; partial, 210, 235, 250, 251, 256–258, 260

Birth control, 99

Bureaucratization. *See* Organizations; Rationalization

Causal processes, 18–23, 248–268; alternative paths, 45, 50; beliefs and, 32, 54, 246, 247; conflict, 20–22; disembedding gender, 211, 249–252; fundamental, 2, 27, 248; historical, 244, 245; historical opportunity, 259; housework's decline, 100; indirect, 4, 22, 126, 260–263; individualism, 172; institutional indifference, 25, 69, 252, 253; international comparisons, 19, 268–270; judiciary, 52; male indifference, 66; meritocratic ideas, 156; multiple, 25, 27, 45, 56, 72, 73,

262, 263; needs of modern economy, 30, 31; needs of modern family, 32, 157; needs of modern society, 29; nonlinear, 73, 248; proximate, 244, 245; resistance to feminism, 211; rising employment, 121; theories of, 243–248; transitional, 28; wage rates, 103; women's movement, 189, 190, 212, 245, 246; women's resistance, 175. *See also* Gender inequality's decline; Interests; Power, social

Childrearing, 85, 99, 100, 131, 180, 236, 251, 252

Citizenship, 21–70; history, 62; meritocratic ideas, 48, 152–154; phases, 61–64; rationalization and, 153; state motives, 62. *See also* State; Suffrage

Civil Rights Act (1964), 35, 50, 51, 60, 200

Civil War, 34, 35

Colleges, 133–142, 144–146, 192–194; acceptance of women, 137, 138; egalitarian policies, 135; graduation rates, 134–136; growth of, 134; motives, 137; rationalization and, 137, 138; resistance to change, 138, 139; students, 9; women's, 134. *See also* Education, women's

Competition: male, 114, 232; organizational, 110, 112

Congress, U.S., 35, 36, 40, 41, 44, 48–50, 58, 60, 82

Destined for Equality was typeset in Adobe Sabon with headings in Fonthaus Tambor Light. It was designed by Gwen Nefsky Frankfeldt, composed in Ventura Publisher by Technologies 'N Typography, printed and bound by Vail-Ballou Press.